BUSINESS COMMUNICATION SKILLS

JANET K. McKEON
DEPARTMENT OF COMMUNICATION
MICHIGAN STATE UNIVERSITY

BUSINESS COMMUNICATION SKILLS

Principles and Practice

second edition

John J. Makay
Ohio State University

Ronald C. Fetzer
Wright State University

Prentice-Hall, Inc., Englewood Cliffs, New Jersey 07632

Library of Congress Cataloging in Publication Data

Makay, John J. (date)
    Business communication skills.

        Bibliography: p.
        Includes index.
        1. Communication in management.   I. Fetzer, Ronald C. (date)
II. Title.
HF5718.M36   1984   658.4′5   83-19243
ISBN   0-13-091959-4

Editorial/production supervision and
    interior design: Linda Tiedemann/Marjorie Borden
Cover design: George Cornell
Manufacturing buyer: Ron Chapman

Printed in the United States of America

10   9   8   7   6   5   4   3   2   1

ISBN   0-13-091959-4

Prentice-Hall International, Inc., *London*
Prentice-Hall of Australia Pty. Limited, *Sydney*
Editora Prentice-Hall do Brasil, Ltda., *Rio de Janeiro*
Prentice-Hall Canada Inc., *Toronto*
Prentice-Hall of India Private Limited, *New Delhi*
Prentice-Hall of Japan, Inc., *Tokyo*
Prentice-Hall of Southeast Asia Pte. Ltd., *Singapore*
Whitehall Books Limited, *Wellington, New Zealand*

to

Leigh, Beth, Kathy,
"Sam," Kristen, David,
J.J., Rhonda, Chuck,
and Michael

CONTENTS

Part Three   Interpersonal Communication

CHAPTER 6   USING THE TELEPHONE   *106*

CHAPTER 7   COMMUNICATING
                 THROUGH THE INTERVIEW   *118*

PREFACE

The role of human communication, both oral and written, is crucial to the success of every business and other professional person who strives for both personal and organizational goals. In response to the recognition of this role by educators and organizational leaders, academic departments are increasing their communication course offerings for today's students.

Those who run the nation's businesses and institutions continually misuse precious human energy through poor communication. Our book aims to help men and women preparing to enter the business and professional world—as well as others currently launched in their careers—to avoid this waste of time and energy. We wish to help the businessperson develop and maintain satisfaction and make significant efforts to meet corporate and institutional goals.

Three major features distinguish our book from others. First, it is comprehensive. Thirteen chapters comprise a theoretically-based and *practical* guide to a wide variety of communication skills. While the emphasis is on oral communication, pertinent ideas are also offered as instruction for written communication. Second, our book offers ideas and illustrations drawn from our experiences both on campus and in a wide variety of organizational settings. Third, it includes not only textual information but instructional activities as well. This information is found at the conclusion of each chapter.

Following the introductory chapter surveying the process of communication in business, where communication is portrayed as transactional, we focus on major activities in which communication needs are found: listening, presentational speaking, telecommunication, interviewing, problem-solving meetings, conference communication, writing, training, use of the speakers' bureau, and career pathing for the professional.

Along with the theory, principles, and concepts of communication, we draw on our work with business and other professional persons for practical applications of all topics covered. Today's students are career-minded and enter our system of higher education to prepare themselves for a satisfying future. Our book has a career focus throughout, and its final chapter allows students to use their composite knowledge and skills in initiating and developing career opportunities.

This book keeps the student in focus in its philosophy, direction, theory, principles, and instructional aids. We provide models and list suggestions for using communication skills efficiently. All of the materials have been tested in our courses, seminars, and workshops. We have sought to combine information from the social and administrative sciences with humanistic knowledge. The settings and illustrations in the book come from our experiences with business and professional communication. In our second edition we have employed new ideas and suggestions given us by those familiar with the first edition.

John J. Makay
Ronald C. Fetzer

ACKNOWLEDGMENTS

We especially want to thank Leigh Makay for authoring the chapter on communicating when using the telephone. Her enthusiasm, expertise, and style of writing, combined, have strengthened this new edition.

We also want to thank Bob Thoresen and Steve Dalphin for their interest and encouragement in working with us.

Finally, we are grateful to all of the students both on campus and in other organizational settings who inspired this book and filled our heads with an abundance of ideas, illustrations, and communicative needs.

PHOTO CREDITS

Photographs are courtesy of the Photography Department of Wright State University, Dayton, Ohio and of ARMCO, Inc., Middletown, Ohio.

BUSINESS
COMMUNICATION
SKILLS

CHAPTER ONE

COMMUNICATION IN BUSINESS

Effective and productive communication in the business organization is tremendously important in the achievement of personal and organizational goals. In fact, if we could peer into the business activities of any organization and take a careful look, we would see that the process of communication is the most consistent and instrumental activity of all. Messages characterize and move the ideas and attitudes of working people as they strive to achieve both personal meaning and financial success in their day-to-day activities.

For the business organization, profit and growth are words that symbolize and encapsulate the members' efforts for success and satisfaction. These efforts are fueled with human desire, talent, educational development, trained skills, and the feelings, thoughts, and dreams that accompany them. Through profit and growth, the quality of life in our nation is ensured, because as a society we depend upon a solid economic base. We cherish and thrive with it, nurtured, stimulated, and protected by a free enterprise system. Even the philosopher who is content to spend life as far away from the board room or business office as possible would be affected adversely without good business. His or her intellectual productivity would be hampered considerably if business were poor, because each of us needs the services and goods of business for the maintenance of our lives, and economic instability would touch us all. We need successful, satisfying, and productive business, and this, in turn, is lubricated and cemented by successful, satisfying, and productive communication.

If we focus on productive communication, we see immediately that effective and satisfying communication in business is complex and difficult, requiring a wide variety of message transactions, in both written and oral forms. Certainly, no one book is able to treat all of these forms comprehensively. For this reason, we shall focus, in this text, on major person-to-person communication principles and practices.

Quite frankly, the need for business persons to study and develop knowledge and skills in human communication is often set aside for the pursuit of other knowledge and skills. Some business people feel that studying communication is unnecessary because communication is something we have been doing throughout our lives, both in school and elsewhere. But a paradox surfaces when we examine the attitudes of persons in the business world, especially executives. On the one hand, we are told by business leaders, "Yes, communication is highly important, and we hire many new graduates who seem to lack basic communication skills. In fact, all of us need to become much better at it." On the other hand, when it comes to investing company time and money in communication development programs, other priorities often seem to take precedence. Action for communication is put off. It is not uncommon for an executive to lament that her or his employees ought to have received basic communication education before joining the company. Nor is it uncommon for business persons to try to "catch up," by participating in communication workshops or by listening to training cassettes on their auto tape players while driving to work.

Of course, there are those who recognize and act on this need, since programs to improve communication skills do occur in the business world. These programs are introduced because management personnel recognize that their employees are not adequately educated in communication skills. One executive made this point recently when she took steps to obtain a course in presentational speaking for the personnel in the department she managed. In a memorandum to a vice-president she stated: "It has become apparent to me over the past few months that there is a great deal of room for improvement in the way most of the staff in our department make presentations. The lack of skill is not a result of indifference, lack of enthusiasm, or a lack of material. Rather, I believe the problem lies in the lack of knowledge of basic principles of communication. Perhaps the colleges and universities cannot be bothered with requiring skill development in such a mundane subject as communication." The memorandum went on to request that an instructor in communication be brought in to help personnel meet their needs for improved communication. In this case, the action was quick—a course was offered for ten weeks—and the employees began to work seriously on improving their skills.

Our purpose is to encourage you to prepare yourself to be knowledgeable and skillful as a communicator. We want you to be able to understand what communication means for the business person and to be able to apply these theories and principles in profitable ways. In a sense, we invite you to think seriously and feel deeply about improving your communication for practical reasons. The quality, efficiency, and productivity in your working life can be enriched if you are able to communicate with ease and excellence.

Certainly, excellent communication can be instrumental in guiding the business person toward developing her or his greatest potential. Two points are important to remember: (1) Communication knowledge and skills are as essential to success in business as any other knowledge and skills; (2) communication knowledge and skills can be learned and highly developed through study, experience, and evaluation.

SPEAKING OF BUSINESS

When we speak of business, we use the term as Zelko and Dance define it: "We like to think of business as including any kind of gainful pursuit by any person or group of persons, regardless of size and numbers, for profit."[1] And Rosenblatt, Cheatham, and Watt remind us that "business communications are the purposeful interchange of ideas, opinions, and information presented personally or impersonally by symbol or signal to attain the goals of the organization."[2] The effort of the business and its individual members should be to achieve efficiency in personal communication, because whether one is speaking to another about a crucial matter in a small office in a huge corporation or whether a large corporation is addressing a vast public audience, business communication is most satisfying when it is personal.

Communication in business can be information sharing or persuasion, verbal play or problem solving. There are numerous times when one person tries to inform or secure agreement from others. In the process, this person may engage in the kind of expressions that can lighten and uplift a human relationship or educate and work on problem solving. Let us use our imaginations of a moment. Suppose we are guests at Automotive Rubber and Plastics Company, Inc., which employs 400 persons and operates three shifts five days weekly. What we see immediately are individuals working with technology and with one another and sending and receiving messages that involve transactions outside the company. These people are using the process of communication as a means to an end rather than an end in itself. They seem to be focused on working with business details and matters, rather than on the process of communication itself.

Imagine some of the typical communication settings and human transactions that are in process:

IN THE FRONT OFFICE

1. The President of AR & P is working with the executive secretary, and most of their work is accomplished through talk, which centers on the substance of ideas to be expressed later in written form.
2. The Director of Labor Relations and Personnel is working with a union official, and they are negotiating (talking) to resolve a labor problem; they are trying to make sense of a written report.
3. The Director of Marketing is making a presentation to the marketing department to show the staff what the latest market research indicates is necessary in order to increase the company's share of the coated-fabrics market.

4. The Director of Regional Sales is drafting a memorandum to her salespersons about new procedures to be followed in entertaining customers in their sales transactions.

5. The Chief Product Engineer is working on a written report to be used by the Director of Corporate Communications, who is in the process of writing the annual report.

6. The receptionist has a visitor waiting for her attention while she is handling two incoming calls.

7. General executives are discussing creating a speakers bureau aimed at lifting the company's profile in the community at large.

This is just a small portion of the front-office activity. Consistently, what we observe is oral and written communication to get "the work done" in ways that bring about both personal and corporate satisfaction. Let's go into the shop.

IN THE PLANT

1. Several people are "on break"—laughing and talking beside the coffee machine.

2. A group of women and men are in a committee meeting, where they are working on suggestions to increase safety measures in the plant.

3. An executive is pointing out a coating process for automobile battery brackets to three well-dressed executives who are customers.

4. Three men on the shipping dock are listening intently to the driver of a tractor-trailer rig filled with bundles of raw rubber.

5. A woman at a huge press is talking with her supervisor about a computer printout she is trying to interpret.

6. A worker is on his way to the front office to interview for a position posted on the bulletin board.

7. A man is on his way to the medical benefits manager to discuss making a claim for benefits for his wife's recent surgery.

Wherever we look, we find communication. It is a lifeline that keeps the company operating and people in touch with one another. Their communication can affect whether or not significant profit is made. Can we assume that all or most of the communication in these fourteen observations was effective, satisfying, and productive? No. Such an assumption is highly unwarranted. Experience and research suggest that some of the communication was probably satisfactory while some was not, because in each situation there was either clarity or lack of understanding, agreement or disagreement. A careful analysis of the communication experiences would reveal that. To understand why some communication was successful and some was not would take us into the complexity of the human communication process. To a considerable extent, this book and your experience in this course should reveal this complexity.

Undoubtedly, to achieve success both personally and for the company, each person needs to know what she or he is talking about, and each must be knowledgeable when giving and seeking information. In order to understand and be understood, to convince or be convinced, to find out what needs to be done or let others know what is to be accomplished, clear meaning must be created and acted on. Each person needs to be an expert in the use of appropriate communication skills in order to complete human transactions. In addition to knowing about their jobs and the goals of the company, these people ought to know about the theories of the process of communication and how to apply this knowledge. Too often, poor communication—careless comments, incomplete ideas, or insensitivity in expression—leads to ill will and unnecessary expense—*only* because knowledge about communication in business was not applied. *Our aim is to significantly assist you to learn how to communicate effectively as a business person.* To further this aim, we should have a common definition of the process of communication. What notions, concepts, and feelings do you find when you see the phrase "process of communication"?

THE PROCESS OF COMMUNICATION

Although the process of human communication is essentially the same, theoretically, in a multitude of settings, the student of business communication can see the basic process and fundamental principles and adapt them to the organizational setting.

We know that there is a great deal of noise around us daily, and most of it is aimed at some sort of communication. But often this noise does not succeed in creating the meaning necessary for effective communication.

What is communication?   The term "communication" today is used in such varied contexts that, in a sense, the term can seem almost meaningless. Ask most executives today where their organization's major problems lie and you're likely to be told, "basically, in communication." Ask these same men and women about their corporate image in the public's eye and the answer is likely to be, "We have a communication problem." Ask what communication is, and you're likely to receive a number of different though related responses. The difference exists because communication affects each component in a business system, and business persons define the term and process as they view it from their corner of the company. For example, in defining communication recently, one vice-president of a huge corporation spoke about the "dynamic interface" between the corporation and the government; another sales executive spoke about "sense of real confidence in the self and the product or service for the consumer"; while a third spoke of "lifting our profile in key markets."[3]

Behind these descriptive phrases, what seems to capture the essence of communication? Communication in business is effective to the extent that meaning is created, goals are achieved, and humans become satisfied as much as possible.

Consider momentarily a statement about communication: *Communication is the creation of meaning through the use of signals and symbols.* Communication is not static. It is ongoing and continuous, so we view it as a process. We can enter into communication, but where and when does the process begin, hold fast, or stop? David Berlo argues one cannot "talk about the beginning or the end of communication or say that a particular idea came from one specific source, that communication occurs in only one way, and so on."[4] Gerald Miller speaks of the process in a broad sense when he says communication "refers to a way of perceiving and responding to the world in which we live"; and that process "implies a universe in constant flux." We cannot view communication as something fixed in time and space.[5] To understand communication, we need to appreciate the complexity of the process, for it is always dynamic—variables and actions interplay, fueled by human energy and force—and at the core is *meaning*. We are part of this process; we are caught up in it; and our success, satisfaction, and growth depend to a great extent on how we function within it.

What is meaning?   When we speak of communication as a process for the creation of meaning, we view meaning as *a recognition of relationship;* it is the perception that takes place when we capture the relationship between two statements or images.[6] In order to understand or create such a relationship, each person must draw on his or her own frame of reference—those feelings, attitudes, beliefs, and values that are part of each individual's understanding of self and social environment. Signals and symbols are assigned meaning by those who send and receive messages in any interaction.

When persons are able to communicate through the creation of meaning, they construct reality symbolically by systematically assigning signals, symbols, and images. When we talk or write, hear or read, we need words (symbols) to make sense, to find meaning, to share it.

Signals and symbols.   The construction of reality takes place within us because of the ways we engage in information processing. For instance, when we decide to communicate, we sort, select, and send signals or symbols as messages that *evoke some meaning* in us and eventually in another person. The other person, in turn, creates within herself or himself a response to these signals and symbols perceived. This communication takes place within a time, space, and cultural context. The context, the signals, the symbols, the world view of each communicator; the individual level of understanding; and the attitudes, beliefs, and values—all enter into communication. It is, then, quite a complex process.

Sorting and selecting symbols can be both conscious and unconscious for the communicator. Signals and symbols provide the components of any message. By signals, we mean the messages "which a communicator feels are beaming from a source, and they suggest very limited but concise meaning. Symbols suggest broader and more complex meanings assigned to the verbal and nonverbal language of the communicators."[7] When a man enters an office wearing a frown on his face and grumbling almost to himself about something, that is a signal that something is bothering him. If we look to the sky early in the morning and see nothing but shades of gray, that is a signal about the kind of weather that the day may bring. The signals only suggest meaning to a limited extent, and the interpreter of the signals makes an inference that may or may not be accurate; the use of symbols can lead to accuracy more directly than the use of signals.

Symbols, though not limited to words, are frequently put into words, symbolic for something else, symbolic for a reality. A word "stands for" an object, an event, or an experience. The referent exists or has happened outside of the self and may be recorded in the memory, which expresses itself in thoughts and feelings. The expressions are in language, both verbal and nonverbal.

If, on a business trip you and a working companion find yourselves in a card game as partners with another couple, you know the possibilities you have of signaling your partner about what cards you are holding. For example, scratching the side of your face could be an attempt to indicate to your partner what sort of play you want him or her to make. If you are playing bridge, however, you can try to tip your partner off with a verbal signal. It is only when a round of cards is completed that the players can use symbols openly to discuss the play in terms of strategy, tactics, and choices, and this complex expression involves symbolic interaction to create understanding.

The business world is filled with verbal and nonverbal symbols which appear as corporate logos. Whether the company is Borden, Nationwide Insurance, Wendy's International, or ARMCO Inc., when we approach their products or business establishments we are greeted by words and pictures that stand for huge corporate enterprises. A great deal of time, effort, and money go into making a decision about what that greeting ought to be. Business people want the verbal and nonverbal greeting of their sign to create quite specific feelings and ideas in the potential or actual customers.

Communication is transaction.   The process of human communication, whether verbal or nonverbal, is transactional. When we speak of the process of communication, we know we are not speaking of a series of static entities. John Stewart provides a useful idea about the transactional nature of human communication in terms of interpersonal communication:

> A transaction is defined as a psychological event in which all parts or aspects of the concrete events derive their existence and nature from active participation in the event. This transactional perspective is important because if one sees human communication simply as an act or interaction [one] is likely to overlook the fact that we construct the persons with whom we communicate. . . . We construct the other with whom we communicate in the sense that we choose from the infinite number of cues [one] "gives off" and organize our chosen perceptions into one configuration that is him.[8]

As communicators, we "put together" what we think, feel, imagine, into language. In this process, the "other" becomes part of us, and his or her messages are really what we create from signals and symbols; thus in communication we have not just transmission, but also transaction.

The transactional nature of communication is more than communicators constructing each other and the messages for meaning; it is also like business. Gerald Phillips and Nancy Metzger speak of the communication transactions that may result from interaction. Their explanation is related to but different from the view explained by Stewart. They see the transaction as being involved with individual goal-seeking in both private or public behavior. In a word, transaction is a quest "for the satisfaction of very personal wants."[9] As we work, using communication as instrumental for achieving success or satisfaction, we do our own sense making, and we make claims about what we think is or isn't or might be or could be or should be; we set up for ourselves what we think we see, hear, touch, taste, and smell. We string words together into what seems to be a logical and meaningful order; and when we do this with other persons, we do so to satisfy a need, a desire—in a word, a goal. And because there is intent on the part of the communicators, as well as some sort of relationship, no matter how fleeting, there is transaction.

In the transactional process, a number of factors or variables are usually involved. In order to account for the most important ones that affect meaning, students of communication frequently use communication models. Models of communication are abundant in the literature, each one an attempt to show something that is important to understanding the process of communication (see Figure 1-1).

Let us examine an encounter between two co-workers in order to illustrate how communication is a human transaction: Working with her office door open, Marion Mason looks up to find Mark Smith, coffee cup in hand, taking a seat near her desk.

MARION: What's up, Mark? What can I do for you? What is it that you need? (Marion seemed pressed in her tone of voice and facial expression, as if she were working on a difficult task.)

MARK: Quite frankly, Marion, what I need is to kill time. I have to go to a meeting with George, Bud, and Sally, and it isn't taking place for another forty minutes.

MARION: Well, I just have to get this report done by five o'clock, and I can't afford to give you the time now. Why don't you catch me later? Please?

MARK: O.K., Marion, I'll slip out and bug someone else for now. Good luck with the report!

In this brief exchange, we can easily see that Mark needs something—a way to kill time. Marion cannot meet this need because she has a greater one to meet. Both needs center in time, and the people work out a transaction through communication. Listen to a similar transaction between Marion and Susan Jones, in which Susan's needs are met in a satisfying way:

FIGURE 1-1   Communication: one with another.

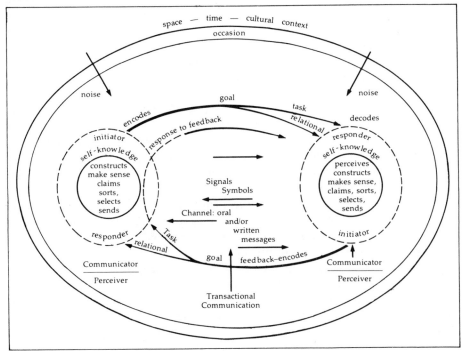

SUSAN: Marion, I suspect you're busy, but I have been assigned to work for you now for two weeks and there is something I just have to tell you.

MARION: You're right, Susan. I am busy now but my work can wait awhile. You sound distressed. Come on in and sit down.

SUSAN: Well, I'm not sure I like the fact that I have been working extra hours on the special project we have to complete. I have even considered quitting my job to find something less demanding, but I don't really want to do that. Can we just talk about this problem for a little while?

MARION: Sure, Sue. I have a meeting in a half hour and I can take the time to to talk with you. If we need more time, before we break up our conversation let's schedule some time to continue talking tomorrow.

Here, clearly, both Sue and Marion have begun a series of transactions aimed at meeting their needs: Sue's need to gain some understanding and perhaps advice so that she can work through what appears to be a double bind, and Marion's need to serve as a caring supervisor willing to help another in a way that can meet their interpersonal needs as well as the needs of the company.

Carefully examine Figure 1-1. This model identifies the major elements in the process of communication as we have talked about it. The communication, person to person, takes place somewhere, some time, and in some cultural context. The place, the time, and the culture help to shape the transactions of the persons. A board room on a Saturday morning in a major city in the South are all important factors in a meeting of business persons. What has brought the people together, the occasion, is equally important.

Goals of communication.   A new manager of a branch bank, Frank Ralston, calls his subordinates together for a dinner at which he intends to introduce his philosophy of carrying out the bank's policies. The occasion is festive, and so the mood among the audience is pleasant when the manager stands to speak. His audience greets the executive's words with positive responses. Frank speaks with both *task* and *relational* goals in mind.

Task goals are those chosen to accomplish a desired act as viewed as a task, and relational goals are those aimed at creating a positive relationship by a communicator with an audience. A positive relationship, one characterized by friendliness, can often aid in the achievement of a task goal (see Figure 1-2). Frank's audience is flattered by the dinner meeting and his friendly manner, and apparently these feelings motivate the listeners to want to do their best to perform the tasks Frank has laid out as goals for the bank. He encodes a message (constructs a message with words and nonverbal expressions), and the audience seeks, by decoding, to make sense of what it hears and sees. The listeners provide Frank with some feedback. His response to the response of the audience reveals communication to be a dynamic and reciprocal process. The internal and external distractions that the communicators experienced in responding to each other can be called noise.

FIGURE 1-2   Communication accomplishes both task and relational goals.

In the pages that follow, we are going to expand our understanding and application of the features in this model, for they are essential in the major forms of communication in the business setting.

A REVIEW OF KEY ISSUES

Successful, satisfying, and productive business is lubricated and cemented by successful, satisfying, and productive communication.

The study and development of the human communication process and skills cannot be set aside as a low priority if a business is to achieve maximum success for both employee and company goals.

Each student of business is not fully trained unless she or he becomes knowledgeable and skillful in business communication.

Business can be viewed as the gainful pursuit of ideas, opinions, and information that are presented symbolically in order to attain the profitable goals of the organization.

Communication in business can be for information sharing or persuasion, verbal play or problem solving.

Communication is meaning-centered. As a process, it is dynamic, ongoing, and characterized by a state of flux.

Meaning is the recognition of relationship, or what happens between two statements or images when recognition occurs.

When persons are able to communicate through the creation of meaning, they construct reality through shared symbols by systematically assigning signals, symbols, and images some sort of meaning. When a person talks, or writes, listens or reads, she or he needs symbolic meaning to make sense of and to share this information.

Communication is transactional, because persons experience as communication psychological events that are constructions of perception in efforts to achieve goals for satisfying various needs. You speak, write, read, and listen to gain something from someone else; in a word, you continually participate in making transactions through communication.

EXPERIENCING EXPERIENCES

This brief in each chapter will discuss experience as a method for developing mastery of skills. We believe activities, when carefully planned, will provide rich experiences for you in developing and mastering skills presented in the text. Therefore, this section is dedicated to specifically explaining why experience with each chapter's activities is important and valuable for learning professional business communication skills.

Communication, like walking, is a daily behavior that all humans engage in. And like walking, it is taken for granted. Communication is a complex activity, and it involves a great number of situational factors.

We speak to other humans every day and often the same humans each day. Some days, the communication is smooth, easy, and enjoyable; but on other days communication with these same individuals is boring, difficult, frustrating, or impossible. Each experience is a learning situation, and over a period of time, the communication effort becomes less difficult. It has something to do with the sequence of behavioral experiencing, observing, evaluating, and then developing when the next opportunity occurs for that behavioral experience.

The activities that follow are designed to provide experience in this four-step sequence with the confident belief that you will master the skills described.

Share our beliefs regarding chapter activities, and we feel you will not only develop specific skills, but have creative fun doing so.

ACTIVITY 1: Analyzing a Communication Act

Select some act of communication that you have observed or been a part of, and try to determine all of the information surrounding this act by filling in the following requested items:

Title of your chosen communication act: _____

_____ Oral communication act   _____ Written communication act

Place/Occasion: _____

Situational circumstances: _____

Time/Length/Date:_____

Persons involved: _____

General subject:_____

Communication purpose goal: _____

Feedback features: _____

Noises or interferences: _____

Communication channels used:_____

Message themes/Contents: _____

Using the information above, design a model that will demonstrate how the communication acts took place. Create the model so that it will show all of the elements of the communication and also the action of the communication.

ACTIVITY 2: The Language of Business or the Business of Language

Select words or phrases that are used in the business environment and try to analyze how and why they communicate messages. These should be "business" terms that you have heard used, heard on TV, or heard others talk about using.

Word/Phrase	Dictionary Meaning	Business Usage Meaning	Possible Alternative Usage or Meaning	Cultural Derivation
put a hold on	1. Keep from going away 2. Restrain 3. Reguard 4. Guard	Stop all action regarding a special issue	Regard some aspect of mailing a contribution	Occurred around the time of the hold button on the phone

EXERCISES

1. In class, discuss public communication and include such subtopics as
   a. growth of population in relation to public communication
   b. growth of technology in relation to public communication
   c. development of communication skills in humans
   d. presentation of communication skills in public education
   e. influences of television, billboards, newspapers, magazines, post office, and modes of travel on public communication
2. Make a list of great speaker/communicators and great writer/communicators. Write down why you put them on your list; share this list with the rest of the class.
3. Discuss such films as *Future Shock* and *The Non-Verbal Agenda* in class, and relate the ideas you find in these words to the field of communication.

NOTES

1. Harold P. Zelko and Frank E. X. Dance, *Business and Professional Speech Communication.* New York: Holt, Rinehart & Winston, 1978, p. 25.

2.   S. Bernard Rosenblatt, T. Richard Cheatham, and James T. Watt, *Communication in Business.* Englewood Cliffs, N.J.: Prentice-Hall, 1977, p. 8.
3.   John J. Makay, "The Communication Analyst Program and Views of Executives," unpublished paper, Speech Communication Association, National Convention, Washington, D.C., 1977.
4.   David K. Berlo, *The Process of Communication.* New York: Holt, Rinehart & Winston, 1960, p. 24.
5.   Gerald R. Miller, *An Introduction to Speech Communication.* 2nd ed. Indianapolis: Bobbs-Merrill, 1972, p. 33.
6.   John J. Makay, *Speaking with an Audience: Communicating Ideas and Attitudes.* New York: Harper & Row Publishers, 1977, p. 8.
7.   John J. Makay and Beverly A. Gaw, *Personal and Interpersonal Communication: Dialogue with the Self and with Others.* Columbus, Ohio: Charles E. Merrill, 1976, p. 9.
8.   John Stewart, "An Interpersonal Approach to the Basic Course." *The Speech Teacher,* January 1972, p. 10.
9.   Gerald R. Phillips and Nancy Metzger, *Intimate Communication.* Boston: Allyn & Bacon, 1976, p. 44.

CHAPTER TWO

LISTENING
ON THE JOB

Of the basic communication skills, listening is given the least amount of attention in public education. The average person assumes that "communication" refers to writing and speaking. Listening is just taken for granted: We all have ears, and so we just naturally use them. We tend to feel that listening is a natural and easy activity to perform. In fact, many people think listening is easy because it can be done while also doing something else. When listening *is* perceived as a complex skill, then mastering it is often thought to require highly specialized skills or techniques—as in training for psychologists or lawyers. Few ever think that these listening skills and techniques are necessary for everyone. The average person rarely views listening as essential for day-to-day communication.

The Speech Communication Association[1] published a document outlining minimal competencies that students should display by the time they graduate from high school. This document, in its section on listening, begin by citing critical needs for essential listening skills in everyone's life:

1. **Occupational**: To assist in obtaining a job; to learn job requirements; and to perform job tasks adequately.
2. **Citizenship**: To provide ability to understand, discuss and evaluate laws, policies and other citizens' viewpoints.
3. **Maintenance**: To form and preserve social relationships; to manage personal finances; to perform consumer tasks; to gain and preserve health; to avoid injury; and to participate in family life and child raising.

15

A significant part of each person's day is spent in listening-related activities. Reading, as well as listening, is considered an information-receiving skill. These two aspects of communication often account for more than 70 percent of our daily communication.

In this chapter we are going to look at a definition of listening, examine some of the major barriers, look at levels and types of listening, and finally, discuss some ways in which we can help ourselves to become better listeners.

LISTENING DEFINED

Ralph Nichols,[2] an expert in listening, states that listening constitutes attention, thought, interpretation, and imagination. Another communication expert, Gerald Goldhaber,[3] believes that listening is a human behavior that functions at one of four levels. The individual can act or operate at any one of these levels:

Level 1 . . . I can hear . . .
Level 2 . . . I can hear and repeat back . . .
Level 3 . . . I hear, can repeat back, and I obey . . .
Level 4 . . . I hear and participate in the communication process. . . .

These two description are the basis for our definition of listening (see Figure 2-1). Listening is a complex behavioral skill that involves preparation, absorption, processing, and feeding back a response to spoken information. This definition has four very important parts or steps. We will examine each individually.

The first step is *preparation.* People must really prepare to listen. This means making a direct effort to focus personal attention. One must deliberately concentrate to clear the mind of distractions. To prepare for listening, an individual must be mentally and physically alert. The human body must make itself ready to listen. This is a conscious effort, and it often involves shifting the body posture or making some adjustment such as turning down a radio or closing the newspaper or book one is holding.

The second step is *absorbing.* The first impression would be to think that the sounds of the speaker's voice must "soak" into the ear. This step, however, is far more complex. Hearing sound is essential, but once the sound is heard, some type of mental identification must take place. This absorbing step often involves the human eye as well as the ear. The eye sees movement or objects along with the sound that the ears hear. When the seeing and hearing occur, a perception takes place. The ears, eyes, and brain work together to create this act of perception. In some ways these three parts of the body operate much like a television antenna. They should work together to pick up a clear signal—or, like the TV and antenna, if the reception is poor, so will be the quality of the picture. This absorption step must be active, accurate, and quick-functioning. If not, it will negatively affect the next step in listening.

FIGURE 2-1   Occupational listening relates directly to productivity.

This third step is *processing.* In short, this is the act of assessing the signals of the previous step. Processing involves interpretation. The individual must create some association with the various signals and symbols picked up in the absorption step. This is a challenging step, because interpretation is a very personal thing. Two individuals hear the sets of sounds but create completely different interpretations. This frequently happens. For example, think back to when you were a child: You are in your bed; the room is dark. You hear some noises while lying there trying to go to sleep. The mind, the ears, and even possibly the eyes strain in the dark room to absorb or perceive what is happening. You make an interpretation: You decide that a monster or ghost is in the room with you. Your older sister hears the same sounds but ignores them, knowing they come from the squeaking floors of an old house. It is this processing step that often leads to listening problems, because something miscues in the interpretation. Even with correct interpretation, listening is not complete. Many people fail to realize there is yet another step.

The fourth and final step is *feeding back a response* to the speaker, to confirm that listening is happening. Again, this feedback is frequently confused with standard communication feedback. It can be quite similar, but it is not the same. When behaving as a listener, one should let the other party know that listening is happening. Listening is not a passive act, nor need it be silent. The listener should let the speaker know that he or she is listening and should do so right at that moment. Leaning forward in a chair, nodding the head, deliberately creating a specific expression on the face, or changing body posture or stance are all examples of this feeding-back reaction. Such behavior is reacting to what has been received from the speaker. It could be responding to the ideas and actions of the speaker. But it should also reflect that the listening lines are open and operating. Feeding back can also be used for regulating the rate or type of listening in process. This active listening occurs only when this fourth step is taking place. It takes deliberate effort, some physical action, and some amount of willingness for interaction with the speaker.

Most people are well trained in "polite" listening which is often little more than facing the speaker and maintaining deliberate verbal silence. This behavior does not constitute listening for many reasons. First, the eyes, brain, and ears can be doing other things without so much as making a movement. Secondly, this is not good listening because the speaker receives no idea of how effectively he or she is presenting the verbal message. This silence is often interpreted that everything is fine, that communication is moving "full steam ahead." Yet, in reality, talking to a brick wall would be just about as productive.

This last step—feeding-back response as a listener—is difficult work. It takes deliberate effort, as well as physical and mental energy. Professionals who get paid to listen, such as psychologists or social workers, will readily share how exhausted they are at the end of a day from sitting at a desk and listening to clients. Unlike speaking, which is more apparent when done improperly, this fourth step in listening can be missing and go unnoticed. Many public speakers have commented on situations in which one person in the audience was asleep in the front row. Yet that silent sleeper made it difficult for the speaker to communicate. Continually glancing down to pick up feedback from the front row and getting nothing from the "sleeper" is most distracting.

The effective listener is active, an individual who enacts all four steps of this listening definition. Complete listening involves constant preparation, absorption, processing, and feeding back reactions in a variety of overt ways.

LISTENING BARRIERS

There are a number of listening barriers. In fact, the numbers would probably go into the thousands. Most of the barriers you encounter would probably fall into one of these categories: mental barriers; emotional barriers; and environmental barriers (see Figure 2-2).

Mental barriers.   Mental barriers to listening are such things as the tendency to avoid subjects that we sense are difficult, ones requiring a lot of mental effort on our part. Often when someone is explaining directions, we tell ourselves that it is too difficult to listen. We can "catch" it later by looking in a book or manual. In the work setting, this frequently happens when employees should be listening for information. They mentally tell themselves, "We can get this 'difficult' information out of a book or ask questions later when we need the information." Some might simply call this mental laziness on the part of the listener, and often it is.

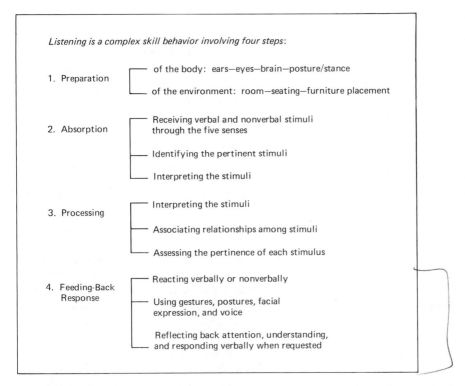

Listening is a complex skill behavior involving four steps:

1. Preparation
   - of the body: ears—eyes—brain—posture/stance
   - of the environment: room—seating—furniture placement

2. Absorption
   - Receiving verbal and nonverbal stimuli through the five senses
   - Identifying the pertinent stimuli
   - Interpreting the stimuli

3. Processing
   - Interpreting the stimuli
   - Associating relationships among stimuli
   - Assessing the pertinence of each stimulus

4. Feeding-Back Response
   - Reacting verbally or nonverbally
   - Using gestures, postures, facial expression, and voice
   - Reflecting back attention, understanding, and responding verbally when requested

FIGURE 2-2 A working definition for listening.

Lack of concentration is another mental barrier. We don't want to take the effort to focus our attention—which is the first step in effective listening. We feel tired, are having a bad day, or maybe are just in a bad mood. In such situations, the energy to focus attention appears to require too much effort. We all have had those experiences on Friday afternoons when we are exhausted and would rather go home to prop our feet up while sitting in our favorite chair instead of listening to an instructor's lecture.

Another barrier is prematurely dismissing a topic: "Yeah, yeah, I've heard all this before." Or, "I've heard enough, I know what it's all about." Mentally, we dismiss the information being conveyed, because we think that we have heard enough or heard it all before.

A third mental barrier is called mental debating. This listening barrier often occurs when we are in a one-on-one discussion with someone and know that we have a different or opposing opinion. While the other person is talking to us, we are setting up contrary evidence in our head for response so we can respond to what is being presented. The listener has all the advantages in doing this. He or she can be formulating some rather sophisticated arguments totally unbeknown to the presenting speaker.

Still another mental barrier is simple daydreaming. This is merely letting our brain take total control of the listening process, excluding the eyes and the ears.

When the brain does this, it not only takes over, it also blocks out the ear's and eye's receiving channels. The brain goes into its own world, doing what it wants rather than concentrating on what is occuring in the communication exchange. This kind of communication interference is dangerous because it goes unnoticed. If someone permits this listening self-discipline continually to break down, eventually that person will not even recognize when this mental "override" control takes place. There is nothing wrong with daydreaming—it is an important part of creativity; but it should not substitute for one's responsibility to listen.

The last major mental barrier is often referred to as a "lack-of-vocabulary dilemma." The speaker uses a word the listener does not know. Rather than express the natural confusion through the face or body posture, the listener goes off on a sidetrack of trying to logically figure out what that word must mean by the way the speaker is using it. If this behavior pattern becomes a habit, the individual using it will build a strong negative barrier that will not only affect listening, but will also eventually affect speaking skills.

To control these mental barriers, we should begin by examining listening-breakdown situations. By identifying the mental barrier, we can often pinpoint the breakdown and how it happened. This is not an easy mental exercise to do in the beginning, but it can help the concerned listener to analyze problems and then do something about these mental barriers as they occur.

Emotional barriers.   Emotional barriers are easier to recognize, both for the listener and for the person speaking. Emotional barriers are usually reflected in the listener's face, gestures, body posture, or sitting position. As a listener you can examine yourself on these actions, but you can also see these barriers within others as they listen to you speak. For effective speaking, we know it is necessary for a communicator to use his or her eyes when checking out the listening level of a receiver. These nonverbal behaviors can often be identified and responded to during the communication process. As listeners we can also perceive these behaviors in ourselves.

The first emotional barrier is anxiety or stress. It is difficult to listen when we are experiencing anxiety or feeling stress. The stress or anxiety uses mental and physical energy that is needed for preparing, absorbing, processing, and feeding back. In such situations, it is necessary to either remove, or at least recognize, the stress or anxiety. If both speaker and listener are aware of such a barrier, each can help the other to compensate for it. Frequently, it makes better sense to recognize it, acknowledge it, and then plan to do the communication exchange at a different time when the listener is more capable of productive interaction.

Anger is another emotional barrier. The greater the anger, the more difficult it is to listen. Anger must always be dealt with before productive listening can take place. The human body uses great amounts of energy experiencing anger, energy that is taken away from the listening process—which prevents the listener from functioning effectively.

Fatigue is another emotional barrier that interferes with listening. Like the mental focus of concentration, emotional fatigue leaves the body's energies drained. When this happens, the eyes and ears may be doing their part, but the brain is not functioning at an effective level. In processing—the third step of listening—the brain takes the major responsibility for interpreting, associating ideas, and weighting or relating independent concepts and facts. If the listener is feeling mental fatigue, the brain doesn't process the information, nor does it cooperate with the eyes and ears. Again, the listener may have to recognize this situation and share it with the speaker. One of the solutions for eliminating this barrier is to take a break or "rest period." Changing gears for just a few minutes can make all the difference. Doing an activity that will let the mind rest for a few moments can usually be productive. We recognize what the coffee break does for the body. Sometimes, the mind also needs such a break. Once the rest or change of pace has happened, it is easier to come back to listening.

As a final thought about this mental-fatigue barrier, we might point out that when the listener takes on an action of rest or change, the speaker should also be involved. Without the involvement of both parties, the listener would merely be employing a version of the earlier-mentioned mental barriers that involve interruption. Under this circumstance, it would be "self-ordained" daydreaming.

A different emotional barrier focuses around personal bias. Listeners may have attitudes, opinions, or values that differ significantly from those of either the speaker or the information being presented. If this is the situation, it is easy to allow bias to interfere with listening. Frequently, when the speaker uses a different accent or sentence structure from the listener, it is easy to lower the level of listening. It is also easy to distract oneself from the listening process because the eye allows clothing style or color to become a barrier. The ears can equally determine some vocal sounds as "unpleasant" or "foreign" and difficult to listen to. Again, the listening level then weakens. Frequently, this barrier is difficult to detect when in process. Few of us want to admit we have bias or prejudices, and we certainly do not easily admit the possibility that this is interfering with our listening ability.

Compared with the mental barriers, the emotional barriers do surface more noticeably when we are involved in listening. We can train ourselves to look for them in ourselves as well as others. Half the battle with overcoming emotional barriers is recognizing them in process. When this recognition takes place, correcting the situation is not all that difficult.

Environmental barriers.   This third category of barriers, by its very nature, is the easiest to identify and work around. Both speakers and listeners can do something about environmental barriers. A sizable part of this book tells you how to deal with these barrier problems as a speaker. Therefore, our purpose here will be to examine them from the listener's perspective (see Figure 2-2).

The first environmental barrier is the faked-attention syndrome—deliberately creating a psychological environment for the speaker by making it appear we are completely absorbed in the behavior of listening. In reality, just the opposite is true. The listener's nonverbal signals—of face, body stance, seat position, or gestures—indicate listening is in action, but the listener's mind is far away. The speaker accepts the created environment and continues giving verbal communication. In a work setting where departments have routine weekly meetings with supervisors, this fake attention is often operating as its best. The meeting leader goes through the agenda in an environment of faked attention as the listeners around the table are "doing their own thing"—from mentally reviewing the morning mail to wondering what is for lunch.

The next environmental barrier is simple physical distraction. As a listener, I should be aware of my distractions. If actions like people passing a doorway or window panel interfere with my listening, then I must learn to seat myself in such a position to visually avoid these situations. Extraneous noise is the most inconsistent barrier. The impact of noise varies greatly from individual to individual. For some, any noise at all in the background interferes with absorption of information by the ear, eye, and brain; others, if they do not have some music or general humming sounds, may find it impossible to absorb and process anything efficiently. Every listener must get to know himself or herself in relation to listening behaviors and environmental barriers. Recognizing what distracts oneself from listening is essential for productive development of listening skills.

When environmental distractions have been identified, solving them then becomes a matter of sharing them with the other listeners present. The next step is to negotiate how to deal with them as a group. This is essential for maintaining a productive work environment: When groups of people are working together in critical listening activities such as problem-solving meetings, they need to recognize environmental listening barriers. This is something most work groups do not give time and energy to. As business organizations carry out such complex activities as quality circles, participative management, and quality control groups, the proper environment for speaking and listening activities must be given consideration.

Another environmental barrier is increasingly being recognized in organizations, owing to some work-group activities. This is the barrier of poor physical arrangements in the room where the listening takes place. Professionals such as doctors, lawyers, and consultants have long recognized the effect of the placement of office furniture, carpet, draperies, and wall hangings in terms of one-to-one communication. Business organizations are becoming more aware of this environmental factor and now consider it in designing conference rooms and shared office space. Not being able to see the speaker makes it difficult for the eyes to do their part in listening. Eyes provide vital information about the speaker's nonverbal behaviors. These clues are essential to carrying out the processing step in effective listening.

Physical discomfort is also a further environmental barrier. It is very difficult to listen when sitting in an uncomfortable chair. Thinking back on any classroom with old hardwood or plastic chairs enforces this point. It appears the ears, eyes, and brain can only absorb as much as the rear area can support. It is difficult to listen if the body is uncomfortable, but it is more difficult to listen if other heads and bodies are blocking the view of the speaker.

The last environmental barrier of major significance is incorrect notetaking. Opinions vary about whether taking notes raises or lowers the level of listening comprehension. Sometimes the speaker provides the clue as to whether the listener should or should not take notes. But more frequently, the listener must make this important decision without clues. Note-taking, unless well planned, will usually interfere with listening. The type of listening being employed is a critical factor in deciding whether to take written notes or not.

Assuming that note-taking is necessary, it is more important to know how to take notes. If notes are to be taken, the listener always will find it easiest to take notes with a small tape recorder rather than with pencil and paper. This, of course, is not always possible. When taking pencil-and-paper notes, keep some of the following guidelines in mind:

1. Use an easy-writing pen, one that does not require a great deal of pressure.
2. Use good, heavy, lined paper to keep the notes in an orderly structure, easy to glance back over for accuracy checking when the speaker pauses briefly.
3. Have a hard surface to write on, such as a table or clipboard.
4. Divide the paper with a vertical line down the middle of each page, with the heading "facts" on the left-hand column; the right-hand column should be titled "personal reactions/questions." When you take notes, use the columns for these two purposes.
5. Write out notes using key-word outlining and brief fact listing (as opposed to sentence or manuscript writing style).
6. Use your own abbreviations or shorthand symbols to save time writing.
7. Use diagrams, charts, scales, and quick-sketch images to summarize thematic concepts or theories.
8. Use a numbering system to get down procedural, directional, or structural units of information.
9. If the note-taking begins to seriously interfere with the listening comprehension, let the speaker know verbally or nonverbally that this is happening.

Before we finish the discussion of listening barriers, two other barriers should be examined. These two barriers do not fall into any specific category. At times, they relate directly to or interrelate with some of the mental, emotional, or environmental barriers already mentioned.

The first one is *defensiveness*. As listeners we often put ourselves into a defensive posture. When involved in listening on the job, people often face the impulse to be defensive. When the listener feels the need to be defensive about the information being communicated, this attitude will negatively affect the listening. The defensive barrier is dangerous because it touches listening at each step of the process. When we prepare to listen, a "self-protective bias" makes it difficult to ready the body, mind, and environment for positive listening. In a defensive situation the receiving step of identification and perception becomes difficult for the eyes, ears, and brain. Processing the information takes on a bias that sets up the listener to feed back false responses, and these directly affect the transactional nature of the communication. At this point the defensiveness has not only affected the listener, but it has posed a barrier for the speaker. Once this cycle has started, it is difficult to stop—which results in an obvious breakdown in the communication.

The second barrier that does not fit exclusively into any of the three previously mentioned categories is the *balance-of-power struggle*. Frequently, in two-person communication a subtle power struggle goes on between speaker and listener. Both parties want or feel a need to dominate the situation. They feel the person speaking has the greater power, and see the listener as holding the weaker position. Of course, this is not true. The act of listening can be very powerful. We only need a few minutes of intense interaction with a good listener to discover how easy this individual makes it for us to talk. The dynamics of oral communication, with its transactional nature, can allow for speaking and listening to be equally powerful and effective. This is apparent when we experience seeing a dear friend after a long separation. We both have much to talk about and yet both want so much to hear what the other has to share. When a superior and subordinate are interacting in the work setting, this struggle for balance of power often becomes a real listening barrier.

In summing up listening barriers, the first action to effectively eliminate these barriers is to recognize them in process. The second step is to make an overt effort to remove the barrier once it is recognized. This strategy takes patience and practical experience before the skills you develop will become apparent.

LEVELS AND TYPES OF LISTENING

Types and levels of listening tend to correspond to one another. There are no absolutes to prove that levels and types of listening always follow specific patterns of correlation. Still, on close examination, levels and types of listening tend to reflect a pattern (see Figure 2-3).[4]

Levels of listening.   The levels of listening can be defined as superficial, intellectual, and emotional. They vary in the amount of energy it takes to listen at each level. Variables such as the length of time, the communication situation, the environment, and the personalities of the parties involved all affect the amount of energy needed at each level. It is logical that a superficial listening level requires less energy than an intellectual level. The emotional level of listening is considered the most difficult, since it requires the most energy and concentration.

Listening at the superficial level takes less effort, because there is no depth of content, and less interaction is necessary between speaker and listener. Little or no exchange exists between the parties involved.

Intellectual listening does require more energy and effort. Not only do the eyes and ears get more involved, but the brain must perform critical thinking. Such listening will have purposeful meaning and will contribute to the communication

LISTENING BARRIERS

MENTAL BARRIERS (based in the brain)	EMOTIONAL BARRIERS (based in the whole body)	ENVIRONMENTAL BARRIERS (based outside the body)
Avoidance of difficult subjects	Anxiety or stress	Faked-attention syndrome
Lack of concentration	Anger	Physical distractions
Premature dismissal of speaker's topic	Fatigue	
Mental debating	Personal bias	Poor physical room arrangements
Daydreaming		Physical discomfort
Lack-of-vocabulary dilemma		Poor note-taking
DEFENSIVENESS		
BALANCE-OF-POWER STRUGGLE		

FIGURE 2-3   Listening-barrier chart.
Fetzer and Byrum-Gaw, *Becoming an Active Listener,* Dayton: Kettering Center, 1982.

interaction. In superficial listening, the four steps do not require the same level of involvement that is essential at the intellectual level.

The third level, emotional listening, is the most difficult. With feelings and mental processes operating simultaneously, a great deal more energy is needed. More opportunity exists for listening barriers to occur. And at this level, the third listening step—association and interpretation—becomes just as difficult as the fourth step—feedback reaction. Listening at the emotional level, a person can experience conflict between the third and fourth steps. For example, suppose that processing the incoming information was upsetting but has been completed. Now the listener deliberately feeds back a response that is different from the one being internally felt. The mind overrules, deciding it is better to provide a modified response. Within the listener, this creates a strained tension that then affects the entire transaction.

This emotional level of listening is hard work. People who do it for long periods of time will often complain of back and neck aches. They can experience headaches and intense muscular exhaustion. The draining of energy can reflect in the facial expression of the listener. The listener can experience physical and mental exhaustion.

Types of listening.   The level of listening frequently corresponds to the type of listening. The superficial level of listening happens in small talk, routine conversational communication. This listening would be typed as appreciative. It is enjoyable by nature and offers visualization to the listener in such activities. Listening to stories or jokes or experiencing enjoyment from hearing people perform or share their life experiences is natural. Conversational listening can often be superficial in nature, but it does require a two-way involvement. A talk-listen-talk-listen cycle takes place. If the cycle breaks, the interaction usually stops or the activity changes.

Supportive listening also corresponds to this superficial level. This kind of listening displays concern or encouragement that supports the speaker and inspires him or her to continue speaking. We experienced this as children, seeking mommy or daddy's comfort for a hurt finger.

The second listening level, which is based on intellectual content, correlates with the evaluative type of listening. In evaluative listening, the process step becomes the focus, requiring additional effort in order to provide useful and constructive feedback response to the speaker. The focus is positive because it is based on creating relationships or associations of the speaker's information after it has been processed by the listener.

At the intellectual level a critical or argumentative type of listening can also exist. The focus here is just the opposite of the focus for evaluative listening. In argumentative listening, the listener is in search of loopholes, or the "weak links." Here, the listener is constructing a relationship based on negative pieces of information. The intellectual listening level involves judgmental action, both evaluative and argumentative. Each is opposite the other, with one focusing on positive information and the other on negative. To be a skillful listener, you must know which type is needed and then deliberately use it.

The third level of listening corresponds with the empathic listening types. The one most recognized is reflective listening. Here the listener's aim is to be totally nonjudgmental. The focus is on the total content of incoming information. Absorbing and processing the whole message must take place first, so that the listener can present it back to the speaker as a means for listening validation.

The other type of listening at the emotional level is interpretative. Listening of this type searches for the implicit meaning in the received information as it relates to the speaker. It is informally referred to it as "reading between the lines." Interpretative listening often occurs at this emotional listening level. It requires a lot of mental and physical energy for the skilled listener. The deliberate effort and hard work is apparent when the listener feels physical tiredness or tension after practicing it over an extended period of time.

The final type of listening—probing—is frequently used at any level, but it's especially needed at the emotional level. Probing is a specialized type of listening that functions well at any level. It is especially useful for the listener wishing to move from one level into another. Probing has a journalistic nature. During the fourth listening step, the listener, by feeding back "who," "what," "when," "where," and "how" questions to the speaker, can initiate the search for more information. "Why" questions are usually not good ones to include, because they can bring out defensiveness in the speaker.

Knowing about types and levels of listening can help the concerned listener *decide how* to listen and *select* the *level* of involvement at which to participate in the communication interaction. As with overcoming listening barriers, practice and patience are necessary in working with levels and types of listening. Proficiency at choosing a deliberate level and type of listening is developed only with awareness and repeated experiences. The growth of these skills is observable in communication behaviors when individuals use them on a regular basis.

HELPING OURSELVES TO LISTEN

Helping ourselves to listen takes deliberate effort and planning. Developing effective listening is an ongoing process of skill attainment. Like the communication skills of speaking, reading, and writing, listening really never reaches a level of complete perfection. That we spend our lifetime working on this skill is a major part of the excitement and challenge in developing it. Since these levels of skill development are unique to human beings, working toward them provides us with constant creative opportunity during our life time.

The formula we present for listening is based on the "three R's." For listening, the three R's represent Readying, Reaching, and Reflecting (see Figure 2-4).

Readying. The first step in listening is preparing, and that is exactly what an effective listener should do. Skilled listeners will detach themselves from what they are doing when the need to listen becomes apparent.

Readying means getting oneself, the immediate environment, one's feelings, ears, eyes, and brain ready for listening. The best way to start preparation is to check for barriers that might easily appear. This readying stage also has a physical dimension: trying to put work and environmental distraction out of the way. There is truth in the old axiom, "Out of sight, out of mind."

Put the body in a comfortable posture, one leaning toward the speaker; sit, or else stand so that you are open to the speaker. Get your eyes working in your listening by focusing them squarely on the speaker's face. It can help to assume the same body posture or stance as the speaker's and to establish a parallel eye level. Maintaining a parallel eye level makes a positive difference. Every adult that has ever squatted down to be on an eye level with a child has discovered the secret of powerful listening. If a door needs to be closed, a phone taken off the hook, or a book closed, the small effort to do it is worth the positive listening results that can follow. Once the readying action is complete, the next R should be put into action.

Reaching. Reaching out to the speaker is a physical and an emotional action, providing nonverbal encouragement to the speaker to continue. Nodding and smiling establish this mood of encouragement. At the reaching stage, verbal silence is truly golden. Let the speaker have the time, floor, and control to present the intended information. If, as a listener, you wish to use verbal encouragement,

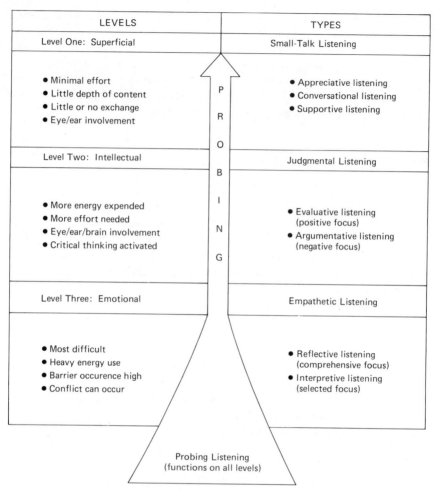

FIGURE 2-4 Levels and types of listening.
Fetzer and Byrum-Gaw, *Becoming an Active Listener,* Dayton: Kettering Center, 1982.

stick to one-word reactions when possible, such as "wow!" "great!" "really?" "wonderful!" Directional short statements might be necessary at times, and when used correctly, they can reach out to the speaker. Some examples would be "Tell me more!" "Go on!" "Sounds great!" "And then?" "What else?"

Sometimes, the reaching may need to be more sophisticated. As a listener, you may have to offer probing questions for more information or to change into a different listening level or type. Some examples would be, "What did you do then?" "How would another person have handled it?" "What did you want to happen?" "How should it be different?" "What was your reaction to the situation?" When you use probing, supplement it with obvious facial expression and hand gestures. Changing body posture to a more open position will add encouragement for more information. And most important, when the probing works, be

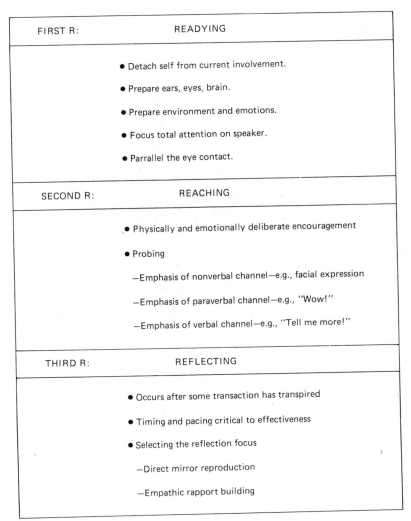

FIRST R:	READYING
	• Detach self from current involvement.
	• Prepare ears, eyes, brain.
	• Prepare environment and emotions.
	• Focus total attention on speaker.
	• Parrallel the eye contact.
SECOND R:	REACHING
	• Physically and emotionally deliberate encouragement
	• Probing
	—Emphasis of nonverbal channel—e.g., facial expression
	—Emphasis of paraverbal channel—e.g., "Wow!"
	—Emphasis of verbal channel—e.g., "Tell me more!"
THIRD R:	REFLECTING
	• Occurs after some transaction has transpired
	• Timing and pacing critical to effectiveness
	• Selecting the reflection focus
	—Direct mirror reproduction
	—Empathic rapport building

FIGURE 2-5   The three R's for active and creative listening.
Fetzer and Byrum-Gaw, *Becoming an Active Listener,* Dayton: Kettering Center, 1982.

pleased with visible reactions to let the speaker know you are listening intently. Display nonverbal compliments in the facial expression and eye contact. Once the reaching-out has been achieved, you as a listener can move into the reflecting stage at the appropriate moment.

Reflecting.   The reflecting stage usually begins after a few moments of communication interaction have transpired. Starting this behavior too quickly or holding back with it too long can make your listening ineffective. The skillful listener has to know when to start this stage. Some variables have to be considered: the other person, the situation surrounding the communication, and the relation-

FIGURE 2-6 Reaching out to listen provides nonverbal encouragement to the speaker.

ship between speaker and listener before, as well as during the communication interaction.

This reflection stage determines the success of the third and final step in the listening process, feeding back accurately. This is letting the speaker know that you, as a listener, are receiving the information accurately. Reflecting involves verbal response along with some nonverbal action. Reflecting can convey empathy to the speaker. You, as listener, should select words that will establish positive rapport between you and the other person. This rapport will encourage a high comfort level for the speaker and suggest you are participating in her or his world of reality. This will display personal concern and interest in the speaker. If there is tension or anxiety within the exchange, the listener's reflection words will help to reduce it. When the interaction is problem-based, this reflection exchange can be so beneficial that the actual listening behavior can initiate the potential solution to the difficulty. The danger at this stage is to reflect incorrect information because you did not listen completely or objectively in order to reflect accurately. Another danger with reflecting happens when the listener completes a verbal feedback response and then, deserting the primary role of listener, continues talking on a listener-initiated topic.

To become a skillful listener, able to use readying, reaching, and reflecting techniques effectively, requires practice. Even more than practice, it requires a willingness to take risks, to trust the other person, to avoid slipping into a defensive position or power-balance role. With some conscious effort, regular practice, and sincerity, every person can be a skillful listener and, at the same time, discover some very beautiful things about life and people that might have otherwise gone unnoticed.

A REVIEW OF KEY ISSUES

Listening is one of the four basic communication skills.
1. It is falsely perceived to be a natural behavior.
2. It is falsely perceived to be a simple behavior.

Listening is a complex, skilled behavior that involves preparation, absorption, processing, and feeding back a response to spoken information.
1. It is deliberate mental and physical preparation of the whole person.
2. It is absorbing with complete ear, eye, and brain involvement.
3. It is processing and interpreting received information and the relationships of symbols presented.
4. It is feeding back verbal and nonverbal responses to the speaker to communicate that listening is happening.

There are many types of listening barriers.
1. Mental barriers are
    a. avoidance of difficult subjects
    b. lack of concentration
    c. premature dismissal of a topic
    d. mental debating
    e. daydreaming
    f. lack-of-vocabulary dilemma
2. Emotional barriers are
    a. stress
    b. anger
    c. fatigue
    d. personal bias
3. Environmental barriers are
    a. faked attention
    b. physical distraction
    c. physical arrangement
    d. physical discomfort
    e. incorrect note-taking
4. Two major barriers in categories of their own are
    a. defensiveness
    b. balance-of-power struggle

The levels of listening tend to correlate with the types of listening.
1. Levels of listening are
    a. superficial
    b. intellectual
    c. emotional
2. Types of listening are
    a. small-talk listening (appreciative, conversational, supportive)
    b. judgmental (evaluative, argumentative)
    c. empathetic (reflective, interpretive)

Helping ourselves to become better listeners requires effort, practice, and genuine concern, using the three R's of listening:
1. **readying** the mind and body for the act of listening
2. **reaching** out to the speaker with physical and emotional deliberateness
3. **reflecting** back to the speaker that total listening and understanding is in process

EXPERIENCING EXPERIENCES

Listening, as this chapter indicates, takes practice and concentration. And most important, developing skill in listening requires a positive attitude. Listening is one communication skill that is very easy to ignore or give minimal attention to in day-to-day situations.

The following activities are designed to create awareness and sensitivity to the listening process. Only after awareness is deliberately present is the individual ready to practice working on the development of the skills described in this chapter. Consider the importance of personal attitude as you are involved in the following activities.

ACTIVITY 1: Listen to My Listening Definition

The class should form into small groups of three. Individual group members should then write down their own definition of listening on paper and, with this definition, provide one example of how it has worked for them. Once everyone has completed the task, then each should share his or her information with the other two. Allow only one minute for each person to share.

At the end of three minutes, have silent reflection of what happened. Class members should write down their own perceptions on a sheet of paper. The class should then form back into one large group, and all students should share their perceptions. Someone should act as recorder and list the comments on the blackboard. Consider:

How many comments were similar?
Did certain ones constantly keep coming up?
Was it difficult to listen while talking? Why?
Was it difficult to listen while writing? Why?
Was it difficult to listen while reading? Why?
Could all of the information and comments be integrated to formulate a group definition for listening?

ACTIVITY 2: Bar the Barriers

Take a videotape recorder and set up the camera to record the class on a particular day. (It is best to have a camera operator who is not a member of the class.) Conduct the class as planned, and ignore the camera taping. The next day, play the tape back for the class. Each student should have a worksheet, and students should record the barriers in the proper column as they witness them played back on the tape.

BAR-THE-BARRIER WORKSHEET

MENTAL BARRIERS		EMOTIONAL BARRIERS		ENVIRONMENTAL BARRIERS	
Type	Evidence	Type	Evidence	Type	Evidence

DEFENSIVENESS BARRIERS	BALANCE-OF-POWER BARRIERS

After the tape has run for about fifteen or twenty minutes, students should compare what they have written on their worksheets.

How many barriers have been identified in the class?

Which ones are the most prevalent?

Are all the barriers that are listed supported with clear documentation?

Can any or all of these barriers be removed?

Which ones can be removed by the speaker (teacher)?

Which ones can be removed by the listeners (students)?

ACTIVITY 3: Life Listening

Take a ride on some form of public transportation. Acting as an observer, watch two other passengers who are involved in a conversation. After the observation period, write down your perceptions. Bring your list of perceptions to class with a brief, one-paragraph description of the situation. Compare findings.

What common listening problems occurred in many of the recorded incidents?

How were they alike?

How was each unique to itself?

What types and levels of listening were displayed?

How did you or could you label the types and levels of listening you observed?

EXERCISES

1. Talk about listening throughout the remainder of the course, each time students do performance assignments in class.

2. Ask a lawyer, psychologist, or other professional to come to class and talk about listening as it is used on a day-to-day basis in his or her work.

NOTES

1. Ronald Bassett, Nilwon Whittington, and Ann Staton-Spicer, "The Basics in Speaking and Listening for High School Graduates: What Should be Assessed?" *Communication Education Journal,* November 1978, p. 296.
2. Ralph G. Nichols and Thomas R. Lewis, *Are You Listening?* New York: McGraw-Hill Book Co., Inc., 1957.
3. Gerald Goldhaber and Estelle Zannes, *Stand Up And Speak Out,* Reading, Mass.: Addison-Wesley, 1978.
4. Ronald C. Fetzer and Beverly Byrum-Gaw, *Becoming an Active Listener,* workshop training manual, Dayton: The Kettering Center, 1982.

CHAPTER THREE

INTRODUCTION TO PRESENTATIONAL SPEAKING

Although presentational speaking may be an infrequent experience for most persons working in organizations, the task of facing an audience with confidence and poise is important. Certainly, there are men and women in positions that require them to speak to audiences regularly, and there are those who perhaps face a group only periodically. In either case, achieving skillful communication is essential. Most executives recognize the importance of public speaking, although many lack the skills that would make them effective at the lectern. Often, indeed, the business communicator feels that speaking with an audience is a duty to be avoided as much as possible. This is because presenting oneself with a prepared message *in front* of an audience appears to be a highly threatening experience. The business world is filled with persons who regard themselves as competent and expert in one or more phases of business but who do not see themselves as competent and expert speakers. "I received a pilot's license at the age of forty; I jumped from a plane as a skydiver a year later; I have tried many dangerous challenges, but I just cannot face an audience," remarked one vice-president who sought tutoring in public speaking. He is not unusual. So, to prepare you for speaking before an audience, we will begin by considering key attitudes.

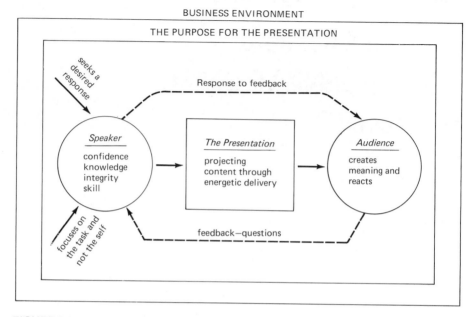

FIGURE 3-1   Model for presentational speaking.

BOX 3-1   KEY ATTITUDES FOR PRESENTATIONAL SPEAKING

The effective business communicator should:

1. want to share information enthusiastically
2. regard herself or himself as *the* expert to speak
3. be primarily aimed at significantly helping each listener
4. feel strongly that presentational speaking is a welcome opportunity
5. nurture, then act on, the belief that speaking can be fun

Each of the points in Box 3-1 is basic to creating a positive attitude toward public speaking and to motivating the reluctant or inexperienced speaker to develop skills.

Although most communication for business persons is informal, there are important occasions that require speaking to an audience from behind a lectern. Researchers conducted a survey of business graduates, a majority of whom stated that they used informal interpersonal communication more frequently than public speaking. But when asked what they would like to have more training in, they often chose public speaking.[1] The study does not offer a clear explanation for this finding. But we feel that though one may not speak often from the lectern, one finds, in business, that when it becomes necessary to make a presentation or a public speech, one must perform with confidence and skill.

A university professor who works in casual clothes recently made this observation: "I bought a very expensive and elegant suit. I don't wear it often but there are occasions when it becomes necessary to look my best in a suit. I am confident that when I go to my closet, take it out, and put it on, it will serve my needs." To the business person, speaking from the lectern is often like the professor and his suit. When the occasion calls for a poised, confident, clear speaker, the business person needs to have the skills available to serve her or his needs.

Perhaps the best place to begin our study of presentational speaking is with a concise view of audience analysis, followed by a focus on the essential qualities of a good speaker. A speaker who wants to develop these qualities must consider them in light of the speaker-audience relationship. The audience can listen most readily to a speaker who projects with confidence, knowledge, integrity, and skill. To adapt to the audience, you must first complete an audience analysis.

WHAT IS AUDIENCE ANALYSIS?

Audience analysis is an investigative procedure. The communicator who wants to relate a message as realistically as possible undertakes an inquiry into the features of the audience. The communicator looks for features that are likely to influence the ways the listener or listeners are going to respond. We use the words *listener* and *listeners* because in the business world, a speaker can make a presentation to an audience of one important listener or to a number of persons. For example, we recently advised an executive trainer for the telephone company about making an important presentation to a single high-level executive who was just coming into her department. "I've spoken as an instructor to a number of classes and I have addressed small groups of executives," she told us, "but this is a first for me—I have an hour with our new vice-president and I have to brief him on the new computerized system we have adopted." Whether you are to address a single individual, a larger group, or a mass audience, you can increase the probability of success by audience analysis.

We will be referring to the importance of being effective with an audience throughout the discussion on presentational and public communication. Affecting the perception and response of the audience, or course, is the speaker's aim—*the specific purpose of a presentation is the precise response sought from the audience!* Box 3-2 contains four primary questions to answer in analyzing the audience. Study

BOX 3-2   BASIC QUESTIONS FOR AUDIENCE ANALYSIS

1. What does the audience know, and how do its members feel, about me and the organization I am representing?
2. What does the audience know, and how do its members feel, about the subject we are to share together?
3. What does the audience know, and how do its members feel, about this occasion for speaking?
4. How does the audience regard itself in this communicative setting?

FIGURE 3-2   Effective speaking from the podium is part of the job for many professionals.

them carefully, and answer them as an initial step in preparing a presentation. Similar questions designed particularly for persuasive communication are included in Chapter 5.

ESSENTIAL QUALITIES FOR A GOOD SPEAKER

Answers to the four basic questions for analyzing an audience can give the business communicator a valuable profile of the group he or she is to face. Answers to these questions can be found by talking to individuals who can provide accurate and current information about members of the audience. A speaker can read survey data, annual reports, or other printed materials to learn about an audience. Once you know whom you are to address, you can find ways to obtain pertinent information to guide you in targeting your presentation to appeal to the needs and capabilities of the audience.

The effective business communicator is a person who possesses the essential qualities of a good speaker: confidence, integrity, knowledge, and skill. The need to "get the facts straight" and make a good case seems heightened today, because business and governmental leaders recognize significant communication problems inside and outside their organizations, problems that are significantly linked to effective presentational and public speaking. A major midwestern corporation recently sent most of its vice-presidents and all of its managers to a plush motel in Florida to spend a week brainstorming and identifying major problems in the effectiveness of the company. At the end of the week, notes were organized and compiled in a huge notebook. Sixteen major problems were identified, and a third of them were specific communication problems. Presentational communication showed up as a major weakness for key personnel. Our experience in working with men and women in business and other professional settings confirms that this weakness is not unusual. Indeed, the business person needs to speak with confidence, integrity, knowledge, and skill.

Confidence. The term confidence, as we use it, refers to being able to speak both with a strong sense or belief in oneself and one's organization and with a specific purpose for communicating. In addition, it refers to being able to speak with minimal anxiety. In a word, good speakers communicate with confidence in what they have to say and with nerves under control. Audiences who feel that a speaker lacks self-confidence and belief in the ideas expressed seem unwilling to pay serious attention to that speaker, and feel uncomfortable about what is being said. Put yourself in an audience for a moment. Are you likely to feel confident about accepting information from a shaky speaker who reflects little genuine feeling about his or her subject and purpose? Can you comfortably listen to the speaker who projects so much nervousness that she or he seems terribly ill at ease and uncertain? Quite often, a speaker appears to lack confidence in what she or he is saying, but actually lacks confidence in the ability to offer a presentation with ease and skill. A great deal of practical advice is available to novice speakers about performance anxiety or speech tension and how to minimize it in order to achieve a high level of self-confidence.[2] Some of these ideas will be developed here on the assumption that the speaker who manifests considerable *self*-confidence when speaking before an audience will reveal confidence in the *ideas* being presented as well.

Students of public speaking have traditionally expressed concern about stage fright. Gerald Miller offers the opinion:

> Probably, the seeds of stage fright are sown when early childhood attempts to communicate are punished by parents. Such negative responses not only cause withdrawal from interaction situations, they also contribute to low self-concept. If the child learns to withdraw from speaking situations, it ensures that when he is trapped in circumstances requiring communication he will experience high anxiety and perform poorly. His poor performance elicits more negative feedback, and the vicious process becomes self-perpetuating.[3]

Miller's view seems to be one generally held by many other communication theorists. Speech tension or performance anxiety is a normal state when one is facing the challenge of having to speak before an audience. Picture a packaging researcher, Judy, for a moment. For eighteen months she has been working for a large corporation that develops, produces, and markets lawn-care products. Judy is reasonably confident in her ability to undertake varied research in the packaging of most of the company's products. Her primary attention for the past six months has been given to a new liquid lawn food and weed control developed to provide competition to the fast-growing use of liquid lawn treatments offered by lawn-service companies. The time has come for the department Judy works in to present its proposal for sound and attractive packages to the Executive Research Board. Judy wants to look and sound good to the board, she wants to represent her department and her individual work in a superior way, and she wants the board to accept the proposal for packaging with complete confidence. She has no guarantee these three goals will be achieved, because the board has a history of turning down about half of the initial products brought before them. Furthermore, she is uncertain about her speaking abilities, for she avoided public speaking in her college studies and her professional life. Still, her department manager insists she is to speak for them. Indeed, for Judy, the performance is important and the outcome is uncertain. What should she do? In the case of Bill Cranston, a useful answer to this question is provided.

Bill Cranston is a vice-president of environmental management for a corporation and he has confidence in himself as a public and presentational speaker. But even though he has been an environmental specialist for twenty years, his "speaking confidence" is a new feature of his behavior. Recently he phoned a private communication consultant and indicated he could no longer continue to avoid speaking in front of his subordinates and in public. "I don't want to be a grand orator," he said, "I just want to be able to speak to the Milwood Rotary or my group in Ridgewood without making a fool of myself, or breaking into a cold sweat. Can you help me?" Bill indicated that although he had served on important committees whose members included persons like the mayor of the city and the governor, he did not have the confidence to give a speech. With practical instruction, dedicated concentration, plenty of practice, and objective evaluation, he has become a confident speaker who actually *enjoys* the challenge and fun of addressing an audience. How did he do it? He learned basic information and techniques about dealing with performance anxiety and speech tension, and he applied what he learned.

Bert Bradley suggests that this kind of behavior is "a normal form of anxiety, or emotional tension, occurring in anyone confronted with a situation in which the performance is important and the outcome is uncertain."[4] "Normal" is here a key word, because it certainly is not unusual or atypical for *anyone,* regardless of status, stature, or experience, to become nervous about having to speak to an audience. Professional performers, skilled business persons, interested citizens in civic groups, persons in just about all occupations and roles experience it. Often, self-occupied and tense speakers feel they are among the few unable to speak with ease. To the contrary, this tension is common! "Performance" is another key word, because most people seem to feel that giving a speech requires a performance (and it does), and that they just simply are not performers. "I'll go to any depths any time in a submarine," one Navy recruiter told his communication instructor, "before I'll go to the high school and make a recruiting speech." He was suggesting that he simply was not a performer. Yet we all perform in our roles each day, and the public or presentational speaking task is just another performance. However, the fact that a speaking performance is both "important" and holds "uncertainty" in its outcome heightens the tension. No one is asked to make a speech or presentation that is unimportant. The audience wants and/or needs information from the speaker. It is important to the listeners. On the other side of the lectern, the speaker wants to look and sound good to the audience, impress its members with the performance and satisfy them that they have gained desirable and necessary information. Clearly, the demands on the speaker are important and thus can cause nervous feelings.

Add to this nervousness the feelings of uncertainty that stem from the speaker's recognition that she or he wants to move the audience to action. If we know for certain that a positive outcome is definitely going to result from our efforts, we can feel secure and comforted. However, a speaker who faces an audience, regardless of the rhetorical goal, has no guarantee of effectiveness; public speaking, therefore, deals with a probability. A teacher hopes that the students will learn certain principles after hearing a lecture; a political candidate hopes to win votes after speaking to an audience; the after-dinner speaker hopes to evoke laughter. But in each case, the speaker must realize that some listeners will not learn; some will not vote; and some will not laugh. The outcome is uncertain. Regardless of anxiety, the speaker's tension can be minimized. In fact, nervous energy can be put to positive use in making communication as effective as possible.

Because the speaker wants to succeed but is uncomfortable and uncertain about what to expect on standing up and looking out into an audience, it is easy to feel pressure from a strong desire to succeed. This can cause a person to experience physiological, evaluational, and withdrawal symptoms. These symptoms are familiar to us all. We have had them. We will experience them in the future. *Physiological* symptoms include dryness in the mouth, flowing adrenaline, quickening heartbeat, and a quivering voice, to name just a few. *Evaluational* symptoms are feelings of inadequacy, and cognitive inner messages such as, "I don't know why I am speaking anyway, when it's the thing I do with the least amount of skill." Evaluative symptoms create a negative and distorted self-image. The third symptom is the *withdrawal*—the desire for *flight* rather than *fight*. The speaker who talks nervously for two or three minutes and then turns out the lights to have the audience focus solely on her slides is withdrawing. The speaker who stares at his shoes, then at the ceiling, is withdrawing. Some executives send subordinates to represent them; they are withdrawing.

These symptoms are not usually exclusive, but are inextricably bound together. We usually find one symptom more dominant than others.

When Judy finally made her presentation on new packaging for liquid lawn treatments, she first noticed physiological symptoms that seemed to bring out evaluational symptoms that then seemed to stimulate feelings of withdrawal. Throughout her twenty-minute message all three symptoms seemed to plague her. She was certainly relieved when she finished the presentation. She vowed to become a confident and effective speaker. She had a strong desire to succeed. But this desire can also cause the symptoms to occur unless the psychology of control is applied. Before discussing this psychology, let's examine some other causes.

Wanting to succeed with confidence but feeling uncertain can generate approach-avoidance behavior. "On the one hand, I want to accept the challenge of speaking (approach), but on the other hand, I have doubts as to my ability and my skills (avoidance)." Such behavior is clearly evident in the efforts of a shy man who wants a first date with a woman he has admired for some time. He approaches the phone courageously with his speech well in mind. Then after dialing two numbers he hangs up the receiver and walks away. Approach—avoid—and then symptoms of tension usually appear.

For the speaker who lacks sufficient confidence, a misinterpretation of the situation calling for the speech also creates speech tension. Michelle is a communications writer for The United Way. When she was asked to make her first appearance before a small group of top executives from local businesses and industries, she was terrified. "My God," she thought, "how can I face all those tough-minded power brokers?" She continued to create a difficult situation *in her mind,* rather than try to create a realistic picture. Once she met the group, twelve men and three women, and found them relaxed, informal, and quite pleasant, Michelle realized much of her anxiety was caused by misinterpreting the speaking situation. The misinterpretation seemed to bring out physiological, evaluational, and withdrawal symptoms.

Judy, Bill, Michelle, and others like them, on careful analysis discovered the primary cause of their lack of confidence, their speech anxiety, was a worrisome preoccupation with "the self." Self-consciousness, characterized by "I" messages, seems to be at the base of nervousness. "I" messages are the inner statements that include thoughts such as, "I don't feel comfortable," "I know my nervousness must really show," "I wish I were someplace else." All the thoughts are directed inward at "I," rather than outward at the audience.

The psychology of control in this case is to focus *solely* on the message and the audience during the preparation and presentation of a speech. A speaker who focuses solely on the message and the audience is not likely to experience any significant degree of self-consciousness, and the three kinds of symptoms of speech anxiety and tension will become minimal. We have used this principle with hundreds of people, not only students on campus but men and women in business, and it works. We say: *Focus on the audience, concentrate on your message and your audience, and you will greatly improve your confidence as a speaker.* Furthermore, it is important to remember several other principles: A confident speaker is one fully prepared, who realizes the audience is friendly, and who communicates with integrity and knowledge. Before turning to integrity and knowledge, remember one more thing. Confidence grows with experience, so the business person who *really* wants to develop confidence will try to speak frequently. Look for speaking opportunities and make the most of them.

Integrity.   More than a thousand years ago, communication theorists noted that the impact of a speaker on an audience was often dependent upon the speaker's ethos. The ethos of the speaker, in the traditional sense, is his or her character, intelligence, and good will, as perceived by the audience. If this ethos is established in the minds of hearers before the speaker begins to speak, we say the ethos is extrinsic. On the other hand, when the ethos is generated and affected by the speech itself, we say the ethos is intrinsic. The point is that ethos affects the audience response tremendously, and so we will devote considerable space to it in this section of the text. Contemporary communication researchers have added to the literature on ethos by completing many studies on credibility, a phenomenon we often use simultaneously with ethos.

Aristotle maintained that the speaker's ethos was a dominant mode of proof and consisted of the listener's evaluation of the speaker's intelligence, character, and good will. Contemporary researchers extended these features of ethos in their studies on communicator credibility. These studies suggest that the ethos or credibility of the speaker includes also the audience's perception of the speaker's expertise, trustworthiness, and dynamism. Other research lengthens the list of factors of influence to include identification, leadership, and charisma—the mystical quality of attractiveness that some persons seem to possess and others do not. The point for us to keep in mind is that *the effect we have on an audience is determined often by the ethos and credibility constructed in our listeners' minds as a result of who we seem to be and/or represent.* This personal "inner construction" is the result not only of predispositions in the listening mind about us and our purpose for speaking, but also of both the interaction with us in the actual speech setting and the evaluation of past communication.

A professor was once employed to conduct a one-day public speaking seminar for corporate executives who were to participate in a new public-speaking program. The program itself was designed to help raise the company's credibility in the eyes of the public. However, the professor knew that the executives were uneasy about having to take a short course in speech from an outside—an "egghead" from the university who was probably insensitive to their needs, positions, and apprehensions. To gain their confidence and trust, the professor asked the company to heighten his credibility by distributing advanced information about his qualifications and experience in conducting this type of seminar. When the seminar began, the public affairs director gave a strong introduction of the speaker. Finally, the professor began by giving information to the audience that could help them to construct him as a person who could be trusted to provide them with an excellent and nonthreatening course in public speaking. His effect was due in large part to their perception and support of him as one who was intelligent, trustworthy, dynamic, and possessed of both professional expertise and good will toward the audience.

One communication consultant received many requests from organizations whose management was aware that their companies suffered an undeserved credibility problem with potential customers. We can see how credibility and ethos become especially important by examining the problem of two businesses who use this consultant's service: The Funeral Directors Association and The Public Utility Company. The FDA was becoming increasingly alarmed because customers were often hostile in their attitudes and beliefs about the funeral business. Because of books on the alleged high costs of funerals and television dramas showing unscrupulous funeral directors, members of the FDA decided they needed to speak up for their business. Their goal was to develop a positive image in the public eye.

In a similar fashion, the Public Utility Company's chief officers felt the company was developing a poor image with the public, and especially with large industrial firms. Many reasons were cited, including energy shortages during peak periods of demand, continuing rate increases, and company insensitivity to customer interests and feelings. the chairman of the board as well as the president and senior vice-president decided to take immediate steps to increase the corporate credibility, the company's ethos. One step they took was to retain the consultant to train speakers to make credible presentations, carefully designed to show the company cared for its customers and tried to place customer interests and feelings first. Both the FDA and the PUC contended, "We have integrity; we can be trusted; we are primarily interested in serving our customers; so we want a positive, favorable image in their eyes." Having integrity in the eyes of your audience, as well as your own, is necessary to achieve success in speaking as a business person.

Every college or university graduate, at some point in life, speaks not only as a representative for herself or himself, but as a representative for some particular business or professional organization. When he or she stands at the lectern to speak, to the audience the speaker possesses the organization's integrity as well as his or her own. One can build on this in audience perception or do just the opposite. Consider the case of Tom, a scientist for the PUC. In spite of Tom's four academic degrees and considerable experience as an environmental expert, when he spoke to audiences both in the company and outside, he was perceived as arrogant, inarticulate, and uninformed. This, coupled with the apparent corporate credibility problem, resulted in one rhetorical failure after another. Tom was about to bow out of any further experiences in public speaking when he began to work with a consultant. Subsequently he began to work at being a good speaker, one who could be regarded as having high image. Ways to develop a message and to project to create high image will be included appropriately throughout this book. An essentially positive image requires a speaker to be a dialogic rather than a monologic speaker in the perceptions of the audience.

Perhaps the most concise distinction between a dialogic and a monologic speaker has been suggested by Johannesen. He writes:

> Dialogic communication is usually viewed as ethical and monologic as unethical. Dialogue is held to be more fully human, humane, and facilitative of personal self-fulfillment than is monologue. Dialogue and monologue represent more of a communication attitude or orientation than a specific method, technique, or format. We speak of dialogue or monologue as permeating a given human communication transaction. . . . In monologue the attitude of the senders toward the receivers is marked by such qualities as deception, superiority, exploitation, dogmatism, domination, insincerity, pretense, personal display, self-aggrandizement, coercion, distrust, self-defensiveness, and viewing the other as an object to be manipulated. The speaker views receivers as objects to be exploited for self-serving purposes; they are not taken seriously as persons. Focus is on the speaker's message,

not the audience's real needs. The core values, goals and policies espoused by the speaker are impervious to influence exerted by receivers.

Audience feedback is used only to further the speaker's purpose; an honest response from receivers is not wanted or is precluded. Often choices are narrowed and consequences are observed. . . . Dialogue in contrast is characterized by such attitudes as honesty, concern for the welfare of the Other, trust, genuineness, open-mindedness, equality, mutual respect, empathy, directness, lack of pretense, nonmanipulative intent, encouragement of free expression, and acceptace of the Other as a unique individual regardless of differences over belief or behavior. Although the speaker in dialogue may offer advice or express disagreement, he does not aim to psychologically coerce an audience into accepting his view. The speaker's aim is one of assisting the audience in making independent, self-determined decisions. While the speaker expresses judgment of policies and behaviors, judgment of the intrinsic worth of audience members is avoided.[5]

Image plays a crucial role in the relationship between a speaker and an audience. Ideally, those who have an ethical attitude towards their audience can enhance their image. And the dialogic attitude is generally regarded by communication theorists and psychologists as highly ethical. To communicate with honesty, empathy, directness, and lack of pretense, for example, is obviously to communicate with integrity, while to communicate insensitively, indirectly, or in pretentious ways lacks integrity.

A business spokesperson can perhaps fool or trick an audience with the clever use of the rhetorical devices of monologic communication, and through deceit increase his or her ethos. This sort of communication behavior was condemned by Plato thousands of years ago and is still viewed as being highly unethical.

Using a dialogic orientation in concert with substantive information and strong communication skills can enhance one's ethos, even among people who hold strong and opposing points of view. And speaking with substantive information means that a business spokesperson must appear knowledgeable to the audience.

Knowledge. Listeners are usually impressed and influenced by speakers who appear to have pertinent knowledge on the subject they are talking about. On the surface, this statement may appear to be too obvious to mention. But often, for a number of reasons, knowledgeable persons do not appear well-informed when facing an audience.

There may be several reasons why people speak in ways that create the impression they not know the subject sufficiently. Perhaps a speaker has not thoroughly prepared for the challenge of speaking. For example, a scientist with a huge corporation dashed into the briefing room to talk about his department's projects for coal degasification. He was scheduled to speak for fifteen minutes. For forty minutes he rambled and rushed through what appeared to the audience to be a great deal of information. But because he could not explain his points clearly and his organization was poor, people in the audience began to feel they were listening to a bright man who was not in command of the information he was supposed to be an expert on. In reality, he simply did not carefully prepare his presentation.

Some business people know a great deal about their work but also have considerable difficulty finding words and ideas to express themselves clearly when speaking from the lectern. In the privacy of their office or even in a committee meeting, they think and manage information quite well. But when called on to speak before a group in their organization, another business, or especially at a press conference, they stumble through statements, and their listeners question their competence.

None of us feels satisfied when leaving a meeting, class, or special event at which the speaker seems not to know what he or she is talking about. Certainly, it is not uncommon on campuses to find students who feel this way about certain professors! "Oh well," one might say, "he may be bright but he certainly can't teach." Perhaps he could teach if he could speak effectively.

The main idea to keep in mind is that appearing to be knowledgeable is an important quality for a good speaker. Careful speech preparation, as well as the development of strong communication skills, can guide the business person to success as an informed communicator.

We have discussed three qualities of good speakers—confidence, integrity, and knowledge. Because the fourth, good communication skills, is so important and affects the others, we will spend considerable time discussing these skills.

SKILLS

In reality, a person speaking from the lectern is a dynamic being generating meaning in a number of ways simultaneously. For academic study, however, we can look at speech behavior in terms of two definite categories—content and delivery. The elements of content and delivery in speaking with an audience are dynamically interwoven as a presentation is being made. In order to learn how to prepare a speech and to develop maximum effectiveness, let's focus on them separately.

Content.   Content is composed of the purpose, organization, and language in a speech. The content of a solid presentation should be developed into a clear and carefully structured outline. We shall examine the steps to achieving control over the content in a public presentation.

1. Determine the specific purpose of the message.

The specific purpose of any message should be the *precise response the speaker wants from the audience.* Generally, speakers seem to know what they want, even though it may be difficult for an audience to figure out precisely the speaker's aim. One businessman, not atypical, dashed into a room filled with listeners, and for thirty minutes he spewed out facts and figures on environmental control, supplementing his verbal barrage with slides of charts and graphs. In closing he declared, "I don't know how much of this makes sense because I just thought I'd throw a lot of stuff your way hoping some of it would stick." What an unfortunate declaration—for his presentation had minimal impact.

This speaker ought to have developed a careful aim at a precise response, one he could have accurately described if asked. Certainly, we waste both our energy and time, as well as those of the audience, with this "shotgun" approach to sharing information.

2. *Determine the core statement and subordinate points of the message.*

The core statement should be the major point or thesis of a message. It should give the audience a clear impression or image of what the communicator wants them to know or believe, and it should suggest how the message is going to unfold.

The core statement should be expressed as a clear declarative sentence. It is a proposition. A proposition can be defined as a sentence that expresses a succinct idea or judgment expressed in descriptive language—that is, neither "loaded" nor highly emotional. The core statement embodies and takes direct aim at the specific purpose of the message. When Pennie wanted the executive board of the Centerville Medical Association to commit their power and resources to the development of a speaker's bureau (the response she wanted—active commitment), she stated unhesitatingly, "I believe the Executive Board should establish and fully support a CMA Speakers' Bureau to create understanding and good will between our professionals and the general public in our community."

When the business communicator begins to develop a core idea and subordinate points to support it, the process of reasoning becomes highly important. We reason to achieve our purpose, and we want the audience to see our reasoning and arrive at understanding and conclusions similar to ours.

The word "reasoning" is used here to mean the process of using the known and believed information to explain or seek adherence to statements as claims that are less well understood or accepted. In brief, it is the process that goes from what we know to what we declare and conclude.

One useful way to consider reasoning is to think about the notion that when we reason, it is either about controversial or noncontroversial matters: The first is argumentation and the second is exposition. Argument is used in the attempt to persuade, and exposition seeks to create objective comprehension.

> Exposition in speech communication is not dichotomous with argument; rather it is communication that is non-controversial to those involved in the communicative or rhetorical situation. That is, they are less likely to be at odds over the claim and more likely to be interested in understanding cooperatively the bases for the claim. . . . Almost every progressive or unifying move by individuals and organizations has been preceded by a period of discussion and/or argument. In the case of argumentation and the controversy it thrives on, history supports the notion that unification and strength are often the result of conflict and intense disagreement. . . . argumentation is the theory and practice of controversial discourse.[6]

In business, we can apply expository reasoning most frequently to oral reporting both within the organization and outside it. We can apply argumentation to persuasive proposals and efforts to influence the customer, client, or general public to buy an image, product, or service effort.

No communicator has a guarantee of achieving the specific purpose, because communication with an audience is a process marked by possibilities or probabilities rather than certainty. We may help a listener to learn or believe or decide. But learning, believing, or deciding takes place within each individual, if it takes place at all. If we aim to achieve a specific purpose and design our message and adjust our delivery with a clear target in sight, we increase the probability of being effective. Ambiguity breeds ambiguity. The task of the business communicator is to *write out* a carefully determined purpose and then develop a message that will achieve it.

The subordinate points the business communicator chooses as the most important lines of reason should be developed to support the core statement. They are important to the creation of clarity and belief in the listener's mind. The number of subordinate points selected for a speech depends on the time constraints the speaker must accept and on what appears to be the most important ideas for the audience as well as the speaker. For example, Thom is a product developer for a large novelty gift company that uses the party-sales concept to distribute, market, and sell its products. When he joined the firm, he worked first on a new gift item for six months. He finally decided the time had come to sell the product to top management, and so he approached his supervisor to arrange for a presentation to the management team. The team leader informed Thom that he could have forty-five minutes at the next Executive Board meeting, and after his presentation the management team would make some decision on Thom's product. Thom's dilemma was how he might develop a thirty-minute presentation and provide fifteen minutes for questions. His office was stacked with notes, reports, diagrams, and mock-up models—it seemed impossible to reduce six months of work to forty-five minutes. After consulting with a speech expert for the company, he decided to build his presentation around the primary business motives of the members of the management team—to organize the message according to lines of reason that would probably have strong appeal for his particular audience. Through researching the background of his listeners, he discovered five motives (see Figure 3-3). After discovering the motives, he developed a core statement aimed at his desired response and lines of reason to represent the primary motives. Thom's approach helped him achieve his goal.

On the way to a Toastmaster's meeting, one of the authors of this book found himself riding with an anxious optometrist who was to give a seven-minute speech after dinner. As he drove, he seemed preoccupied until at last he said, "I need some help with my speech. I timed it this afternoon at work and it came out at twenty-eight minutes. What can I do to cut it down?" He had been planning to develop ten subordinate points about how the municipal officials of New York City in concert with the business and professional communities could dramatically solve most of the city's financial woes. In the car, he decided to select the three most

FIGURE 3-3   The speaker should carefully select the major points that will be most effective with his or her audience.

important lines of reason for the particular audience he was to address and to build his speech around those points. By the time he had completed his speech that evening, sound organization had helped him a great deal; he spent a half minute on the introduction of the message, two minutes on each line of reasoning, and a minute concluding.

Choosing subordinate points to support a core statement is not an easy task, especially when there appears to be so much worth talking about. But focusing on the most important ideas and limiting the presentation to the time allowed is necessary for effectiveness.

3.   Choose words carefully for meaning.

The management of a nationally known research foundation decided that its image in the community was poor for a number of reasons. In an effort to lift its profile, the foundation's leaders decided that a speakers' bureau would help, so a training program was begun to prepare scientists to accept speaking engagements that would inform the community's audiences about the foundation's important work. The greatest problem the speakers experienced was a problem of words—most found that translating the language of science and research to layperson's talk was tremendously difficult. They would work on their message construction and delivery, but find themselves talking as scientists to an audience of other scientists. The solution to the problem was found in the challenge "Choose words carefully for meaning."

Meaning, as we stated in Chapter 2 is what happens between statements. The speaker at the lectern wants meaning created in the minds of the audience that is identical with the meaning in her or his mind. The identity can never be achieved if the words of the speaker do not create the recognition of relationship that is necessary for meaning to be achieved. The challenge for the speaker is to find ways to express ideas and facts with words that clearly symbolize meaning for the audience and at the same time maintain the accuracy and precision required to explain the material. People assign meaning to words, but the words themselves are of little or no meaning; the meanings come from within the users, both speaker and listener. The subjects of semantics, general semantics, and linguistics provide some basic principles we can use effectively in word choice. When we focus on persuasive communication, informational communication, and communicating with the broad public, we are going to introduce concepts and principles that can be instrumental in making choices to create clear meaning. At this point, it is important to understand that speakers often believe that once the message is complete in terms of reasoning, support, and organization, then it is time to move on and work for effective delivery. Before the message construction is complete, however, the speaker can examine *all* of his or her words with the audience in mind. If you and the audience are not sharing meaning because too many of your words register little or nothing in your listeners' minds, then the result is a rhetorical failure.

Outlining is essential for effectiveness.   The purpose, the core ideas, the subordinate points, and the language of a speech are to be developed in the form of an outline. Outlining is essential for effectiveness.

Developing a useful outline can help you keep on target with your persuasive message. The outline can help you say what you want to say without careless straying from your plans. It can also keep you from being tied mechanically to a manuscript—which, among other things, usually inhibits one from natural and direct delivery. A detailed outline can be easily prepared. Once a speaker has analyzed the audience and settled on the points to develop, a detailed outline can be easily prepared (see Box 3-3 and Box 3-4).

There are two kinds of outlines for the speaker to prepare, and we argue that both are necessary for thorough preparation and delivery. The first is the *full-content outline,* and the second is the *key-word outline.* The key-word outline is

BOX 3-3   OUTLINING GUIDES

1. Each unit in the outline should contain one idea.
2. Less important ideas in the outline should be subordinate to more important ones.
3. The logical relationship between units of ideas should be shown by proper identification.
4. A consistent set of symbols should be used throughout the outline.

BOX 3-4   *WHAT SHOULD AN OUTLINE LOOK LIKE?*

I. Introduction (begin with an attention-getter)

A.
B.

II. Core Statement: The body of the speech begins here.

A. Subordinate point
  1. Support
  2. Support
B. Subordinate point
  1. Support
  2. Support
C. Subordinate point
  1. Support
  2. Support

III. Conclusion: Restate the core idea.

A. Final summary
B. Closure

---

developed from the full-content outline. The full-content outline is detailed, with all the information to be presented. Each idea, with its supporting data, is expressed in a complete sentence. The speaker can examine the sequence of ideas, pattern of organization, and the balance in the relationship of points and can test the data once the outline is complete.

The full-content outline does not restrict the speaker to a word-for-word message as a manuscript does. The full-content outline does, however, include ample detail so that the speaker can work through the message carefully and check it out for logic, organization, and particular persuasive appeals. It facilitates speaking in an orderly fashion.

Delivery.   Constructing the message carefully with precision and clarity for the intended audience is not sufficient for a skillful speaker at the lectern. The business person must also project herself or himself with force and animation, in a way that is not distracting to the eyes and ears of the audience. There are key principles to keep in mind for an effective delivery of a message, one that will enhance the communication transaction that can take place in a speaker-audience relationship.

1.   *Project your voice naturally and fully with emphasis.*

At a public-speaking seminar for business persons, an anxious executive queried, "What can you do to help some of us avoid sounding like hicks when we address financial communities in New York?" The questioner used a strong regional dialect as he spoke. The advice given him first was, Do not apologize, do not assign yourself an unfortunate stereotype because you *sound* different to audiences outside of the region of the country you call home. Be yourself! There are several ideas and principles to keep in mind and put into practice to increase the quality of vocal production.

First, the voice is a miraculous product of organs that serve both vocal production and other functions important in the maintenance of our life system. Knowing how sounds are produced can give one an appreciation of one's own vocal ability and insight into how the voice can be fully used. Basically, there are two major kinds of speech organs: those for sound production and those for articulation. The sound-producing mechanisms include the motor (the lungs and breathing muscles), the vibrator (the vocal chords), and the resonators (the sinuses and other cavities in the head and chest), while the articulatory mechanism is made up of the tongue, teeth, lips, jaw, and the hard and soft palates. We must use these organs consciously and with control if we are to create sounds that are pleasant, appropriate, and attractive to an audience.

Breathing is important for speakers, since improper breathing can adversely affect strong, clear, and articulate vocal production. The breathing apparatus we possess serves as the motor and energy source for vocal production and is responsible for bringing oxygen into the lungs as fuel for the body, as well as for expelling waste material. The person making a presentation and experiencing a great deal of tension because of the stress from performance anxiety (stage fright) will become caught with a rapid inhalation-exhalation cycle, and hyperventilation is likely to occur. To gain control of the motor, the speaker must breathe deeply and naturally with slow and deliberate efforts. Remember: *The key to the control of speech tension is to focus on your task and not your self. Be centered, then, in your message and audience instead of being self-centered.*

Proper breathing can be instrumental in helping a speaker to control the essential features of good vocal projection for speaking with an audience: volume, rate, pitch, pronunciation, and pausing (see Box 3-5). No matter how much substance you have in the content of your presentation, if the audience cannot hear the message, it is of little value except to you. So to be heard completely, to produce adequate *volume*, you must bring the air up from your diaphragm as you would in playing a wind instrument in an orchestra. As the air passes through your vocal cords and resonators, it is to be articulated sharply by your tongue, teeth, lips, jaw, and the hard and soft palates that are your tools to modify the production of speech sounds. Select a few words right now and speak them several times, varying the volume and articulation—become momentarily conscious of your vocal production. If you have a tape recorder handy, experiment with yourself to learn more about how you sound.

Rate and volume are very important to achieving success with your voice. Presentational speakers who race through their material (because of nervousness or for any other reason) are likely to lose the audience's attention. So also are slow-paced speakers whose voice seems to make the speech drag on and on. As with volume, you can control and regulate the rate at which you speak. Fast speakers can *learn* to vary their rate, just as slow talkers can *learn* to pick up the pace. One should speak with the volume and rate appropriate for the occasion and the purpose. A recent

BOX 3-5   *KEY IDEAS FOR VOCAL CONTROL*

1. Project your voice out, and use enough volume to enhance the message and gain your intended response.
2. Control your speaking rate, and use a rate that is consistent with the verbal meaning of your presentation.
3. Speak in a pitch that is normal and relaxed for you, and keep from putting strain on your voice by an inappropriate pitch.
4. Attack words sharply and use proper pronunciation—when in doubt, check it out!
5. And finally, remember to pause—silently—so that ideas can sink in and you can breathe properly as well.

study reported that a presidential hopeful suffered in part during the 1980 race by shouting too frequently at his audiences. Sometimes shouting is appropriate but certainly not all the time. Effective speakers learn to adjust their rate and volume as part of controlling the voice.

Pitch is a level of sound that depends on the frequency of vibration of the vocal chords. A speaker can control his or her pitch by raising or lowering the level of vibration. Poor control of pitch can result in an unnatural sound, creating monotony and distraction. You should operate witin a range of pitch that is comfortable, normal, and pleasing to you *and* the audience.

Pronouncing words properly and carefully can assist the listener to construct meaning from what the speaker is saying. Because regional and cultural dialects vary in our country, we would not advocate one standard for pronounciation. We do urge that the business communicator articulate in such a way that audiences can hear and understand every word spoken. Do not hesitate to refer to a dictionary when a question of pronounciation arises. We should be familiar with the words we use for any presentation and should know how to express them for an effective presentation.

Knowing *when to pause* is also important to speech delivery. Some nervous speakers will talk without taking a breath, while others will pause so long in the middle of a word or unit of thought that the audience is distracted. When the train of thought is disrupted, the loss of an important idea may result. Furthermore, the quality of the communication suffers considerably if a speaker not only pauses inappropriately but pauses vocally so that the message projection is characterized considerably by sounds of "aaahhhh," "err," "uuuummmm" between words or sentences. A slow speaker pausing frequently becomes monotonous, and a rapid speaker who only pauses for breath does not allow ample time for important ideas to sink in. Part of the control we can have over our speaking skill is to be fully in charge of both proper pronunciation and appropriate silent pausing.

If the business communicators are familiar with how their voices work and deliberately use their voices in ways appropriate to themselves, they will be able to establish a meaningful listening and responding relationship with the audience.

We can do some things to bring the voice up and out, to enhance our words and gestural behavior. The first task for the business communicator to work at is volume control. No matter how important and crucial the ideas are for an audience, if some of the listeners cannot hear what is being said, the speech is rhetorically unsuccessful. Moreover, if the audience can hear the speaker but tries to create meaning from words expressed in either a monotone or a screeching pattern or un-necessary shouting, the distraction can be significant enough to impair effective communication (see Box 3-5).

2.   *Observe your audience for feedback.*

Many people have trouble looking out and into an audience. They face the audience with their bodies, but they also cast their eyes above the audience, in a downtown stare, or at a visual aid being used to support main ideas in the speech. Somehow, the audience is being avoided. Looking into the eyes of another is not easy in many settings, whether riding on a bus, standing on an elevator, experienc-ing an important interview, or standing up to speak. But research tells us that looking directly into an audience is a powerful signal expressing interest in estab-lishing contact or sustaining social interaction. And the business person seeking success with an audience must create a transaction through direct contact with the listener—visual directions through eye-to-eye contact can greatly assist this goal. Furthermore, visual directness can give the spokesperson important information about the audience's response.

We often say that communication is the speaker's response to the listener's response, so that a reciprocal process is underway. The meeting of eyes and the genuine attempt to see something of each other's ideas and attitudes by *looking* for feedback can be beneficial to both speaker and audience as each tries to create meaning in pursuit of mutual understanding and the attainment of a goal.

3.   *Maintain good posture and use appropriate gestures.*

Any sort of physical behavior, no matter how appropriate it may be, can prove tiring to an audience if there is no variation. The business communicator needs to provide meaningful activity when appearing before an audience. But the activity must not be hampered by poor posture at the lectern or by distracting gestural behavior.

There is a general principle that applies to the posture of speakers and to their gestures as well. Purposeful posture and gestural behavior is that movement which does not draw attention to itself and away from the meaning intended by the speaker. Gestures are the movements of any part of the body to convey some emotion and/or reinforce ideas. To ensure against monotony, a speaker should change his or her position in front of the audience from time to time during a presentation and should use gestures of hands, arms, head, face, and eyes. But the effective speaker is fully aware of his or her total physical presence in concert with the words being spoken and the ways in which they are being vocalized. In a word, control is necessary for the business communicator who does not want to have physical behavior prove to be distracting.

Picture a man attempting to sell a roast-beef franchise to fast-food investors. In contrast to the strongest competitor, while presenting the comparative advantages of the chain he represents, he aimlessly wanders about in front of his audience, he waves and strokes his visual-aid pointer when not using it on the bar graphs, he needlessly clears his throat, and his eyes are looking everywhere but into the audience. Frequently, during the presentation he leans against the lectern and shifts his weight, again suggesting discomfort. Such discomfort and distraction is felt not only by the speaker, but by members of his audience as well. Their attention on his information and point of view is interrupted by the distractions of his awkwardness. There is a contagious tenseness in the speaker-audience relationship because of the distracting signs of the speaker and their effect on the audience. This speaker should use meaningful gestures and movement.

Posture (whether the speaker is standing still or using some movement) and gestural behavior must be natural, easy, and purposeful. It can also provide a way to relieve physical tension. There are several things one can do to work for posture and gestures that contribute to the meaning of the message (see Box 3-6).

BOX 3-6   POSTURE AND GESTURES

1. Apply the principle of controlling speech tension we suggested in this chapter when we discussed confidence in speaking.
2. In a practice session, extend the arms full length and turn completely around several times to identify a "speaking space" for movement (you are not limited to this space but you can find it a comfortable area within which to move).
3. Plan to use facial expressions and arm and hand movements as gestures, but do not plan specific gestures (practice in animated ways to loosen up and become familiar with ways you can use your physical presence to your advantage).
4. Remember, a lectern is to hold notes and not you; it is an aid and not a crutch, so work with it but not on it.
5. Above all else, remember that any movement, posture, or gesture that draws attention to itself and away from the intended meaning of the speech is a distraction and ought to be avoided.

In our classroom work and consulting experiences with men and women in business and industry, we have developed a list of the ten most frequently occurring nonverbal distractions:[7]

1. Nervous pacing
2. Frozen posture with no movement
3. Leaning on the lectern
4. Hands and arms locked tightly in front of or behind the body
5. Scratching (oneself, the lectern)
6. Rubbing hands, twisting rings or other jewelry
7. Gesturing with a pen or pencil

8. Covering mouth
9. Jingling objects in pockets
10. Looking down or away from the audience

At first glance, you might feel that this is a list of minor matters. And perhaps, in the context of a total speaking transaction with an audience, it is. But when distractions occur, important parts of a message are not likely to be processed by the audience. When a listener is consciously or unconsciously annoyed by awkward speaking behavior, in terms of voice or other physical distractions, neither speaker nor listener gains anything.

THE QUESTION-AND-ANSWER PERIOD

Presentational speaking usually includes a question-and-answer period. We have compiled a concise list of ideas to help and learn to effectively respond to questions from the audience. The information is in Box 3-7. Examine it carefully, learn it

BOX 3-7   ANSWERING QUESTIONS

1. Make any question period an integral part of your speech presentation.

    A. This period provides the audience with an opportunity to clear up any uncertainties or to raise doubts or objections that you have not satisfactorily answered.
    B. Do not view this period as an ordeal to be survived—the prepared extemporaneous portion of your speech has ended, but this portion is a challenging extension that is often necessary to create mutual understanding between the speaker and the audience.
    C. Aim for the response you sought in the prepared speech—your specific purpose should always be kept in mind!
    D. This question period can give you feedback and at the same time reveal you as a sincere person with concerns similar to those of your audience.

2. A major element in answering questions successfully lies in your skill in providing answers that relate to what you stated in your speech and that emphasize your specific purpose.

    A. Listen careful to the question, making every effort to understand the intent of the questioner—you can go wide of the mark in your answer if what you think is quite different from the questioner's intent.
    B. Make sure the entire audience hears and understands the question—repeat it or have the questioner repeat it loud and clear (usually it is better if you repeat it for everyone).
    C. Make a quick appraisal of the question to yourself—see it in terms of the value you feel it has and the real feelings of the questioner; make your response controlled, direct and honest.
    D. Keep in mind always:
        1. Answer directly and to the point.
        2. Relate your answer to the response you seek.
        3. At the end of the question period, make a final summary.
        4. Don't be rattled by the unexpected—maintain your poise.

completely, and apply the principles appropriately in any situation in which you must respond directly to the audience.

Our chapter has now introduced you to essential information for achieving success in presentational speaking. The next two chapters are also guides to being an effective speaker; the information you have studied so far is material you will need in order to understand and apply the ideas to follow about technical and persuasive presentations. It is also key information to use in carrying out the ideas in Chapter 12, which focuses on communicating with the public through a speakers' bureau and a dialogue with public audiences. To review in your mind the essentials of presentational speaking, study Figure 3-1 and discuss it with others in your class.

A REVIEW OF KEY ISSUES

Five key attitudes are necessary for success in presentational speaking:

1. Share enthusiasm about your information.
2. Regard yourself as *the* expert.
3. Aim to genuinely help each listener.
4. Believe presentational speaking *is* an opportunity.
5. Nurture then *act* on the belief that speaking can be fun.

Audience analysis is an important procedure in preparing a presentation. There are four major questions to guide you in completing an audience analysis:

1. What does the audience know, and how do they feel about me and about the organization I represent?
2. What does the audience know, and how do they feel abut the subject we are about to share?
3. What does the audience know, and how do they feel about the occasion for speaking?
4. How does the audience regard itself in this communicative setting?

With the knowledge gained from completing an audience analysis, adapting to the audience becomes necessary.

Four qualities are essential for an effective public speaker:

Confidence is communicated, both in oneself as well as in the ideas presented.

Integrity in the image of a speaker is determined by one's use of dialogic rather than monologic communication behaviors.

Knowledge is displayed in the amount of preparation as well as the quality of the ideas expressed.

Skills are evidenced in the six steps fundamental to successful speaking from the lectern—

Skills pertaining to content:
1. Determine the specific purpose of your message.
2. Determine the core statement and subordinate points for the message.
3. Choose words carefully for meaning.

Outlining is necessary for effective speaking:
1. Developing a useful outline keeps a speaker on target.
2. Speech outlines are of two types: full content and key word.
3. A valuable outline follows four basic guidelines:
    a. Each unit contains one idea.
    b. Less important ideas are subordinate to important ones.
    c. Logical relationships between ideas should be identified.
    d. A consistent set of symbols should be used throughout.

And skills in delivery:
1. Project your voice naturally and fully for appropriate emphasis.
2. Observe your audience for feedback.
3. Maintain good posture and use appropriate gestures.

EXPERIENCING EXPERIENCES

Speaking to the public from the podium is a performance skill. The principles are heavily based on a variety of tested theories, but the real test of learning comes from practicing the skills. Memorizing the guidelines for employing the skills is helpful but certainly not necessary for mastery. The experience of practicing the skills in specific situations, followed by serious analysis, is the best way to learn. This experiential learning will carry far beyond the boundaries of the classroom and infiltrate your professional work habits and entire career. With this kind of a philosophy in mind, we offer the following activities to make this practical kind of learning meaningful to you now as a student. Give this some serious thought as you begin involving yourself in these activities.

ACTIVITY 1: Assess Your Qualities as a Speaker

Directions: Answer the following questions about yourself.

1. What do you think are the best assets in your voice?

_____

2. What do you think are the worst weaknesses in your voice?

_____

3. List your most used and favorite

    Gestures: _____

    Facial expressions: _____

    Body movements: _____

    Kind of posture: _____

4. How would you rate your ability to

Organize ideas.	poor	average	good
Write solid sentences	poor	average	good
Use colorful descriptive words	poor	average	good
Create good introductions.	poor	average	good
Find transitions to bridge different ideas	poor	average	good
Find proper words to summarize your ideas . . .	poor	average	good
Create ear-catching endings to speeches	poor	average	good

ACTIVITY 2: Have a Classmate Assess Your Speaking Qualities

Directions: Ask several classmates to evaluate you. Compare your self-assessment with the assessments provided by your classmates by using these forms. Note the similarities and differences in your self-perceptions and those of others. You should have a clear picture of where you are at present with your speaking skills, so that you will have some definite direction in which to proceed in this developmental learning process.

Name _____, as I perceive, has

1. The following good voice qualities:

_____

2. The following weak voice qualities that need improvement:

_____

3. Most frequently used

    Gestures: _____

    Facial expressions: _____

    Body movements: _____

    Posture habits: _____

4. Ability to

Organize ideas.	poor	average	good
Write solid sentences	poor	average	good
Use colorful descriptive words	poor	average	good
Create good introductions.	poor	average	good
Find transitions to bridge different ideas	poor	average	good
Find words to summarize ideas	poor	average	good
Create ear-catching endings to speeches	poor	average	good

ACTIVITY 3: Organizing a Public Speech for Performance

Directions: Select a subject and prepare a speech using the following format. (This is designed for a 3- to 5-minute speech.)

Speech Subject: _____

Speech Purpose: _____

Speech Audience: _____ Speech Situation: _____

Length of Speech: _____ Location to deliver it: _____

Introduction

Attention-Getter: _____

_____

Core Statement: _____

_____

Transition to 1st main point: _____

_____

Body of the Message

1st Main Point: _____

    Subpoint: _____

    Example: _____

    Subpoint: _____

    Example: _____

Transition: _____

2nd Main Point: _____

    Subpoint: _____

    Example: _____

    Subpoint: _____

    Example: _____

Transition: _____

3rd Main Point: _____

    Subpoint: _____

    Example: _____

    Subpoint: _____

    Example: _____

Transition: _____

Conclusion

Summary

    1st point: _____

    2nd point: _____

    3rd point: _____

Final Thought: _____

EXERCISES

1. After you have prepared your speech, practice it in front of a mirror and then deliver it to your classmates. Ask them for comments after the speech.

2. Have the classmates fill out anonymous written analyses so that you can compare various personal opinions.

3. Prepare a speech using the same format but adding more than three main points and form a public-speech community bureau. Pick topics of interest to your local community. Type up a brochure with the speakers and speech titles plus the days and times the speakers are available to go to local clubs and organizations. Then go out to engagements that can be booked. This is excellent experience, and it will be the very best learning experience you can have in preparing you to look and act like a professional.

NOTES

1. Vincent DiSalvo, David C. Larsen, and William Seiler, "Communication Skills Needed by Persons in Business Organizations." *Communication Education,* 1976, p. 275.
2. John J. Makay, *Speaking With an Audience.* New York: Harper & Row, 1977, p. 22.
3. Gerald R. Miller, "Speech: An Approach to Human Communication," in Richard W. Budd and Brent Ruben, *Approaches to Human Communication.* New Rochelle, N.J.: Hayden, 1972, p. 384.
4. Bert Bradley, *Fundamentals of Speech Communication: The Credibility of Ideas.* Dubuque, Iowa: Wm. C. Brown, 1974, p. 270.
5. Richard L. Johannesen, "Attitude of the Speaker Toward the Audience: A Significant Concept for Contemporary Rhetorical Theory and Criticism." *Central States Speech Journal,* Summer 1974, p. 96.
6. John J. Makay and William R. Brown, *The Rhetorical Dialogue: Contemporary Concepts and Cases.* Dubuque, Iowa: Wm. C. Brown, 1972.
7. Makay, *Speaking With an Audience,* pp. 37-38.

CHAPTER FOUR

TECHNICAL PRESENTATIONS

Communicating technical information is an extremely important function of the professional business person. It is an important part of most jobs, and in many situations it is written into the job description as a required skill. If for no other reason than to explain a job assignment or procedure, many employees must often provide technical information to a new employee as a part of an orientation. Executives and managers often assume that because employees know their jobs, they should be capable of communicating this technical information to others. Unfortunately, this is often not the case. Knowing how to do the job well does not automatically mean that a person can communicate the information to another. These are two completely different tasks and they should not be confused. Perhaps you have had the experience of teaching someone how to drive a car. You know perfectly well how to drive, but when you try to explain this complex procedure to a nondriver, you quickly realize the importance of accuracy and clarity in communiation. In the work environment, thousands of individuals face this communication task almost daily. Nurses explain procedures to new hospital employees; teachers explain technical data in the classroom; salespersons inform clients about new products. The list of examples could go on and on.

In this chapter, it is our concern to explain how to use oral communication in order to communicate technical information. This oral communication must be clear and specific to achieve the intended purpose. Our focus will be on selecting the correct technical information and planning, organizing, and presenting it in a format that is efficient and effective. It is important to select and organize the pertinent data in such a task, but it is also necessary to adapt the data to specific audiences. Technical presentations use skills that are basic and vital in the business and professional world.

DEFINING THE PURPOSE IN TECHNICAL COMMUNICATION PRESENTATIONS

We have found in our consulting that many professional people have problems completing this first step: defining the purpose of the presentation. They often have an idea for the purpose of a technical presentation, but most frequently, they speak around the purpose rather than addressing it specifically. This first and extremely important step in communicating technical information requires careful reflecting. This first step establishes the focus for the rest of the process.

The process in presenting technical information depends on the situation, and this is all the more reason why the purpose must be specifically defined. When business people are asked why they make technical presentations, they usually respond, "I tell people how to perform certain job skills," or "I explain how to operate special types of equipment," or "I explain how to act in certain professional situations." If you look closely at these statements, what do they really say? These statements have not actually described anything. Technical communication requires specific descriptive information. This certainly is the case if we are teaching someone how to drive a car. A simple mistake or omission of one bit of technical information could make the difference between life and death.

This principle of specific descriptive information applies to defining the purpose for a technical presentation. Some type of assessment must be made at the very beginning of this process, before the information is collected and outlined. Answering the questions in Box 4-1 should help you to determine your specific purpose for making a technical presentation. You may feel that this is a time-consuming way to determine the purpose for a technical presentation; however, when you become aware how necessary it is to establish a focus for this kind of communication, you will value the time spent on this first step.

BOX 4-1   PURPOSE ASSESSMENT FOR A TECHNICAL PRESENTATION

The general purpose of my technical presentation is to	
_____ Inform	(present technical data in some specialized format)
_____ Suggest	(persuade through the use of technical information)
_____ Instruct	(train technical data or processes)
_____ Acquaint	(introduce technical process or products)
_____ Appraise	(evaluate technical processes or products)

_____ Announce or   (introduce/explain some new technical data)
               update

This presentation is for an audience made up of
_____ New employees	_____ Experienced employees
_____ Promoted employees	_____ Old clients
_____ New clients	_____ Professional peers
_____ Nontechnical laypersons	_____ Others _____

The expected general audience attitude is
_____ Receptiveness	_____ Biased
_____ Negativism	_____ Noncommitment

This presentation is a
      _____ Routine situation
      _____ Unusual situation
      _____ One-time situation

Purpose statement:
I will present technical communication about (topic)_____
for the specific purpose of _____

Having completed the assessment of purpose, you have designed a road map, or more specifically, you have determined your own goal to follow as you continue preparing your technical presentation.

COLLECTING THE PERTINENT TECHNICAL INFORMATION

Unlike speech writing, in which selecting the topic becomes a major part of the process, a technical presentation often has a topic that is defined by the speaker's area of expertise. Because someone is believed to be a professional or expert in the subject area, this person is requested to do the presentation. It is assumed that doctors know medicine, lawyers the law, teachers education, accountants accounting.

In this step of collecting pertinent technical information, the real issue is for the expert to select and specify *precise* data. The professional knows the subject well and can usually talk on, around, above, over, and in great depth about it. The qualified professional understands the importance of selecting the proper information and should be able to decide what information is appropriate—as opposed to what is interesting but certainly not necessary. With little difficulty, the specialist can ramble on, moving in many fascinating directions. In reality, this creates an information overload, and the listeners become confused or unknowingly turn off their listening comprehension. Experienced professionals may quickly sense when listeners get confused, but rarely are they immediately aware that the listening is turned off. Repeating technical information already known to listeners—or constantly elaborating to the point of getting sidetracked or off-target—does not encourage positive listening comprehension or achieve the pre-planned purpose.

Information for a presentation should be technically accurate and should be taken from reliable sources. A professional must know how to locate the proper sources and use specialized material containing the needed technical data. In a business or professional environment, resources must also be up to date. A person preparing a technical presentation should be aware of the professional journals in her or his area. If there are, in the field, magazines, conventions, workshops, or highly acclaimed books written by recognized scholars, the professional or expert should know of their existence and should be able to locate them easily.

Availability of technical information is a major concern. When one is preparing a technical presentation, the time is best spent planning and organizing the data. Spending large amounts of time locating the sources of information is a luxury not so frequently permitted in the professional work world as it is in the academic environment. No doubt you have already had the frustrating experience of having spent hours in the library at work on a term paper, only to discover that one vital book is missing from the shelf. Browsing in the library and leafing through pages of interesting but not always pertinent books takes time the employed professional cannot afford. Organizations and employers rely on the ability of the professional to know where to begin an immediate search for the needed data.

Another important aspect of collecting information is the format that is used in gathering technical data. If you think back to your first term paper or speech assignment, you very possibly remember note cards and pages of yellow legal pad scribbles. After hours of searching for the information in the library, you headed home with reams of notes, only to discover that a page number, a copyright date, or some footnote that you need is missing. No doubt, you also remember that in retracing your step you lost precious writing time. In order to help you collect technical information, we will make some specific suggestions later in this chapter.

Many organizations provide research assistance for their employees: private libraries, media centers, or research facilities. With or without the luxury of such facilities, you will need to know how to search for and collect technical information. Knowing how to use the card catalog, journal indexes, microfilm, periodical file, computer-stored data, and computer information searches is imperative. These valuable tools will be helpful in the pressured world of a professional. The availability of the quick copy machine is another important tool in making technical data conveniently available.

To prescribe a particular system for collecting data, such as the use of 3 × 5 index cards, is unnecessary. For one person, note cards may be the ideal system, while another may find that legal pads or looseleaf notebooks work better. Most people find their own system, one that they feel works best for them. For some professionals, with the availability of the computer, the organized collection of data and easy access to large amounts of information may be only seconds away. Thanks to this sophisticated information-retrieval system, computer printout sheets can be easy to read as well as time-saving.

ORGANIZING THE TECHNICAL INFORMATION
FOR A PRESENTATION

The writing style. Oral technical presentations do require a certain amount of organization on paper, requiring some writing skills. However, the product in its final form is the spoken presentation, and that form of communication uses a somewhat different written style in organization and presentation. There are some basic differences between the written and the spoken communication style. In order to organize the technical information effectively, it is very important to have a clear understanding of these differences. In choosing vocabulary when organizing ideas and preparing information from which to speak, one should keep in mind the guidelines in Box 4-2.

BOX 4-2 SPOKEN/WRITTEN VOCABULARY COMPARED

Spoken vocabulary uses:	Written vocabulary uses:
1. many personal pronouns	1. few personal pronouns
2. familiar (common) words	2. less familiar; more word-choice variety
3. concrete and strong words, visually descriptive	3. more abstract words
4. specific words, unique to their usage	4. general words that adapt creatively to literary figures of speech

Sentence structure and organization are also different in oral and written presentations. Box 4-3 points out the differences in the two styles.

BOX 4-3 SPOKEN/WRITTEN SENTENCES COMPARED

Sentences in a spoken presentation use:	Sentences in written communication use:
1. short and simple construction	1. longer and more complex structure
2. questions, exclamations, commands—dramatic, colorful	2. statements, straight approach to the subject—formal
3. few dependent clauses and modifying phrases	3. more dependent clauses with variety of modifiers
4. repetition for emphasis of ideas	4. deliberate variety to avoid repetition of words, phrases, and ideas

In a technical presentation, the data are organized around major points or ideas. Usually each idea is carefully outlined independently, and when that point has been sufficiently communicated, the speaker moves on to the next idea. This style of organization requires careful outlining, but this format can create a problem. A speaker must not only organize each point of the technical information adequately but must also be able to mentally move the listeners on the next piece of data without losing them in the process of this "mental journey." Much like the professional writer, the technical speaker must have some method of organizing all the individual pieces of information to give an image of wholeness or totality. A writer does this with carefully composed transitions. These transitions can be single words but more often are complete sentences, paragraphs, or even a series of paragraphs.

Unlike the writer, the technical speaker has to look at transitions with a different viewpoint when organizing information, since they will be heard, rather than read on a printed page. The speaker should use brief transitions—single words or short phrases—as a means of pulling together the technical data into some organized framework. The transition should serve as a connection between one point of information and the next, in order to maintain an organized flow. Often the speaker will not write all transitions into the written notes, but will add them during the actual delivery. For the novice, this can be difficult to do. The successful use of transitions depends on the purpose the transition is to serve. Box 4-4 lists transitions frequently used in technical presentations, according to the intended purpose for which a speaker might wish to use them.

BOX 4-4   TRANSITIONAL LINKS FOR TECHNICAL INFORMATION
PRESENTATIONS

Speaker's purpose:	Suggested transitional words:
to define . . .	that is to say; according to; in other words
to explain . . .	for example; or specifically
to add . . .	furthermore; also; in addition; likewise
to change direction . . .	although; on the other hand; conversely
to show both sides . . .	nevertheless; equally
to contrast . . .	but; still; on the contrary
to indicate cause . . .	because; for this reason; since; on account of
to summarize . . .	recapping; finally; in retrospect; summing up
to conclude. . .	in conclusion; therefore; and so; finally

Effectively organizing technical information in this manner requires thorough understanding of the information. Furthermore, you must understand the purpose for including each major item within the total content. The constant focus on the purpose of the presentation is a good check system to prevent you from overloading information or straying too far from the original purpose of the presentation. Simply put, applying the purpose of the presentation to each main point of the presentation and connecting these main points with solid transitions will keep you on target.

Structuring concepts.   Another major concern when organizing the technical presentation is the structure and placement of ideas and concepts. Since we have seen the difference between the verbal language style and the written, it will be no surprise that structuring ideas into outline form is also different for a technical presentation. A great deal of time and effort can be saved by learning rules for this organizational step.

The organizational format you use for pulling your technical data together should be based on three factors: (1) It should be a system that you understand how to use; (2) it should be a system that will work effectively with the type of technical data being presented; and (3) it should lend itself functionally to the type of audience to which it is presented. Occasionally, a situation may call for some special kind of presentation format. For example, for a safety presentation using a specially designed set of color slides and meant to be delivered to 300 employees, the speaker may want to organize the major concepts around a particular type of outline. (We shall examine this kind of presentation a little later.)

The basic outline format shown in Box 4-5 has proven to work well for many business professionals in a variety of different situations. This organizational format can be varied for specific topics or speaking situations. The introductory items set up the delivery for the technical presentation. The organizational abstract focuses on each major piece of technical information. Once the concept has been introduced, it then should be explained. Once it has been explained, a verbal example should be given to support the explanation. It should be followed by a visual example, which can be explained verbally or by using material in the visual aid or by pointing to parts of the actual object. Once the concept has been completely communicated, some transitional thought, word, or phrase should bridge the thinking of the listeners to the next concept to be presented.

The actual number of concepts to be presented in a single technical speech must be based on the subject, audience, the time limits, and the purpose for giving the presentation. This outline format is flexible enough to provide the speaker with optional planning.

The conclusion is organized to provide a summary of the main pieces of technical information presented. The application of the information should be dealt with, and the presentation should end with some concluding thought that ties into the theme of the presentation, very possibly relating to the original purpose.

You will find this outline model helpful in pulling your thoughts together as you collect the data and in providing continuity in evaluating and selecting specific data. The more informed you are about the subject, the easier it will be to work with this basic outline format. If you have an organizational pattern in your head as

BOX 4-5   *SAMPLE OUTLINE FORMAT FOR A TECHNICAL PRESENTATION*

Specific Subject: _____ **Specific Purpose:** _____

Introduction

Interpersonal Attention Focus: _____

Introductory Proposition: _____

Audience Role/Purpose Statement: _____

Organizational Abstract of Technical Information

Concept One: _____

- Explanation: _____

- Verbal example: _____

- Visual example: _____

Transitional idea: _____

Concept Two: _____

- Explanation: _____

- Verbal example: _____

- Visual example: _____

Transitional idea: _____

(Follow Concept pattern for all succeeding concept statements; then
    summarize all important concepts in Conclusion.)

Conclusion
Summary Listing of Major Concepts:

One: _____

Two: _____

(Include all major concepts in Summary.)

Application of Technical Data: _____

Thematic Concluding Thought:_____

you research your data, it will be easier to collect the data in a format from which
the delivery can be made.

There are other ways to organize technical information for a presentation.
One such system is designed around using color slides as a focal point of the presentation. Many organizations and businesses prefer the delivery of a technical
presentation with slides. This technique is becoming more common for some very
practical reasons (see Box 4-6).

BOX 4-6   *SLIDE PRESENTATIONS*

1. Slides can give a presentation a very professional look.
2. Slides are easily provided in organizations that have their own inhouse facilities and resources, such as photographers and darkrooms.
3. Slide presentations can be easily stored for repeat presentation.
4. Slides provide a way of keeping formal records for future legal or commercial reference.
5. Slide presentations can provide accuracy of technical content when more tan one person must present the same information.
6. Slide presentations can maintain a level of consistency in large organizations that have many locations in different parts of the country.
7. Slides permit the translation of content to other languages with a minimum of communication problems.

The organizational format in Box 4-7 is designed for professionals who know from the beginning that they are going to be using slides as the main source of their technical presentation.

BOX 4-7   *BASIC ORGANIZATIONAL FORMAT FOR A TECHNICAL SLIDE PRESENTATION*

Greeting

Introduction of Technical Theme: Slide # _____ Title: _____

_____ Slide # _____ Title: _____

_____ Slide # _____ Title: _____

_____ Slide # _____ Title: _____

Purpose of Presentation:

_____ Slide # _____ Title: _____

_____ Slide # _____ Title: _____

Abstract of Procedure or Process

Step One: _____ Slide # _____ Title: _____

     Explanation: _____ Slide # _____ Title: _____

     Application: _____ Slide # _____ Title: _____

     Evaluative Comment: _____ Slide # _____ Title: _____

     Transition: _____ Slide # _____ Title: _____

Step Two: _____ Slide # _____ Title: _____

     Explanation: _____ Slide # _____ Title: _____

     Application: _____ Slide # _____ Title: _____

Evaluative Comment:_____   Slide #_____   Title:_____

Transition:_____   Slide #_____   Title:_____

(Continue with as many steps as are necessary.)

Conclusion

Summary: (repeat key slide for each step)

One:_____   Slide #_____   Title:_____

Two:_____   Slide #_____   Title:_____

(Include all preceding steps in Summary.)

Recommendations:

_____   Slide #_____   Title:_____

_____   Slide #_____   Title:_____

Closing Remarks:

_____   Slide #_____   Title:_____

In addition to this format, several other methods can function well in technical presentations. *Chronological order*, sometimes referred to as time-order sequence, will work when you are trying to provide a historical approach to some technical area.

Spatial order, commonly called "parts of a whole," is a popular format for technical presentations. For example, if the subject of the presentation is the operation of an office copy machine, explain each part of the working machinery. Once each part is identified and explained, the operational process can be explained step by step.

Presenting technical data in *order of importance* is another convenient organizational pattern. For example, a sales manager may find this the most workable format when trying to explain a new product to a group of salespeople. Explaining the product features and specialities in order of importance provides the listeners with perspective on the marketability of the product. Depending on the marketing campaign, a descending or ascending order of importance could be used in organizing the technical information.

When some organizational pattern cannot be found to work for a particular technical area, there is always the *topical approach*. This is simply a matter of taking the subject and subdividing it into minitopics. This pattern, although less structured than others, does function well in some situations. When a new product or procedure is being introduced into a large business, the topical pattern of organizing the information may work very well. A novice speaker may discover that more time is needed in this method, since it is less structured than some of the others.

Most of these organizational formats have proven to work well for individuals preparing technical presentations. We have found that the first two organizational patterns presented in this chapter—the basic outline format and the slide outline format—are the most popular and most adaptable to a variety of situations. They appear to save busy professionals planning time when preparing their technical presentations. Examine and experiment with these various organizational formats. You will have to practice and experiment to determine which structures work well for you in specific situations.

MAKING A TECHNICAL PRESENTATION VISUAL

Visual aids are an important part of spoken technical presentations. Donald Bryant and Karl Wallace write that "although speech is the principal medium of any communication act, it is often profitable to employ visual aids."[1] As a student, you have probably found that the eyes more often than the ears assist you in acquiring information. The blackboard and chalk bring a great deal of information to all of us through our eyes. Many times the barest of scribbles clearly communicates an abstract concept that is ever so difficult to put into words. Donis Dondia states that we seek visual reinforcement of our knowledge for many reasons, but primarily because of the directness of the information, the close approximation to the real experience.[2]

Military departments have been using visual aids for many years in their training programs, and they have done so because they claim that as much as 40 percent of the time needed for instruction can be saved by the use of visual aids. Information is comprehended with a higher percentage of accuracy when visual aids are used, and during the crisis of World War II, the military forces discovered this fact.

In order to use visual aids successfully in your technical presentations, you must have a clear understanding of what they are, how they relate to a listening audience, and how they relate to you as a speaker, and you must be aware of some basic guidelines for ensuring their successful use.

There are three basic types of visual aids. The first group is *actual objects,* the real things. If you are talking about a calculator and have one in front of you as a visual aid, you can refer to the real object as you speak. The second type of visual aid is called *pictorial realism.* Rather than the real object, the presentation uses a picture, sketch, or slide of the real object. This is a practical aid, and it makes sense for some technical presentation: A salesperson making a presentation on the latest model car or a steel punch press would find it difficult to carry the objects themselves to the presentation. The third type of visual aid is the *symbolic figuration.* This is a simple rendition of the object or some abbreviated form of the real object. This is the type of visual aid that quite often is used by the teacher who is trying to communicate an abstract idea on the board with chalk. The symbol may not look at all like the real object, but the simplified sketch stimulates the human mind to fill in the details.

Visual aids can be most effective for the audience. Harold Weiss and J. B. McGrath[3] summarize some specific benefits for the audience when the speaker presents information with visual aids (see Box 4-8).

BOX 4-8   VALUE OF VISUAL AIDS

1. Visuals help the audience to retain and recall technical information.
2. Visuals will help to attract the attention of the listeners.
3. Visuals will help to simplify complex information.
4. Visuals, when used throughout the entire presentation, will help to maintain a constant interest in the technical material, especially if the information is of a repetitious nature.
5. Visuals help to improve the level of understanding of the technical information, especially for a nontechnical audience.

Visual aids are extremely important to you as a speaker. They are most helpful in the actual delivery of the presentation, because they help you keep your place in the thought process during the delivery. They can also help you to reduce your nervous tension. For many beginning speakers, gestures feel and look unnatural; but when using visuals, speakers often find that many gestures just "happen naturally." Visuals give the speaker a reason to move about in a natural manner. Visuals can also aid the technical speaker with the content of the message. Transitions are often difficult during the presentation, since most speakers do not plan every transition they intend to use. In an effort to look and sound natural, most speakers attempt to insert transitions as they move along during the delivery. This is where the visual aid can be helpful, since it can serve as a physical transition. As the speaker moves from one aid to the next, this visually cues the audience that the next piece of information is about to be presented. Changing the visuals gives the speaker a second or two of "breathing time" to prepare for the next point in the presentation. Many professional people specifically comment on the benefit of having this little bit of time between visuals to collect their thoughts. Visuals, when used correctly in technical presentation, can provide a poised, professional image.

It is important for you to be aware of some basic guidelines when you make your first attempt to incorporate visual aids into your technical presentations. The practical suggestions in Box 4-9 have proved to be most beneficial to those who employ many visual aids in their delivery.

The use of visual aids is encouraged in most professional organizations and businesses. Most organizations are very positive about providing equipment and photographic and graphic-art services to their employees who are expected to present technical information. With fast processing of color slides, the easy accessibility of videotape equipment, the availability of company-produced 16 mm films, and portable easels and flip charts, the use of visual aids can be a creative and excit-

BOX 4-9   GUIDELINES FOR SELECTING VISUAL AIDS

1. Be sure that all your audience can see the visual material. Take into account the size of the group and size of the room.
2. Speak to the audience and **not** to the visual aid.
3. Use simple, clear visual aids.
4. Use visual aids that are colorful and eye-catching.
5. Use visual aids that are appropriate to the intellectual capabilities of the audience.
6. Remove the visual aid from sight after using it during the delivery.
7. The visual aid should be pertinent to the subject of the technical presentation and contribute to the information rather than detract from it.

ing addition to any technical presentation. Some businesses specialize in creating and selling visual aids; many of these companies, on request, will make aids to order.

Even though such services are available, however, you must know how to organize your information and find the technical data in the proper resources, and you must practice your speech delivery, if you intend to communicate effectively. Visual aids are no substitute for the basic skills.

DELIVERING THE TECHNICAL PRESENTATION

Chapter 3, "Introduction to Presentational Speaking," contains the basic information for presenting a public speech. You may find it convenient to review that material before reading this section. This section is focused on delivery skills in technical presentations, with the assumption that the student is thoroughly familiar with the information in Chapter 3.

First, you will need more volume and force in your voice in a technical presentation that uses visual aids. If the room is darkened for showing slides, a speaker will soon discover that the voice must work harder to compensate for the lack of eye contact, facial expression, and body movement. A dark room does not physically impede the audience's listening, of course, but their attention is focused on the visuals. You will quickly discover the need for vocal clarity and inflection. You may have to slow down a little. Many speakers have found it beneficial to pause for a brief second after they present the visual to their audience. This provides listeners with a moment of "visual absorption," and having done this, they are ready to listen.

Gestures are also important for the technical speaker. Sometimes a simple hand gesture can get lost if the speaker is showing slides on a large screen. In some situations, the visual contains a lot of detailed information, and in this case, the speaker may need a pointer. This instrument will extend the gesture and provide the speaker with an opportunity to point out small but important details. The danger with a pointer is that it can become a source of distraction in the hands of an unaware speaker when it is not in use. Some speakers have found it is better to use a small penlight. This compact flashlight works well in darkened rooms when slides, films, or overhead projectors are used. In fact, some of these lights have an arrow-light projection that will show direction as well as point out detail.

Eye contact, a very important part of delivery, can be most effectively incorporated into a technical presentation. The major complaint we hear from professional people is that they have trouble looking at all of their notes and still trying to look up at the audience without losing their place on paper. A well-designed set of visual aids can serve as the outlined notes. When planned carefully, these visual aids can completely eliminate the need for written notes. Then, the speaker is free to use more and improved eye contact with the audience. Many speakers, showing slides in a darkened room, think that eye contact is not important. On the contrary, whenever possible, a speaker should try to have some light in the room—even a small podium light will do—so that the audience can still see as well as hear the speaker. With high-quality projectors available today, it is rarely necessary for the audience to sit in total darkness during a technical presentation.

Visual aids should contribute to the image of expertise for the technical speaker. For those who feel insecure and uncertain of the subject, visual aids will not serve as a substitute. We do not endorse visual aids as a way of compensating for a lack of skills. They should be looked on as a way of enhancing the delivery and increasing the clarity of the technical data for the audience.

AUDIO-VISUAL EQUIPMENT
AND THE TECHNICAL PRESENTATION

A great variety of audio-visual equipment is available to the technical speaker. In recent years, such equipment has become increasingly lightweight and compact. Much of the equipment is small enough to fit inside a briefcase. Even when heavy and bulky equipment must be used, there are all types of collapsible wheel carts and carries to make this equipment portable. In fact, one type of cart will roll into the trunk of a car; the legs fold up on much the same principle as on the roller cots designed for emergency vehicles.

Because audio-visual equipment and aids are becoming more and more popular with professionals, it is easier to find them. For example, if you have to make a technical presentation, chances are that the place where you are speaking will have the type of equipment you desire. Many hotels provide audio-visual equipment as a part of their convention services, and most business organizations have audio-visual departments to take care of their needs. You must, however, plan in advance.

As a technical speaker, you should be aware of the different types of basic audio-visual equipment that are available. And you should have some idea of the advantages each offers.

The film projector. Either 16 or 8 mm, it is compact and weighs little. New ones are designed for easy insertion of film cartridges. If a sound film is used, a speaker should not try to talk over the sound. If a silent film is used, a speaker can be talking as the projector operates.

Most projectors can be stopped on a selected frame. When using a film projector, most speakers prefer to have someone else operate the projector, since this piece of equipment is usually at the back of the room.

The slide projector. Fast becoming one of the most widely used pieces of audio-visual equipment, it comes in many varieties. Most have interchangeable lenses and slide trays. It is very easy, in long technical presentations, to change the slide tray when necessary. Most projectors have a remote-control switch so that speakers can change their own slides. This is an important feature, because the speaker then has total control of the pacing of the presentation. Most newer models have an automatic focus device. The real caution when using slides is for the speaker to check them over carefully prior to the actual delivery. It is distracting and very unprofessional when slides appear upside down, reversed, or out of sequence. Previewing the slides will eliminate these errors. It is also a good idea to check the lens of a slide projector to make sure it is clear. It does little good to have professionally designed slides, only to have them viewed through fingerprints and dust.

Film-loop projectors. These are designed in compact cases for convenient handling. These projectors work very well in small-audience presentations. For a technical presentation that is repeated for several small audiences, the film-loop projector is an ideal piece of audio-visual equipment.

The cassette tape recorder. This is a convenient piece of audio-visual equipment. Some speakers like to use it not only for technical data, but also to provide background sound for a presentation. You should be cautioned that using background music is not an easy thing to do. Selecting the proper music, and setting it at the proper sound level is most challenging. This is something that the novice technical speaker should not attempt without help.

The overhead projector. This another popular piece of equipment. For technical speakers who wish to demonstrate their information, this projector, using plastic sheets and special colored grease pencils, is an ideal aid. This type of projector will operate well in a fully lighted room. It can be right next to the speaker; it adjusts easily to accommodate any size of screen. You should be cautioned, however, that using this machine takes a special skill of its very own. The speaker must be able to speak and write or draw at the same time. For beginning speakers who are concerned about their accuracy with the content, using this machine takes serious practice. Speakers must be verbally fluent and confident about their information, so that they can write or draw images without confusing this process with what they are speaking. Many speakers have the plastic sheets drawn up before the delivery and merely project them as they speak, and this is certainly the appropriate way for the novice speaker to use the machine. Some specially designed models have a roller device, so that the speaker can change the plastic, draw, and speak at the same time. The speaker who can use this piece of audio-visual equipment well can communicate to the audience the image of an expert.

The videotape recorder. Definitely one of the newest and most popular developments, it can be one of the most helpful aids for communication of technical information. This machine, owing to the design of compact cassette tapes, is great for information storage as well as for repeated delivery of the same presentation. It can be stopped at any moment during its operation; it can provide "instant replay," a feature that is often very important in technical presentations. Furthermore, it can use color as well as black-and-white material. Businesses and professional organizations like this equipment because it permits them to create visual support material designed to their specific needs. In training, which is one of business's most important uses for technical presentations, the videotape recorder is the most important piece of audio-visual equipment available.

Easels and flip charts. These have been around the longest of all visual aids, and adapt to almost any situation. Charts can be designed to accommodate big audiences as well as small ones. With a little bit of colored paper and a few colored felt-tip pens, even artistically naive speakers can create very practical yet visually exciting aids. This is an excellent way to make a highly technical subject both comprehensible and personal for a specific audience. In large organizations, the layout of such visuals can be planned by specialists in graphic-art departments.

FIGURE 4-1 Video tape equipment is frequently used in technical presentations.

FIGURE 4-2   Easels and flip charts are simple and inexpensive, and afford interaction between speaker and audience.

TECHNICAL PRESENTATIONS AND THE PROFESSIONAL

Technical presentations are very common in the life of a professional. Anyone in the professional world today can safely assume that at some time he or she will be called on to make some type of a technical presentation. Whether someone is working with employees, customers, or clients, or as a part of public relations to the community at large, basic skills for presenting technical information are valuable.

In addition to job orientation and training, there is in the business world an increasing focus on providing technical data to consumers. More and more professionals are finding the need to have well-developed skills for communicating technical information for the financial success and growth of an organization. Not only do salespeople and maintenance/repair specialists need these skills, but engineers, draftspersons, designers, and researchers are finding these skills a necessary part of their work. These professionals quickly discover that job success revolves around competence in communication skills. Often such professionals are called on to communicate information to laypersons in their field of speciality, and the challenge of effective communication becomes all the greater.

Such professional demands make it necessary for you, when functioning as a technical speaker, to be organized, to understand the purpose of a presentation, and to relate it to the audience and the occasion. In order to do these things in a presentation that looks professional, you need to be able to remove the unnecessary extras. It is important to learn how to compact loosely structured ideas into an organizational pattern that communicates the proper technical information. When you are able to do these things, you will realize the value and advantages in having these verbal communication skills.

A REVIEW OF KEY ISSUES

Presenting technical information requires the use of selective skills in collecting, organizing, and preparing technical data in order to communicate this information to others. When the use of these skills is planned around a basic process, the speaker will create a professional image of competence as well as maintain an efficient level of verbal communication.

First step: Define the purpose
1.   in general terms
2.   in relationship to the specific audience
3.   in relationship to the attitude of the audience
4.   in relationship to the circumstances surrounding the presentation

Second step: Collect the pertinent technical information
1.   Select the information with care.
2.   Be specific with information in regard to detail.
3.   Know where to look for the technical information.
4.   Use reliable sources.
5.   Organize the collection procedures in order to save research time.

Third step: Organize the technical information
1.   Select vocabulary appropriate to spoken communication.
2.   Use sentence structure appropriate to spoken communication.
3.   Create verbal transitions appropriate to spoken communication.
4.   Develop and employ an organizational format appropriate for the information and the speaking occasion.
     a.   basic outline format
     b.   slide outline format
     c.   chronological order
     d.   spatial order
     e.   order of importance
     f.   topical order

Fourth step: Make the technical presentation visual
1.   Select the type of visuals; real, pictorial, or symbolic.
2.   Realize how visuals relate to the audience.
3.   Realize how visuals relate to the speaker.
4.   Follow the seven basic guidelines for effective use of visual aids.

Fifth step: Deliver the technical presentation
1.   Volume, speech rate, vocal inflection, and emphasis require special attention.
2.   Eye contact, gestures, and body movement should be incorporated into the presentation.

Audio-visual equipment and the technical presentation
1.   film projector
2.   slide projector

3. film-loop projector
4. cassette tape recorder
5. overhead projector
6. videotape recorder
7. easel and flipcharts

EXPERIENCING EXPERIENCES

Presenting technical information to a specific audience about a specialized topic requires the use of highly developed communication skills. These skills, like the other skills presented in this book, require practice. Knowing the skills makes one wiser, but experiencing these skills in practical situations is what will make your presentations professional. Your professionalism is reflected in the confidence you convey as you deliver the technical information in a formal or informal presentation. The poise and smoothness of your behavior is the image you present to your audience. Actual speaking circumstances are not the times to practice these skills; rather, those are the times for concentration on achieving your communication purpose. The time for practicing should come in less formal surroundings, less pressured situations. Your opportunity is here. In the activities that follow, we have tried to set up situations that will provide you with simulated professional experiences in a controlled environment, with you and your classmates under the direction of your instructor. You should use these activities to develop solid verbal communication skills for presenting technical information.

ACTIVITY 1: Orienting the New Employee

Directions: Select one of the following situations and prepare a 10-minute technical presentation for a group of 10-15 persons. [Give your completed presentation in class, followed by your classmates' analysis.]

Situation A: Select a piece of office equipment and explain its technical operation, step by step.

Situation B: Develop a three- to five-step procedure for establishing a new office policy in an organization.

Specific Subject: _____ Specific Purpose: _____

Step 1:

    Explanation: _____

    Application: _____

    Evaluation: _____

Step 2:

    Explanation: _____

    Application: _____

    Evaluation: _____

        (Continue with all steps necessary—usually from three to five.
        Be sure to include all steps in your closing summary.)

Summary and Conclusions: _____

ACTIVITY 2: Presentation to the Board of Directors

Directions: Prepare an oral presentation to the board of directors of a local business organization. Collect as much information about this organization as possible before you plan the speech. Use some form of visual aid. Base your organizational format on one of the patterns suggested in this chapter. Use one of the following situations.

Situation A: Design a public-relations campaign for this organization to improve community relations.

Situation B: Prepare a technical procedure for your organization to negotiate a contract for a product, services, or materials with some other local organization or business.

    When these presentations are delivered in class, use role playing by classmates, so that after the speech a question-and-answer session can follow. After a discussion by the board members, a vote should be taken on whether or not to accept the design or proposal.

EXERCISES

1.   Bring into the class some pieces of office equipment, and present formal technical presentations on how to clean and maintain the machinery. Give a brief written test after the presentation, to test your communication skills when working with the technical information.

2.   Invite to class a professional who does regular technical presentations for groups of people. After the speaker gives the presentation, critique the presentor, using some type of written critique. The students should prepare specific questions concerning the speaker's problems and expectations when traveling around doing this type of communication.

3. Do Activity 2: Presentation to the Board of Directors. Fill out the following Audio-Visual Checklist form the day before you deliver the presentation in class, to test for professional preparedness.

AUDIO-VISUAL CHECKLIST

Visuals:
_____ Are all the visuals labeled correctly?
_____ Are all the visuals in correct order with the text?
_____ Do all the visuals communicate the intended message?
_____ Do the visuals logically follow one another?

Equipment:
_____ Did you check the running parts of the machinery for operation?
_____ Did you clean exposed parts of machine? For example, lenses, tapes, heads, reflectors.

Slides:
_____ Slides all mounted straight?
_____ Slides free of dirt and fingerprints?
_____ Slides project on screen in correct direction?
_____ Slides focused on screen (is the projector the distance from screen)?
_____ Slides fall into projector correctly?

Transparencies:
_____ Placed in proper sequence?
_____ Overhead placed proper distance from the screen?
_____ Projected image on screen with no screen-edge spill?
_____ All overlays fit properly in correct order?
_____ Is image straight on the screen?
_____ Do you or the overhead block the view of any of the audience?

Films:
_____ Film checked for breaks or tears?
_____ Film threaded on projector correctly?
_____ Film set to start on the first picture frame past the leader?
_____ Film focused on screen for the proper distance?
_____ Picture large enough?
_____ Film sound level tested and present?

Tapes:
_____ Recorder heads clean?
_____ Running speed set correctly?
_____ Sound level tested and set?
_____ Tape cued up to start in exact place?

Posters:
_____ Clearly printed in large enough lettering for audience?
_____ Check each chart for spelling, grammar, etc.
_____ Charts in correct sequence?
_____ Easel to hold charts setting level for easy flipping of material?
_____ Easel placed for all of the audience to see it?
_____ Easel placed at proper angle for you to use a pointer?

Location: _____   Is there electrical power in the room? (Need an exten-
                                sion cord?)
                  _____   Is the screen placed so all the audience can see it?
                  _____   Do you have a podium or table to speak from?
                  _____   Can you operate your equipment and see your visuals
                                as you speak?
                  _____   Can the room be darkened?
                  _____   Will you need an assistant for operating equipment and
                                light?
                  _____   Did you check your voice level for the room with the
                                equipment running?
                  _____   Do you need a stool, pointer, reading light for notes?
                  _____   Do you have your entrance to the speaking area
                                planned?

NOTES

1. Donald Bryant and Karl Wallace, *Fundamentals of Public Speaking,* 5th ed. Englewood Cliffs, N.J.: Prentice-Hall, 1976, p. 119.
2. Donis A. Dondia, *A Primer of Visual Literacy.* Cambridge, Mass.: MIT Press, 1973, p. 2.
3. Harold Weiss and J. B. McGrath, *Technically Speaking.* New York: McGraw-Hill, 1963.

CHAPTER FIVE
PERSUASIVE PRESENTATIONS

"We blew it, Gary, I feel we just blew it!"

"What do you mean, Dan? I thought we were doing just fine."

"Somehow I felt throughout your presentation, Gary, that you were simply not being very persuasive. I'm sorry to have to say this, but I have to be honest with you. Then in the question-and-answer period, I kept getting the sinking feeling that both of us were not really expressing what the audience needed to hear in order to be persuaded."

"Well, Dan, we will know later this afternoon because Dave, the director of personnel, told me the Executive Board would discuss our proposal and then vote on it once our forty-five minutes was over. They are talking it over now. Let's keep our fingers crossed because we have a good idea for the company. You know, it isn't easy to be persuasive, is it?"

The discussion between Gary and Dan is not fiction. These two men worked out a proposal to conduct a personnel analysis for a major corporation. Because the corporation was nonunion, and because Gary and Dan were outside consultants asking to come in to do research for the company, their entry was looked at with great caution. On the one hand, the company's top management felt that a new analysis of personnel placement was necessary to ensure that the right person was in each middle-management position, especially supervisory positions. But on the other hand, none of the high-level executives wanted to create such a stir that employees would feel insecure or angry. Moreover, the company had always maintained itself with minimal assistance from outsiders. A decision was made—the company would not accept the proposal made by Gary and Dan. And they let Gary and Dan know that they could have been persuaded by a stronger presentation. There were simply too many ambiguities in what was said, too many questions left unanswered in the forty-five minutes given the two outside consultants. Gary was right when he said: "You know, it isn't easy to be persuasive is it?"

This chapter is designed as a guide to constructing and presenting a persuasive message in the business setting. The foundation for the chapter has been set in the preceding two chapters. We remind you that our goal is to help you feel comfortable and competent in making a presentation to an audience, whether technical or persuasive, within the business community or outside.

KEYS TO PERSUASION—ATTITUDES, BELIEFS, AND VALUES

Persuasion requires having an effect on the attitudes, beliefs, and values of the intended audience. Before we examine the nature and characteristics of attitudes, beliefs, and values, a common understanding of what we mean by "persuasion" is necessary. There are many definitions of persuasion, from many research studies on the subject. The literature deals with the communication variables that appear to be instrumental in creating a change within a listener in response to messages designed to be persuasive. For persuasion to take place, the listener experiences some change in behavior that arises from a shift in attitude, belief, or value. These psychological variables are within each of us and are inextricably bound together.

Definition of persuasion.   When a listener changes a personal attitude, belief, or value in response to a message or series of messages, the change and action of that listener is the "effect" created. Wallace Fotheringham points out that "persuasion is that body of effects in receivers, relevant and instrumental to source-desired goals, brought about by a process in which messages have been a major determinant of those effects."[1] For a presentation to be persuasive, the speaker must share information in ways that are instrumental in bringing about action. The action is the desired response sought by the speaker.

This definition suggests that the message is not the sole determinant for persuasive effects, although it is a major one. We know that intervening variables can also be instrumental in the creation of change. Before hearing a presentation, a listener could have been exposed to other information similar to what the present persuader offers. Some listeners may have previously heard another, less attractive, presentation that encouraged them to take action, and they may act after comparing the two presentations. Or a listener may be under serious time constraints and feel that action cannot wait for another speaker to come forth with an acceptable presentation. We could list many other examples; however, the point to remember is that *if a decision follows a presentation, the speaker's message has been a major instrument affecting the attitudes, beliefs, and values of the audience; if the effects are favorable, the speaker can take a great deal of credit for being persuasive.*

Insight and direction for being persuasive can result from understanding the characteristics of attitudes, beliefs, and values. These psychological features of human beings are the keys to action. As a persuader you must know what attitudes, beliefs, and values are and how they operate in people. Then when you are developing a presentation, you must take the pertinent attitudes, beliefs, and values of your intended audience into account as you select information and develop a strategy for achieving a desired response. We will talk about persuasive strategy and supporting information later in this chapter.

Attitudes, beliefs, and values.   What exactly is an attitude? This question has occupied the minds and research of theorists for generations. A satisfactory answer, based on research, is that an attitude is a mental and neural state of readiness, organized through experience, exerting influence on the individual's response to objects and situations to which it is related. Think for a minute. As you approach this book to study, you have attitudes that come into play; they are organized within you as *predispositions to think, feel, and perceive—in a word, to behave.* The chief characteristics of attitudes are shown in Box 5-1. Furthermore, communication researchers believe that an attitude consists of three fundamental dimensions: (1) cognitive, (2) affective, (3) behavioral.[2] The cognitive dimension of an attitude is the knowledge associated with it or the information about an object, event, issue, situation, or person. But interwoven with the cognitive dimension are feelings or emotions about an object, event, situation, or person. And our knowledge and feelings are springboards to action.

BOX 5-1   CHARACTERISTICS OF ATTITUDES

1. to be aimed at an object, situation, event, issue or person.
2. to be characterized by direction, degree, and intensity.
3. to be a learned response.
4. to be generally stable and enduring.

Ruth, a new executive for the phone company, has been thinking about joining The Forum, a self-improvement speakers' club associated with the company. She has hesitated because, until recently, the group was all male; women were not even approached about becoming members. Through the efforts of affirmative action in the company, accompanied by changing attitudes, women are increasingly moving into management positions, and The Forum is changing, too. Whether they want it or not, male executives can no longer ignore women as they did in the past. Among other things, women are now invited to join the speakers' club.

Ruth, herself, has acquired a new attitude about what it means to be a woman. Furthermore, she has increased the positive strength of this attitude because, since she joined the company, its policy has encouraged more and more women to grow professionally. There is no longer supposed to be any sexual discrimination. Emotionally as well as intellectually, Ruth's attitude toward learning to be an effective speaker is highly positive. She attended a meeting of The Forum at which the officers of the club urged the guests to become members. Her predisposition before entering the meeting room was favorable, so she was highly receptive to becoming a member. It was up to the speakers to encourage the growth of this attitude so that she would make a final decision to join.

Dick is a representative of the Rate Department at the Gas Company. He spent weeks with his peers and supervisors preparing a presentation for the Public Utilities Commission. The company believes it is necessary to obtain a sizeable rate increase. They have completed an audience analysis of the attitudes of the Commissioners toward any rate increases. The analysis has indicated to Dick and others in his department that his job of persuasion will be difficult. Apparently, the commissioners have a strong attitudinal pattern of opposition to any increases. So Dick *shapes his presentation* with this pattern in mind.

Attitudes result from beliefs, and the student of persuasion ought to understand how beliefs operate. A belief represents a mental and emotional acceptance of information and the creation of a particular kind of internal state that acts as a degree of faith. Milton Rokeach has written exhaustively on the subject of beliefs, and he defines belief as "a simple proposition, conscious or unconscious, capable of being preceded by the phrase 'I believe that . . .!' "[3] Rokeach described three kinds of beliefs: (1) existential—those capable of being demonstrated as true or false; (2) evaluative—those in which the objective of the belief is judged to be good or bad; and (3) proscriptive—those which lead to an action that can be judged desirable or undesirable. Rokeach argues that these beliefs have cognitive, affective, and behavioral components, just as attitudes do. According to Rokeach, the beliefs we have can be identified according to a centrality-peripherality model that has five classes. The first class is most central, while the fifth is most peripheral:

1. *Primitive belief 1.* One learned through a direct experience with an object and supported by social consensus.

    George *believed* that money was to be spent cautiously. Throughout his childhood he had earned most of his expense money and observed the conservative, frugal ways in which his parents managed their money. He came to manage his in similar ways.

2. *Primitive belief 2.* One that does not depend on social consequences but, rather, on deep personal experiences.

    Sherry was an outstanding salesperson for a textbook publisher. She refused to drink alcoholic beverages with customers or sales personnel. While in college she had a deep religious experience when vacationing alone. A decision she made as part of a total religious commitment was to avoid eating or drinking anything she *believed* could be harmful to the growth of her mind and body.

3. *Authority belief.* One in which who or what to trust and who or what not to trust is supported by negative or positive authority.

Mary had a great deal of difficulty trusting other people in her social interactions, especially men. She *believed* she could not trust people in general. Quietly struggling with her inability to trust most people, she met several times with a psychoanalyst, and together they decided that she had been taught as a child by her mother not to trust other people unless they were close members of her family. Her mother had always been the major authority in Mary's life and has influenced her in ways which are beyond her conscious comprehension.

4. *Belief derived from authorities.* One that is assimilated from sources with which an individual identifies.

When Al went to work at the First National Bank, he found himself identifying strongly with the high-level officers in the bank. His dress, his political views, his notions about the state of economy, and his activity in selected service organizations were determined largely by his perception of the images and views of these others. He found himself reconstructing his views of such realities in line with what he *believed* these banking authorities believed.

5. *Inconsequential belief.* One that directs behavior but is not highly significant when compared with other beliefs.

Beverly did not gamble and generally she did not *believe* that gambling was a good thing to do. Shortly after she took a business position, Esther and Tony came to her desk selling spots in a football pool. Bev hesitated to get into the pool, but the cost was only a dollar and she did not feel strongly opposed to it. Furthermore, she believed she would be more readily accepted by Esther, Tony, and others around the office if she played as well as worked with them; joining the pool had socializing benefits for her.

All these people in our examples have beliefs that range from central and primitive to peripheral and inconsequential. We all do. And in order to persuade someone, *the person making a presentation must be accepted as someone to believe—someone who offers a highly attractive message. What the listener accepts depends upon how the persuader's message attractively interacts with the listener's psychological makeup.* We cannot know most of what is going on inside another, but we can learn through audience analysis the prevailing and primary attitudes, beliefs, and values that have a bearing on our specific purpose—the precise response we want from the audience.

To be persuasive, the communicator must take into account the shared as well as the particular attitudes, beliefs, and values within an audience. A group of seven members of a board about to make a final decision on a proposal may share in common positive attitudes about the introduction of creative new products into the market, and at the same time they may have differing beliefs about how to develop and introduce such goods. And their attitudes and beliefs are centered in both personal and shared values. If you have a personal value that good health is your most important possession, then your beliefs about exercising and your attitudes toward eating are most likely going to support this value. *Values may be defined as deep-seated standards or central psychological anchors that serve as a basis for ethical guidance and approach-avoidance behavior.*

Carl Rogers tells us that values direct us in prizing.[4] If we prize a relationship with another person, we place value on this friendship. On the other hand, if we can take or leave the presence of another, we place little value on the relationship. If you treasure the free-enterprise system, freedom of speech, and a high level of competitiveness with others, then these are values that are quite enduring and rooted deep within you.

Attitudes, beliefs, and values are woven together within us as interrelated internal variables reflecting human personality and guiding human behavior, especially communication. We engage others for persuasion, and we allow ourselves to be persuaded according to attitudes, beliefs, and values. Therefore, we cannot adequately respond to the question, What is persuasion? without giving attention to them.

PERSUASION AND THE AUDIENCE

A business speaker once appeared on campus as the guest of a student who arranged with the professor to have him speak. The class was a large communications course at which it was common practice for guests suggested by students to appear and share ideas about communication. The guests were to speak about some feature of communication in the texture of the world each experienced professionally. This particular speaker had not asked about the class in advance; so, shortly before he was to be introduced, the instructor began to brief him on the nature of the audience about to be faced. "Hell, I am not even quite certain where I am today— I've been on the run so much this week," the speaker declared. He signified that even though his pace was fast, he was at least going to try to fulfill his commitment to appear. Without any apparent sense of the audience, he worked well with it from the beginning when he said, "I'm not going to make a formal speech! Can we just talk for the hour?" The response to his question was immediate; hands went up and he fielded questions without hesitation. He and the audience seemed continually to adjust to each other, and the immediate response of both speaker and audience was that this hour was a success.

Occasionally this kind of speaker-audience relationship takes place with a sort of communication magic in the event. In general, however, for a speaker to achieve success with an audience, an analysis for adaptation is a necessary part of the effort to be persuasive. The president of one huge corporation will not even think of venturing out to face more than one kind of audience—one made up of persons much like himself. He apparently does not have the flexibility and confidence possessed by the speaker in our first example. He is unwilling to make a strong effort to become effective with a variety of audiences. Once, he sought advice on overcoming his difficulty in facing audiences made up of financial experts and investment counselors. After some initial discussions, he balked at suggestions for audience analysis and adaptation—the adjusting of self and ideas to others to achieve the desired response. "I'm usually fine with audiences at my management seminars," he boasted. "We're having one this week. Stop by the Hilton Tuesday at 3:00 and you can see me in action!" Indeed, he was successful with this particular audience, for the members seemed to view him as some sort of folk hero. To them he reflected the realization of the American Dream: a man with only a high-school education who used the free-enterprise system and hard work to become a corporate giant. There was a strong identification between this speaker and his audience of new managers. This identification was good, and with this audience he was influential. What he needed to learn to do was to be as successful with other kinds of audiences!

A successful route to persuasion begins with analysis for persuasion. How much more could this corporate leader expand his world as a visible business leader? We want to help you achieve success in persuasion with any kind of audience. One important step to take is to learn to develop a clear image of that audience (whether it is one, several persons, or a large organization). Then, in the construction of the message, adjust ideas to the audience, so that the audience can adjust to the ideas. Make yourself and your ideas as attractive and compelling as possible.

In order to make the ideas compelling and attractive, a communicator must conduct an analysis and construct a profile of the particular audience to be addressed. Suppose you work for a high-technology corporation developing, manufacturing, and marketing computational machines for retail stores. You have been asked by your division to make a presentation in order to be awarded research-and-development money, and the awards in the company are competitive. You have the subject, your general goals, and you have determined the specific purpose—the precise response you want from the decision-making audience. You are going to call for a decision to award your group the money for undertaking the research and development of a new product your group believes can make the company far more competitive in selling equipment to discount department stores and fast-food stores stores. You write out what you want from the audience. Then you make a useful analysis of the audience and apply a persuasive strategy to obtain this response. In conducting the audience analysis, you want to discover those characteristics of an audience, including values, beliefs, and attitudes, that are most likely to affect the ways in which its members will listen to—and act on their perceptions of—you and your message. This analysis can be achieved by discovering answers to three basic questions:

1. What does the audience know, and how do its members feel about me and the group, department, or organization I am representing?
2. What does the audience know, and how do they feel about the subject and purpose of my presentation?
3. Are there prevailing and powerful attitudes, beliefs, and values in the audience that are necessary to attend to in order to gain satisfacton?

In order to answer these questions, you are going to have to read about an organization, its divisions, or particular executives within the organization. You are going to have to interview persons who can tell you about the audience, and you may even talk individually to members of the audience before the formal presentation. You search for pertinent information that answers these questions, and this guides you in constructing a profile of the audience.

Let's consider each of these questions now in more detail. The first audience-centered question is one designed to help you learn about the image and credibility the audience assigns to you and the group you represent. As you remember, we spoke of image and credibility in Chapter 3, for they are among the most important elements in the process of persuasion. Decisions are often partly made by how clearly and positively the listeners see, hear, and feel about you and your organization. When Jim was assigned by his company's owners to manage an investment newly acquired as an addition to a rapidly growing chain, he formally addressed his new staff two weeks after assuming his managerial position. The employees had been extremely fond of the person Jim replaced. They knew little of Jim. They only knew he was young, that he had a reputation of being able to manage a restaurant in highly profitable ways, and that apparently he was both a fair and demanding employer. In the two weeks before he met with his staff, he learned all he could about what his audience knew about him and how they felt about him, so that he could consider this information as he constructed his message as their new boss. He discovered that this knowledge helped him to obtain the desired effect, his specific purpose.

The second question concerns the subject for the speech. Georgia discovered how important it is to use this question for audience analysis. She became the new chairperson for an academic department. She had been chosen for the job because the college dean recognized that she possessed skills for managing funds and budgets. Georgia discovered that the faculty in her department were extremely sensitive on money matters and knew little of the constraints the department had to work within. So, in several ways, she surveyed the faculty and pertinent other administrators before constructing her presentation for her meeting. She needed to speak about the budget for both the current and the upcoming academic years. As in the case of Jim, she felt that the information she gained about the audience's knowledge and feelings was instrumental in preparing and presenting her message.

The third question focuses your attention on particular features not uncovered or highlighted in answering the first two. For example, suppose your audience consists of five decision-makers who hold top management positions within your company. Because you discover they collectively hold a strong belief in effective use of current manufacturing equipment, you need to refer to use of this equipment in your plan for the production of the product under consideration. Two of the five, you discover, are firm managers of corporate budgets. One particularly favors products capable of less complex marketing strategies, while another values products that directly compete with those of the major competitor. The attitudes, beliefs, and values about these matters must be dealt with if you are to be effective.

Information about the audience cannot help you achieve success unless you use it wisely. *Therefore, audience adaptation is the necessary extension of audience analysis.* As we stated earlier, the successful speaker must adjust ideas to an audience, so that an audience can adjust to ideas. Moreover, the audience is likely to feel positively toward the speaker and the ideas expressed if its members can relate to what they hear with interest and understanding. This is true even when an audience is gathered for a message on an unpleasant subject or occasion. The challenge for the speaker is to learn how to capture the audience's attention, maintain it, and encourage the audience to listen fully.

We have spent considerable time talking about audience analysis, because to be persuasive, you must motivate the audience and get it to act favorably on your ideas and proposals. You can accomplish quite a bit with carefully structured persuasive messages tailored to the desires and needs of the audience. In Chapter 3 we reviewed the fundamentals of speaking before an audience, and as a persuasive as well as informative communicator, you must use these fundamentals skillfully. As we proceed in the present chapter, we will treat some of these fundamentals again to reinforce their importance.

A STRATEGIC DESIGN FOR PERSUASION

The persuasive communicator designs a message strategically, to motivate the audience to act. Armed with an audience analysis and a specific purpose, the speaker has a number of options open for selecting, arranging, and supporting ideas with the utmost effort to be persuasive. One option we have found effective is to combine organization, reasoning, and supporting materials in a persuasive pattern.[5] Figure 5-1 shows the pattern.

The first feature of the persuasive pattern is the introduction. Using one or two *appeals for attention,* the communicator seeks to establish a positive relationship and a good feeling toward listening as she or he begins speaking to the audience. You can choose from at least six options: (1) a personal warm greeting; (2) a startling statement; (3) a dramatic illustration; (4) a relevant quotation; (5) perti-

FIGURE 5-1   The persuasive pattern.

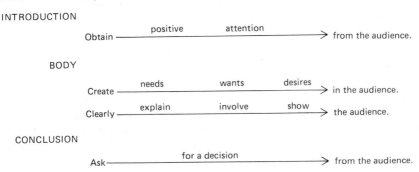

nent humor; (6) or a rhetorical question. The rhetorical question is perhaps the most frequently used attention-getter, although the others can equally effective. In any case, it is important for the speaker not to spend a great deal of time obtaining positive attention. Most of the presentation should be devoted to the body of the message, which includes the second and third features. Along with gaining attention, the communicator can enhance the chances for effectiveness by including in the introduction some information that helps the audience to "feel good," "positive," and "warm" toward the speaker. This feeling can be created through a friendly, sincere, and enthusiastic delivery from the onset, as well as through the use of information the audience is likely to find attractive or thought-provoking.

The second feature of the persuasive pattern is the effort to *create in the audience a need, want, or desire* for an idea, goods, service or plan. When you begin to make a strong effort to affect the attitudes, beliefs, and values of your audience, you have several choices about the path you must take.

Sometimes in persuasive communication we speak as if a message gains its thrust from only one of three kinds of proof: appeal to emotions, appeal to logic, or appeal to ethics. For instance, a business executive was once heard to remark, "Well, Herb tells a good story in his presentation, but it is all emotional appeal." In contrast, a listener can say of a speaker, "She sounds so rational, but there is no real feeling in what she says to us." Or "He's a good man, even though what he claims does not make much sense if you look at it logically." In each comment, the listener acts as if the speech is characterized by one major mode of proof, whereas in reality this is not the case. Ethical, logical, and emotional appeals are bound together in a communicative relationship, but one mode may dominate over others.

A speaker who is trying to get the audience to make a decision to purchase a computer system may use lines of reason (logic, sense-making) that at the same time appeal to the audience's *feelings* about security, success, and good will. The message has emotional as well as ethical impact.

In the second feature of the persuasive pattern, the speaker develops ideas that can lead the audience to recognize a need for something or a desire for something. The communicator does this by appealing to the emotions. At the same time, this appeal can be developed according to sound logic that makes a "great deal of sense" to the listeners. And if the listeners feel attracted to the speaker's ideas and the ideas make sense, the speaker also is seen as having high credibility or ethos. In this portion of the message you want to be credible and logical and to have the listeners experience feelings, too. We remind you that in order to accomplish this, you need to carefully and realistically analyze your audience before you plan and construct your message.

Some listeners may be aware of a need you can satisfy, while others may not. Therefore, in your analysis, you must determine the extent to which you feel the audience understands its need and can define it. A troubled man entering a church to hear a religious speaker may sense something is missing in his life but may not see the depth and extent of the need. The speaker can help him to see the need quite clearly. Other listeners are aware of the needs they face, but they are uncertain how to satisfy those needs. The persuasive communicator can express a strong desire in a way that brings out a similar desire in the audience. For example, one growing business needed a number of new vehicles for transporting both products and people. Uncertain of what they really wanted, the management team scheduled a series of presentations with automotive businesses. The communicators tried to get this audience to want their vehicles. In another case, several investors told a franchise representative of a fast-food corporation, "We feel we need to invest our money in several franchises in this region of the state, but we are uncertain whether we want to go with hamburgers or roast beef." In this case the sales representative's task was to persuade her audience to want to invest in roast-beef franchises. She wanted this audience to experience an intense desire to invest their money in her firm's franchises. She presented herself, her data, and her major points to the audience in such a way that they came to see her as highly credible and a representative of an extremely profitable industry. At the onset, the audience *knew it needed* a product, and by the time this representative completed this presentation, the audience felt *it wanted* what her firm could provide.

To make the audience reach a decision, the representative relied on the other part of the second feature of the persuasive pattern. First, she carefully *explained* the ways her franchise operated in comparison with competition, and then she distributed some of the products. She also demonstrated some of the technology used by her company, and she tried to get the audience to actually see themselves as satisfied customers. When she was almost out of time, she *moved for closure*—the final feature of the persuasive pattern—by directly asking the audience to make a decision.

PERSUASIVE SUPPORT CONTRIBUTES TO SUCCESS

The persuasive message ought to have attractive and sound supporting material. Supporting material is the evidence used by a communicator to clarify or prove claims offered for the audience to understand, accept, and act on. Sometimes an audience needs little or no proof of the issues the speaker focuses on, but other times, a considerable amount of clarification seems necessary. A thorough audience analysis suggests to the speaker how much clarification and how much proof seem to be needed. A rule we use frequently when working with supporting material is that clarification precedes proof. If, for example, an audience is to accept new rate increases for meeting the growth of the electric company, the speaker may have to discover how much the audience knows about the way a rate increase is determined and the underlying causes of such an increase. However, if the audience knows enough about these matters, the speaker is wasting precious time in review. A knowledgeable audience may become irritated if it is told something it already knows!

Usually most of the effort in a persuasive speech is aimed at obtaining proof—

information that leads to a high degree of probability that the members of the audience will act according to the request. Most audiences in business are unlikely to accept unsupported statements, and reasoning based on evidence becomes necessary for the speaker. Furthermore, audiences in the business world prefer documented to undocumented claims, and the speaker must show or be prepared to show where the evidence was found or how it was determined.

In making a persuasive presentation in the business setting, perhaps the three most effective kinds of supporting material are *reliable research findings, expert testimony, and detailed illustrations.* The first kind of support is usually found in special reports and surveys of intensive, well-designed research. After determining the point or claim to be made for the audience, the speaker reviews the studies that were the basis for making the claim and draws information the audience is likely to understand and accept. Both the data and the claim are given to the audience. The same construction is necessary for the use of expert testimony and factual illustrations. The support must be information the audience is likely to understand, accept, and be moved by. This is another reason for the importance of audience analysis.

Additional supporting material includes nondetailed illustrations, analogies, and explanations. Analogy, or comparison, points out similarities between something that is known, understood, or believed, and something that is unknown. An explanation is a concise statement that clarifies an obscure term or concept or describes the relation between a whole and its parts. The nondetailed illustration is similar to the detailed illustration, but it is best used with a number of similar instances to back up a factual illustration.

When your research brings you support you believe can be effective in a persuasive presentation, you can check out the potential of the support by applying the six questions presented in Box 5-2.

BOX 5-2   SUPPORT CHECKLIST

---

1. Is the support accurate and reliable?
2. Is the support directly related to the claims?
3. Is the support the best available?
4. Is the support information I can understand, accept, and believe?
5. Is the support relevant to the needs of the audience?
6. Is the support information the audience is likely to recognize, understand, and accept?

In the business setting, supporting material is often provided through the use of visual aids. We treated the development and use of visual aids extensively in Chapter 4, "Technical Presentations." The information found there, however, also applies to the use of visual aids in persuasive presentations. Remember: *Vivid, clear visuals can be the most effective way to present support in using a persuasive strategy.*

To illustrate the kind of support that can be used by a persuasive speaker, two examples are provided. Examine them carefully, and consider them first from the view of the speaker and then from the view of the persons who might be in the audience. Can the support contribute to persuasion? To what extent?

Consider, for example, the business person arguing before a select audience of city planners that the installation of nuclear power plants for generating electricity is safe. To support her point, she tells the audience:

> The Reactor Safety Study is the most recent and by far the most compre-
> hensive of the studies available. You have heard detailed presentations on the
> subject, but let me underscore its importance. It required some seventy man-
> years of effort and about four million dollars, using experts from around the
> country. The draft was published for comments more than a year ago, and
> eighty-seven sets of responses were received and factored into the final report.
> After this public scrutiny and input, the conclusions remained that nuclear
> power is much less hazardous than many nonnuclear risks common in our
> society. In fact, many nonnuclear events, such as airplane crashes, dam
> failures, and explosions, are about 10,000 times more likely to produce large
> numbers of fatalities than nuclear plants.[6]

In this particular setting, the audience found themselves giving careful thought to what they heard in relation to their attitudes and beliefs. Nuclear power and its risks have always been something to fear, but each listener was familiar with the study, and reference to it along with the use of nondetailed examples contributed to an eventual persuasive outcome.

An executive of a large supermarket chain addressed a group of consumer advocates. His task was to persuade them that the inflation in food prices was not the result of the supermarkets significantly increasing their profits. Using statistics in a careful explanation, he told his skeptical audience:

> Out of the typical dollar paid by the shopper for food in the average super-
> market, about seventy-nine cents is paid out by the stores to cover farmers'
> and middlemen's costs for growing, processing, and transporting the food.
> These are the costs that occur before the food ever reaches the supermarket.
> In other words—of a typical dollar you spend in our store, approximately
> seventy-nine cents goes back to a supplier or manufacturer to pay for the
> product. The remaining twenty-one cents of your typical food dollar is the
> average amount added by the retailer to cover the expenses of performing the
> "endman" function of gathering together a variety of products, preparing
> those products, and offering them in a clean and attractive store for final
> selection by our customers. It is where this twenty-one cents, often called
> the retail margin, goes that I want to examine with you at this time. Margin
> reflects expenses—not profits. The first bill paid out of that twenty-one cents
> is fourteen cents for employees' wages. In other words, sixty-seven percent
> of the cost of operating a store goes for labor. Next to the cost of the mer-
> chandise itself, wages represent the largest part of your food dollar. Add
> about six cents for other operating expenses—rent, insurance, supplies, adver-
> tising, the trucks to bring the food to the store, and of course, taxes and
> utility bills. We've all gulped a bit at our gas and electricity bills. What's left

of course is profit. After all the bills are paid, the typical American supermarket company today has a little less than a penny left over as profit.

Again, we have an example of a speaker attempting to persuade his audience. If his
supporting material was carefully selected and tested in advance, he could stand
firmly on it and offer a claim for the audience to accept and act on. However, the
audience will interpret and evaluate both the support and the claim on the basis of
their attitudes, beliefs, and values. If the support is qualified to the audience and is
concrete, in line with the six questions about support, then it can have real impact
for persuasion.

Know your audience, research the subject thoroughly, and reason carefully
with sound supporting material. An audience is not likely to be persuaded by
ambiguous, unsupported statements.

VOICE, MOVEMENT, AND APPEARANCE— AIDS TO PERSUASION

The credible communicator is one who appears confident about speaking ability
and about the specific purpose, or response sought. We discussed delivery in
Chapter 3, covering speech tension, gestural behavior, and the use of the voice. You
may want to review this information, for the most carefully constructed message
can sometimes turn a listener off if it is delivered in a dry, monotonous manner by
a person who lacks animation.

The persuasive speaker is one who is *in control* of her or his delivery. Control
is a key word here. You have to know how to use your voice, your body, and your
appearance to increase the attractiveness of your total presentation.

Capturing and projecting a vocal tone (volume, rate, pitch, pronunciation,
pauses) completely in the spirit of your intentions is extremely important. Persuasive communicators do not have to be great orators to be effective, but they do have
to know their vocal strengths and weaknesses and build on the strength. An important executive once tried to persuade other high executives in his company that
they should purchase a company airplane. Although his case seemed attractive on
paper, when he spoke before his superiors, his droning voice, slow pace, stumbling
pauses, and a nervous chuckle all contributed to their difficulty in listening to him.
He appeared to lack confidence in himself. Only after several additional presentations was a plane purchased. Did his voice improve, or did he wear them out? We
think improved delivery helped.

Physical presence is equally important. The speaker who paces aimlessly,
stands frozen like a statue, or gazes anywhere but at the audience makes it difficult for the audience to hear and to listen to the presentation. Often, distracting
cues draw attention to themselves and away from the meaning of the speaker's
words. The persuasive communicator must control his or her movement and gestures and visual directness so that these behaviors work effectively with the content

of the message. There is no substitute for ample practice by yourself and with a "practice audience" so that you can become comfortable, sincere, and enthusiastic in the projection of ideas.

Along with effective use of the voice and body, we need to be in control of our appearance so that it is appropriate, attractive, and certainly not distracting. We all know that we cannot easily modify our physical characteristics. We can accept ourselves and dress in a way that enhances who we are, who we represent, and what we are to say.

A story about John F. Kennedy states that the President was on an elevator a few minutes before making an important speech. He suddenly noticed he was wearing brown shoes. He is said to have remarked angrily that the shoes would not do, and one of his aides made him relax by declaring that it was "O.K."—he could be addressing a "brown-shoe audience." Select your apparel carefully so that if contributes to your overall effort. A woman once appeared before a business luncheon wearing a blouse that was colorful, its print patterned with cocktails, lit cigarettes, and romantic couples. Throughout her presentation, many members of the audience seemed to focus on her apparel more than her ideas.

Clothing can be distracting. Both clothing and other nonverbal factors in appearance can also help to draw and maintain attention to a credible speaker with a sound, attractive message. The point is, dress to look your best and in ways consistent with your specific purpose in talking and the occasion for the communication.

HANDLE THE QUESTIONS— PERSUASIVELY

We have now studied analyzing the audience with persuasion in mind, designing a speech with the persuasive pattern and strong support, and determining a delivery that can enhance the persuasive effort. But in all business speaking, both in organizational settings or with an audience from the public, there is one additional task— handling questions from the audience. Chapter 3 explains how to handle questions from the audience. Now is an excellent time to carefully review this material. For some speakers, the Q-A responsibility is a relatively easy task, and for others it is extremely difficult. Moving from the security of the prepared outline often frightens the speaker, who may fantasize about the tough questioner in the audience—the one with an ax to grind, a speech to make, or who does not easily accept or understand anything new.

The speaker should look forward enthusiastically to this part of the presentational experience.

Persuasive presentations are ones creating a favorable decision to act on what the speaker needs and wants. The effective communicator will—with the knowledge of attitudes, beliefs, and values—analyze and adapt to the target audience. A persuasive pattern combining organization, reasoning and support centered in audience motives is necessary for success. The persuader will use skillful delivery and attractive visuals to enhance the spoken presentation. Finally, the question-and-answer period must reveal a strong persuader who does not shrink back from her or his purpose but instead remains assertive, confident, and in control until the entire presentation is finished.

A REVIEW OF KEY ISSUES

Persuasion is the act whereby a speaker causes a listener to believe in a way that furthers the speaker's goals; it is largely accomplished through the speaker's messages.

Attitude is a state of readiness, organized through experiences exerting influences on individual responses to objects and situations with which it is related.

Belief represents an acceptance of information, mentally and emotionally, and the creation of a particular kind of internal state that acts as a degree of faith.

Value is a deep-seated standard or central psychological anchor that serves as a basis for ethical guidance and approach-avoidance behavior.

Audience analysis is an investigative procedure, beginning after the subject, general speech goal, and specific purpose have been chosen; its purpose is to discover audience beliefs, attitudes, and values.
1. Approach audience as listeners who sense, interpret, evaluate, and respond.
2. For persuasion speakers should approach audience analysis with three basic questions:
   a. What does the audience know, and how do its members feel about me and the group, department, or organization I am representing?
   b. What does the audience know, and how do they feel about the subject and purpose of my presentation?
   c. Are there prevailing and powerful attitudes, beliefs, and values in the audience that are necessary to attend to in order to gain satisfaction?

A strategic design is necessary for persuasion:
1. introduction—to gain positive attention
2. body—to create a need and clearly explain why the audience should want that need satisified
3. conclusion—to ask for the listener to make a decision

Persuasive support materials contribute to the success of the speech:
1. Obtain proof supports with
   a. reliable research findings
   b. expert testimony
   c. detailed illustrations
   d. nondetailed illustrations
   e. analogies
   f. explanations
2. The following should be applied to each proof support:
   a. Is it accurate and reliable?

    b.   Is it directly related to the claim?

    c.   Is it the best available?

    d.   Can I accept, believe, and understand the support information?

    e.   Is the support relevant to the needs of the audience?

    f.   Is the support likely to be recognized, understood, and accepted by the audiences?

Voice, movement, and appearance are vital as aids in persuasion.

Handling questions and answers is important to the persuasive presentation.

1.   Questions are an integral part of the speech presentation.

2.   Answering questions is successful when responses relate directly to the speech content and purpose.

EXPERIENCING EXPERIENCES

Persuasion is something that we see around us every day in newspaper ads, television commercials, roadside billboards, mailers, and painted panels on trucks and vans. We live with this constant bombardment of persuasive strategies. Therefore, we do not give it our primary attention; we tolerate it. It is only when we begin to think about how much influence and power this persuasion has on us that we give serious thought to it. This use of persuasion is powerful and well-planned. We need only look at the products we use in our homes to become aware of this fact. Persuasion strategies do not come naturally; they are carefully designed before they become a working reality. It is our purpose, with the following experience activities, to make you aware of the careful planning and detailed effort that go into persuasive strategy operations. Once you understand this planning effort, you will see the value and ethical obligations that are part of developing skill in persuasive speaking presentations. Use these structured activities to experiment with planning, organization, and ethical standards as you persuade others.

ACTIVITY 1: Planning Your Persuasive Presentation

Directions: Use this form to plan a persuasive presentation for delivery in class.

Persuasive Subject: _____

Audience considerations:

    What do they know about me? _____

    Feel about me? _____

    What do they know about the subject?_____

    Feel about the subject? _____

    What do they know about the occasion?_____

Feel about the occasion? _____

How does the audience regard this communication act? _____

Introduction:

Positive attention-getter: _____

Speaker/audience relationship? _____

Body—core statement: _____

_____

Create a need:

Support #1: _____

Support #2: _____

Involve audience with need:

Support #1: _____

Support #2: _____

Answer the need:

Support #1: _____

Support #2: _____

Conclusion:

Restate core statement: _____

Summarize:

Need: _____

Need involvement: _____

Answer to need: _____

Closing thought: _____

ACTIVITY 2: Testing Your Proof Supports

Directions: Include an example of each of the six support types in your speech, and use this form to analyze each support before you try it out on your listening audience.

Support Type: Researcher Fact

Describe it: _____

Source? _____

Purpose? _____

Timeliness? _____

Probability audience reaction? _____

Personal opinion—Why? _____

Support Type: Expert Testimony

Describe it: _____

Source? _____

Purpose? _____

Timeliness? _____

Probable audience reaction? _____

Personal Opinion—Why? _____

Support Type: Detailed Illustration

Describe it: _____

Source? _____

Purpose? _____

Timeliness? _____

Probable audience reaction? _____

Personal opinion—Why?

Support Type: Nondetailed Illustration

Describe it: _____

Source? _____

Purpose? _____

Timeliness? _____

Probable audience reaction? _____

Personal opinion—Why? _____

Support Type: Analogy

Describe it: _____

Source? _____

Purpose? _____

Timeliness? _____

Probable audience reaction? _____

Personal opinion—Why? _____

Support Type: Explanation

Describe it: _____

Source? _____

Purpose? _____

Timeliness? _____

Probable audience reaction? _____

Personal opinion—Why? _____

ACTIVITY 3: Classmate Persuasive Reaction Reply

Speaker: _____

Speech: _____

I (was, was not) persuaded by the presentation because:

_____

Audience Analysis:	poor	average	good	Reason:
Introduction:	poor	average	good	
Core Statement:	poor	average	good	
Creation of Need:	poor	average	good	
Audience Involvement with Need	poor	average	good	
Answer to Need:	poor	average	good	
Conclusion:	poor	average	good	
Summary:	poor	average	good	
Closing Thought:	poor	average	good	
Quality of Supports:	poor	average	good	
Organization:	poor	average	good	

My suggestions for needed improvement are: _____

Your most effective persuasive quality was: _____

Your least effective persuasive quality was: _____

Your delivery style (was/was not) effective because: _____

_____

EXERCISES

1. After having given these speeches in class, go out into community organizations and give these speeches in revised form. Have a classmate or two go along and do audience observation reports based on your presentation.

2. After doing the presentations in class, stand before the class and have them ask you questions. You can role play this situation and make it revolve around a news conference.

3. Listen to a video-tape speech from some professional speaker or public figure. Do a written analysis of the tape. Classmates can then compare and contrast their opinions of how they "viewed" the persuasive ability of the speaker.

4. Invite a professional business person to come to the class and do his or her persuasive presentation that they have already performed for an audience. Then have them tell about their planning of it, the delivery, and how it was received by their audience.

NOTES

1. Wallace C. Fotheringham, *Perspective on Persuasion.* Boston: Allyn & Bacon, 1966, p. 7.
2. Ronald L. Applebaum and Karl W. E. Anatol, *Strategies for Persuasive Communication.* Columbus, Ohio: Charles E. Merrill, 1974, p. 9.
3. Milton Rokeach, *Beliefs, Attitudes and Values.* San Francisco: Jossey-Bass, 1968.
4. Carl Rogers, *Freedom to Learn.* Columbus, Ohio: Charles E. Merrill, 1969, pp. 83-87.
5. For a similar but alternative persuasive strategy, see Douglas Ehninger, Alan H. Monroe, and Bruce E. Gronbeck, *Principles and Types of Speech Communication,* 8th ed. Glenview, Ill.: Scott, Foresman, 1978.
6. Excerpts from speeches are drawn from the authors' files of material collected while consulting in business and industry.

CHAPTER SIX

USING
THE TELEPHONE

While the telephone has always been an important asset to business communication, today it has become an absolute necessity. Unlike the typewriter or microphone at a podium, we grow up with the telphone. As soon as their first words are uttered, children begin to grab for the telephone in order to imitate their message over the phone. Unfortunately, few people have actually been taught the most effective way to use the phone. Most of us grow up learning how to speak or converse with a friend, but that does not mean we can deliver an effective speech or presentation. Likewise, effective use of the telephone requires some knowledge: It, like public speaking, is a skill that can be easily mastered.

All businesses depend on the use of the telephone. Some are more dependent than others. Organizations whose major goals involve sales often base an entire strategy around the telephone. No doubt you have probably received a phone call welcoming you into the neighborhood and offering to test your water to see if you are a candidate for a water softener. That solicitation is an attempt to set up an appointment with a customer to present a persuasive sales campaign. The telephone message provided just enough information to persuade you to allow a free visit and water test. If you accepted the invitation, the solicitor was effective in presenting the case and persuading you to accept the free visit. If you did not accept the invitation, then probably that solicitor did not learn the skills involved in telephone communication.

Each department in a corporation uses the telephone for a variety of reasons. Sometimes the phone is used to clarify or inform. Personnel may telephone various departments to announce a last-minute important policy update. Marketing may conduct an entire campaign via the phone to determine the acceptance and effectiveness of their latest product. A random survey can quickly ascertain whether people who use Product X have purchased that product because of television advertising or on the basis of a friend's reference. Research and Development can find out what their customers like or dislike about Product X to enable them to implement changes for the upcoming year's revisions. No matter which department is utilizing a telephone strategy, they all have a common purpose: to maximize profit.

Particularly in today's difficult economic situation, any strategy a company can employ that will maximize profit is a necessity. Because of that, the business community is taking a fresh look at the telephone. With technical advances, telephone methods have improved and, in addition, the number of ways in which we use it has increased. Changes in method come to us through experience, refinement, and the increase in knowledge of how to communicate. The increased variety of uses for the telephone has developed by improvements in technology, satellite communication, and microchips. Now we can talk, not to just one person on the other end of the line, but to several groups of individuals in many locations at the same time.

DEFINITION OF TELEPHONE ACTIVITY

What is telephone activity? Telephone communication involves the immediate transmission and reception of audio responses. It is a process of communication that, like any other, involves the creation of meaning and achieves a goal. Unlike face-to-face communication, however, the telephone allows only for auditory transmission of the words that create the message. Except in the case of video teleconferencing, neither party is able to see the other party with whom the conversation is conducted.

This absence of visual stimuli can create a problem in the dialog, because even though the sender uses body language to emphasize a point, the receiver only receives the auditory message. For example, when rapidly giving a company representative telephone directions on how to drive to a local plant, the office manager told Harry Jameson to turn at the second traffic light, which would bring him directly to the plant in two miles. After hanging up, Harry realized that he had no idea which way to turn. The office manager, on the other hand, felt a sense of accomplishment at having given such explicit instructions. Both individuals perceived their situations correctly. The office manager did give thorough instructions, but when he told Harry to turn, he gave that instruction while pointing to the left. He *thought* he told Harry to turn left, but Harry could not receive this visual instruction. This limitation of the telephone must be recognized in order to communicate effectively. Any body language used during a phone conversation must be translated into words in order to be perceived by the receiver of the message.

REASONS FOR DEVELOPING
TELEPHONE SKILLS

Imagine that you are a young sales executives who has just received the latest, updated piece of equipment from corporate headquarters. This equipment represents years of innovative research on the part of R & D Corp. Your company is the first in the world to develop a rapid-speed printer that will enable quick ink change and print at ten times the speed of anything currently on today's market. You have several important clients in need of this printer, but time is a critical factor. It used to be that sales representatives would hop the next jet to present their wares over an imprsssive lunch designed to "loosen up" the client before the close. While face-to-face selling is effective, many organizations are discovering that phone sales are just as effective but at a fraction of the cost.

There are a number of advantages to telephone communication. Besides reducing business operating costs, the telephone often allows you an opportunity to contact individuals who would be unreachable for a private appointment. Officials in high positions have little free time but are usually willing to spend a few moments in phone conversation. Another advantage to telephoning is that a phone call demands attention. How many times have you allowed the phone to ring without answering it? Someone who is speaking on the phone is less likely to be interrupted. In contrast, it is surprising how many face-to-face dialogs are interrupted by a phone call. People do not expect lengthly phone calls. Because of that, it is easy to quickly come to the point of the call without appearing to be insensitive. This, of course, saves time for both parties. Finally, because the listener cannot see the speaker, the speaker can mask any tension or anxiety. One can also deliver the presentation from notes or take notes during the conversation. This is particularly effective when dealing with difficult, technical material.

DEVELOPING SKILLS

Most people do not associate the similarities between giving an effective speech and talking on the telephone, but both have several characteristics in common. If you needed to present a persuasive sales talk to the chairman of the board, the chances are great that he would not be persuaded if you did not spend time in preparation. Likewise, in order to speak effectively on the telephone, you must take several preparatory steps.

1. *Identify the purpose of the call.* Telephone calls are made for reasons. Some of those may be persuasive—such as telephone sales or soliciting. Others calls may be informative—to divulge information such as upcoming meetings or schedul-

ing changes; calls may be seeking information—such as data collection or marketing surveys.

2. *Plan who is to be called.* In some cases only one individual need be contacted, but in the case of a market survey a strategy is necessary. Is it important that the individuals surveyed be chosen randomly? Perhaps the respondent comes from a list of customers who purchased Product X in 1983. For whatever goal the call is designed to achieve, you will avoid a great deal of time and frustration by predetermining who will be called.

3. *Plan to follow up the call if necessary.* If you are introducing a new product on the phone to a potential client, perhaps a direct mail illustration of that product would best accomplish your goal. When you are informing supervisors of a meeting, it might be helpful to plan a call to remind each supervisor on the morning of the meeting.

4. *Plan the main points.* Plan the main points you wish to cover in order to accomplish your goal. Just like a presentation in person, a telephone call should be planned ahead of time. It may also be necessary to have appropriate supports for the main points. If a technical product is being discussed, the customer will want to know how you, as the sales representative, can make such bold claims about your product. Data to support statements will answer the customer's objections.

5. *Execute your plan.* Execute your plan by putting the "three R's" into effect: ready, reach, and react. In the chapter on listening we learned about being ready to listen, reaching out to the other, and reaching. These "three R's" are also useful with the telephone.

Ready. John Bloom has just left a trying meeting with his boss, who appeared to be angry because of some seemingly unimportant details. John is responsible for the creation of window displays in a leading department store. With Valentine's Day approaching, he had several displays changed to red and pink color accents with cupids and hearts to symbolize the occasion. John's boss does not like to see red with pink. He showed visible signs of being angry at John's work, accused him of incompetence as a decorator, and threatened to fire him. At this moment John is tense and preoccupied, but the clock does not stop to permit recovery time. He must make some calls to place orders for St. Patrick's Day decorations by 10 o'clock, or it will be too late to make the order. He rushes to his desk directly from his boss's office and begins dialing. The phone is answered by a young clerk, Miss Jensen, who is very competent at her job but whose father died suddenly two days previously. She is preoccupied with grief. John barks out his order and proceeds to tell Miss Jensen that she had better get it straight this time or her head is going to roll. Miss Jensen is upset. She repeats the order to John, who is still preoccupied with his anger over the treatment he received from his boss. The order is incorrect, but John does not catch the error, and they close the conversation. What went wrong? Basically, John was not "ready" to make his call. Following the meeting with his boss, he did not take time to prepare himself mentally to use the telephone. The result was an unnecessary error. John has not achieved the purpose of the call.

"Readying" to telephone is preparing oneself psychologically to accomplish the purpose of the call. To accomplish any ask, there must be full concentration on the goal. John was preoccupied with anger and possible loss of his job. Before you pick up the phone to dial, concentrate on letting go of outside distractions and relax. Take a minute to think about the phone call you are about to make. These few moments of focusing on the task at hand will pay off in the end by helping you achieve the results of the call. Had John spent time letting go of his anger and thinking about what he would say before rushing to dial, he would have heard the mistake and corrected it immediately. If he had been under control the mistake might not have occurred. He will spend much more time undoing the problem caused by not readying himself than he would have spent in preparation. So, before dialing, take a moment to relax, let extraneous problems go, and focus on the message to be delivered.

Reach.   By this point, the goal and message are clear and the speaker is ready to deliver it to the listener. As in any oral presentation, it is important to be clear, concise, and to the point. Clarity, however, is particularly important in telephoning because, again, the speaker and listener cannot see each other. The only way to judge the listener's reaction is through verbal response. Make certain that you have the listener's full attention. Take a look at the following example:

Jim Brown is a purchasing clerk. He has just received a demand for flywheels from the Chicago branch. He knows that he can fill the order from existing stock in the warehouse. The problem is that his company has been hit dramatically by the economic crunch, and a directive issued three weeks ago by the company president stated that all parts were to be shipped by truck, not by air. If Jim follows this directive, Chicago will not receive the part it needs in time, and that office will lose this account, which is a large one. The only one who can accept responsibility for a decision of this type is the president himself. Jim prepares to make a call to the president and knows exactly what his goal is and how he will achieve it. Mentally, he takes a moment to block out outside distractions that could hinder his effort. He picks up the phone, dials and asks the president's secretary to put him through. She replies that the president is in a meeting and has asked not to be disturbed. This call is very important to Jim and to the company. He tells the secretary it is urgent, cannot wait, and he must speak with the president immediately. She puts the call through. The president is engrossed with two young accounts who have just presented him with some projected cost overruns which are alarming. He is annoyed by the ringing of the phone. When he answers and Jim begins to speak, his mind is still running over the figures he has just seen, attempting to figure out what he can juggle to make everything fit next quarter. He is not really paying attention to Jim or what is being said. Jim, who has just railroaded his call through, is nervous and is getting through his rehearsed presentation as quickly as possible. He does not pick up that the president is preoccupied and is not in a position to listen to Jim's dilemma.

How can this be avoided? Make certain that both you and your listener are prepared to converse. In this situation, it would have been helpful for Jim to first acknowledge that he is interrupting the president, who is busy, but he has something very important that he needs a decision on, and can he take just a few moments to present the issue. This gives the listener psychological time to make the transfer from one situation to the next: in this case from participating in a meeting to listening to Jim.

React. Probably the most important stage in telephone communication is listening and reacting to the respondent. Tune in to how the respondent is perceiving what is being said. Many kinds of responses can be given, and some of these can be interpreted either as showing understanding or as possibly showing confusion. Sometimes a mere grunt on the other end of the line will demonstrate that the listener is paying attention to what is being said. The most accurate way to tell if the listener is perceiving what is being said in the way you are attempting to say it is to rephrase back to the listener the statement of understanding he or she just made to you. The following example should clarify this stage.

Joe Calloway is a first-line supervisor at the Akron Rubber Plant. His superior stopped by his desk and asked him to contact the other ten first-line supervisors in Joe's unit. Joe felt that the fastest way to accomplish this task would be to use the telephone. The purpose of the telephone call is to notify the other supervisors of a meeting to discuss a change in the benefit package Akron will be offering all employees in the future. Joe retrieves a roster of his peers from a desk drawer. Since the meeting will not occur for one week, Joe decides that it would be best to place reminder calls the morning of the meeting to ensure attendance. In this case, Joe only needs to cover one main point, so his conversation will be short. With the list in front of him, he takes a moment to focus on the task of making the phone call and block out the other issues that are on his mind. He dials the first supervisor in his group on his list, Ann Sommers.

JOE: Hello Ann? This is Joe Calloway.
ANN: Hi, Joe. What's up?
JOE: Listen, the super asked me to call and tell everyone in our unit that there will be a special meeting at 2:00 next Tuesday to announce some changes in our benefit package.
ANN: O.K.
JOE: Then we will see you at 2:00 on Tuesday?
ANN: Right, Joe. I'll see you at 2:00 next Tuesday.
JOE: Thanks Ann. Goodbye.

After Joe delivered his message concerning the meeting, Ann replied, showing that she was hearing. But with only the response of "O.K.," Joe could not be sure that she did get the message. As was mentioned in the chapter on listening, hearing and listening are not the same thing. By reacting to Ann's response, Joe clarified with her second response that she did understand about the meeting. Barring any unforeseen consequences, the follow-up call should ensure her presence.

TIME MANAGEMENT

If used correctly, the telephone can be an important tool in effective time management. On the other hand, unplanned or unstructured telephoning can be one of the largest time-wasters in the workday. How many times can you recall dialing someone you plan to discuss two major points with, and ending up talking fifteen minutes longer? Those fifteen minutes should have lasted only five. By lunch time you are wondering, "Where is this day going? I have so much to do!" Let's take a look at what probably stretched those minutes out and how proper planning can increase the amount of work that can be accomplished in a day.

First of all, it is crucial to plan and jot down the purpose of the call, the main points to be stressed, and any follow-up activity that will be needed. Just "thinking" about these points, but not placing them in writing, leaves room for error. It is easy to become engrossed in an interesting dialog and forget to cover a main point of the call. By actually writing this down, you can avert a possible oversight. Secondly, keep in mind that when telephoning an acquaintance, as with anyone else, it is important to establish rapport in the initial stages of the conversation before moving into the main points—but this is one place where it becomes necessary to watch the time. This is an area that causes five-minute calls to last fifteen. Another time-waster is digressing from the point; this can be avoided by glancing occasionally back to the paper that outlines the call. Box 6-1 shows an example of a possible telephone diary to help effectively manage time.

BOX 6-1   TELEPHONE DIARY

Name:	Appropriate Time:
Phone Number:	
Purpose of Call:	
Main Points:	
1.	
2.	
3.	
Follow-up:	

Remember, to avoid wasting time, it is important to preplan who will be called. At the beginning of the work day, it is helpful to make a list of persons to be telephoned. The people to be called will depend on the purpose of the call. For instance, if the purpose is a sales message, the names of the clients can come from a file of individuals contacted previously or from probably one of the most helpful but often most neglected sources in the business world: the Yellow Pages. By looking at the index at the back of this directory you can pinpoint new businesses.

PARALANGUAGE

As we mentioned earlier, the one feature that makes a telephone call different from a face-to-face dialog is the lack of visual contact. Earlier we talked about Harry Jameson and his difficulty with instructions given over the telephone because he could not see the office manager's body language or movements. (This scene was presented to show that you need to be aware of how much we say with our bodies as well as with words.) At first, this lack of visual contact may be seen as a drawback to using the telephone. The way to compensate for this is through paralanguage. Paralanguage is the intonation, pauses, and inflection in the voice when we speak. Because the body cannot be used to express meaning over the phone, it becomes very important to learn to use voice inflection as a substitute for the body. Telephoners who sound enthusiastic about the topic they are discussing will create enthusiasm in their listeners. It's somewhat analogous to being in a room with several people laughing, while you attempt to not laugh.

Enthusiasm is contagious and can be portrayed through voice modulation. In phone solicitation, phone workers are taught to dramatize their presentation. What may sound "overdone" to the face-to-face listener sounds normal to the phone listener because that visual medium is lost. The telephoner must learn to translate the emphasis relayed through body language (squinting the eyes, pointing, smiles and frowns) into an emphasis through voice modulation.

Planned pauses can also be very useful. In sales there is an expression, "He who talks first buys." Just like we find it practically impossible to allow a ringing phone to continue ringing, we also find it uncomfortable to allow silence. If you need your listener to respond and he or she does not seem to be following your "game plan," try just being silent. A pause following a main point can also serve to dramatize that point. When you are listening, you can help the speaker by giving some utterances to convey that you understand the speaker's message. Those "mm's," "uhs," and "ah's" affirm the speaker's belief that he or she has created understanding.

TELECONFERENCING

One of the most dynamic innovations in industry today is teleconferencing. With the press of economic hard times, businesses are taking a careful look, not only at how to increase productivity, but also at how the cost of running an operation can be streamlined to maximize profit. One major expense to any company is the cost of meetings that require travel. In 1980 alone, more than $25 billion was paid by U.S. industry in travel costs, including air fares, meals, auto expenses, and lodging.[1] When one considers the amount of time lost in productivity when the traveling business person is "on the road," an even greater cost to industry must be assumed. In recent research on meetings, it was discovered that 80 percent of the meetings conducted have a useful time of only 30 minutes or less. The rest of that time is present in either formalities or small talk, and half of those meetings did not even need to be conducted face-to-face.[2]

Today's technological advances have made teleconferencing a reality for more and more businesses, both large and small. The teleconferencing industry has literally exploded in the past ten years. In 1980 a representative from Exxon announced that his company had been successfully using teleconferencing for seven years.[3] This explosion is due to several factors, one of the most important having already been mentioned: the economic climate. Increased travel costs have forced the business world to take a close look at conferences and workshops demanding travel. Also, many executives have become more conscientious about effective time management. Finally, new, fast-paced technology has increased the need for rapid information flow. Where businesses compete for their share of the market, speed in the transmission of information can often determine whether or not an organization remains in first place.

What is teleconferencing? "Teleconferencing combines the resources of a complete broadcast environment with the interactive communications requirements of any business organizations."[4] There are several types of teleconferencing to choose from; obviously, an organization's need and fiscal ability will dictate which

FIGURE 6-1   Teleconferencing a meeting to several locations at the same time makes communication more useful in complex organizational settings.

type is best suited to accomplish that organization's goals. Basically, the options fall into either visual or audio categories, and there are several types in each category. Audio teleconferencing can be as simple as the speaker-phone, which allows several people to speak from and be heard in one facility. Another type is call-transferring, which allows two parties to add an additional party in another location or, though a type of chain reaction, to add several other locations. The difficulty with this arrangement is loss of quality with the addition of each new party. The quality of audio teleconferencing can be enhanced by using a full-time audio facility that has lines that function only in the capacity of teleconferencing. To extend the capability of audio teleconferencing, corporations can add a second audio connection to transmit graphics from one terminal to another. These graphics can either be simple character displays, or charts and graphs, or even handwriting. Actual textual material can be transmitted though facsimile. Visual teleconferencing includes slow-scan video, freeze-frame video, and finally, live, full-motion video.[5] Slow-scan and freeze-frame video can both be transmitted via telephone lines. Slow-scan allows for the completion of one picture frame in about 60 seconds. The camera begins scanning at the top of the picture and completes at the bottom. The replication at the other end follows the same pattern. Freeze-frame is a similar process; however, each frame is frozen at the point of transmission and sent in this completed form. Full-motion video teleconferencing is obviously the most natural and, therefore, the most desirable form of teleconferencing. Unfortunately, it is also the most expensive, because transmission requires a larger band width and use of satellite transmission. Also, the room utilized must have specific atmospheric conditions. Many businesses are finding, however, that the benefits of satellite teleconferencing far outweigh the cost. Obviously, it saves time and travel costs. Because of the time limitations, meetings are well planned and do not include wasted time. Important speakers can be brought to a large number of viewers—a much greater number than could be contained in a convention hall. Also, teleconferencing improves employee morale by increasing communication between distant facilities. It gives the employees and the public a positive image of the company as being one that moves with today's technological changes.

Several forms of teleconferencing are being utilized by many of today's public and private concerns. In 1981, Greater Southeast Community Hospital in Washington, D.C., adopted a Telemedicine System. The purpose of this system was to improve the speed of reading X-rays by allowing radiologists to read and interpret radiographic images sent via telephone lines from the hospital to the radiologist's location.[6] In 1980, Aetna Life and Casualty added two teleconference rooms to provide a full-motion video system. The system links a satellite site in Windsor, Connecticut, with the home office in Hartford. Aetna feels this link decreases time loss from travel and increases productivity.[7] Another example of teleconferencing can be seen with Republic Airlines. Maintenance managers coordinate their activities daily, using telephone conferencing. This gives personnel access to key people and an ability to discuss problems occurring the previous day.[8] The benefit that this free flow of information brings to the airline is invaluable.

The list of examples of current-day teleconferencing is endless. These are just a few examples of how this technique is being used by a number of businesses. We cannot take telephone communication for granted, in any setting. As with any other kind of human communication, telephone communication requires preparation and concentration. Now, carefully work to develop your telephone skills for business and professional needs.

A REVIEW OF KEY ISSUES

Telephone skills can be taught and mastered.

Telephone communication involves immediate reception and transmission of audio responses.

Reasons for developing telephone skills:
1. more economical than face-to-face communication.
2. ability to contact individuals who would be difficult to contact under other circumstances.
3. phone calls demand attention.
4. phone calls less likely to be interrupted.
5. less time necessary to make crucial points.
6. ability to mask speaker tension.
7. ability to take and use notes.

Steps to making successful telephone calls:
1. Identify the purpose of the call.
2. Plan who is to be called.
3. Plan follow-up activity.
4. Plan main points.
5. Execute plan:
   a. ready
   b. reach
   c. react

Effective time management:
1. *Write down* purpose, main points, and follow-up activity.
2. Make a list of individuals to be called.

Paralanguage is the intonation, pauses, and inflection in the voice when we speak.
1. Voice inflection is a substitute for body language.
2. Enthusiasm can be shown with voice modulation.
3. Silence causes listening tension, which demands to be broken.

Teleconferencing combines resources of a complete broadcast environment with the interactive communication requirements of any business organization.
1. audio
   a. speaker-phone
   b. call-transfering
   c. graphics
   d. facsimile

2. visual
   a. slow-scan
   b. freeze-frame
   c. full-motion

Benefits of teleconferencing
1. cost effective
2. time efficient
3. large audience
4. improvement of employee morale
5. public relations
6. increased information flow

ACTIVITY 1: Voice Modulation and Paralanguage

Visit a telephone marketing division of a nearby business. Talk with the director of solicitation to see how voice modulation is taught to trainees. Monitor several calls to see the effectiveness of voice inflection.

ACTIVITY 2: Time Management

Start a normal business day by planning your telephone strategy. Make a list of individuals to be called. Using the telephone-diary approach and the points for planning outlined in this chapter, identify the purpose, main points, and follow-up activity for each call. Be prepared to discuss your strategies in class.

ACTIVITY 3: The Three R's

Choose a partner for classroom role-playing. With the three R's—Reading, Reaching, and Reacting—in mind, act out several phone conversations for class discussion and critical analysis. If your class has access to a video recorder, tape the role-playing for the purpose of analysis through replay.

NOTES

1. A. Miura, S. Michael Stevenson, and David Linker, "Video Teleconferencing Brings New Direction to Business in the 1980's." *Communication News,* February 1982, p. 52.
2. Thomas Cross, "Teleconferencing is an Important New Tool for Business Productivity." *Communication News,* February 1982, p. 49.
3. ____, "Teleconferencing in the Satellite Age." *Marketing Communications,* October 1980, p. 95.
4. Willard Thomas and Cinda Thomas, "Teleconferencing Reaching a Critical Pivotal Stage in Growth and Development." *Communication News,* February 1982, p. 46.
5. Greg Paulsen, "The View from VideoNet." *Video Systems,* April 1982, p. 17.
6. Wallace Munsey, "First Phase of Telemedicine Program is Prescription for Improved Health Care." *Communication News,* February 1982, p. 62.
7. Elliot Gold, "Aetna's Successful System Designed Around User Needs." *Communication News,* February 1982, p. 50.
8. ____, "Republic Airlines Coordinates Its Operations Via Phone Conferencing." *Communication News,* February 1982, p. 65.

CHAPTER SEVEN

COMMUNICATING THROUGH THE INTERVIEW

The interview is a common communication tool in the business world. Often, this communication activity holds serious consequences for the individuals involved. An interview could be the launching point of a client-company relationship or, conversely, the end of what could have been an important start for a client-company relationship.

Usually we think of an interview as that single great moment in our career when we apply for the big dream job. Contrary to this common belief, interviewing is frequently a communication activity in our professional work. It is an activity we experience routinely in our daily communication with fellow employees. Every time we seek information from another person, provide information, demonstrate how to do a job-related activity, evaluate someone, are ourselves evaluated, receive professional advice or provide it for others, we are engaged in various types of interviewing activities.

When learning how to walk, a child places one foot in front of the other, and it isn't very long before that child takes walking for granted. Interviewing is similar. Since we talk and have been doing so from childhood, we tend to take it for granted. Unfortunately, we quickly assume that interviewing is just a form of talking. It takes a great deal of practice for the child to become poised and skillful at walking. This child has to experience hills, rough surfaces, and an array of strange-shaped footwears in order to become a skillful walker. It is only after many experiences in numerous situations that this child progresses from walking into dancing. This "elaborate walking" provides the child opportunity for rich creativity and great personal satisfaction through personal achievement. We can experience a similar development with interviewing. The fundamental skills are mastered quickly with experience, but they should not be taken for granted. After basic mastery of the fundamentals, you should be ready for more complex experiences. Interviewing, as a communication activity, can lead you into opportunities for success on the job that can provide you with great personal satisfaction.

In this chapter we will focus on defining interviewing and understanding its basic skill requirements; and then we shall examine how to put these skills into practical use for productive communication on the job. Performing with these interviewing skills in your work environment should encourage success and provide you with great personal satisfaction.

DEFINING THE INTERVIEW

In an effort to gain a better understanding of *interview,* we will look at what some experts perceive this specialized communication activity to be. Goyer and Sincoff[1] contend that the interview is a form of communication involving two parties, at least one of whom has a preconceived and serious purpose, and both of whom speak and listen from time to time. The fundamental communication skills of speaking and listening are emphasized in this definition. The transaction of the communication process is here emphasized—that is, a dyadic quality of two parties involved in the activity. This could refer to two individuals, or it could mean two groups of individuals. For example, three representatives from a consulting firm could be interviewed for expert information by a group of executives from a private company. The deliberate intent in the term "preconceived" is central to this definition. It suggests some type of preparation and planning on the part of the individuals or parties involved. The term "serious purpose" separates this communication activity from the social, interpersonal kind of dialog used when two friends are sharing experiences.

We wish to focus more on the importance of the process of selecting information for the interview, which places a high priority on speaking and listening. It is the speaking and listening skills that will affect how much and what kind of information it will be successful to select for and use in the interview.

Steward and Cash[2] consider interviewing as a dyadic communication process with a predetermined and serious purpose designed to interchange behavior, usually involving the asking and answering of questions. This definition specifies the speaking and listening behavior, the asking and answering of questions. It is certainly an interchange of behavior, because both parties ask and answer questions. Therefore, we believe the parties in an interview are constantly changing communication behavior roles, and this affects several of the basic elements contained in interview activities.

THE INTERVIEW

A communication model.   For our purpose, we define the interview as a communication process used to seek or provide information based on a preconceived purpose open to a unique dyadic relationship influenced by the behavior roles of interviewer and the interviewee. The purpose is important in this definition, but the emphasis is placed on the communication behavior roles as they change and operate among the parties involved in the activity. Figure 7-1 clarifies this emphasis.

This model illustrates how the role of interviewer and interviewee can fluctuate during the interview. The communication role of the interviewer is described as questioning behavior; the communication role for the interviewee is characterized by responding behavior. Regardless of which role either party assumes, the relationship between the parties is transactional. This means the relationship is constantly changing, owing to the stimulation of the questioning and responding behaviors. Such things as the wording of the question, the context in which it is asked, the tone of the voice, the words especially stressed in the question, and the timing of the question are factors that influence change. The same factors also apply to responding behaviors.

The awareness of this changing communication role behavior has a direct effect on what information, out of all that is available, that one selects to present. If a problem occurs during the course of the interview, it very frequently is stimulated by one of the factors that can affect these behavior communication roles. For example, an office manager calls in an employee for a job appraisal interview. She is seeking information in order to make a decision about whether to promote this employee. Therefore, she asks him to talk about his job. He interprets her questioning behavior as his opportunity to ask about some new equipment that he had

FIGURE 7-1   The interview: a dynamic model.

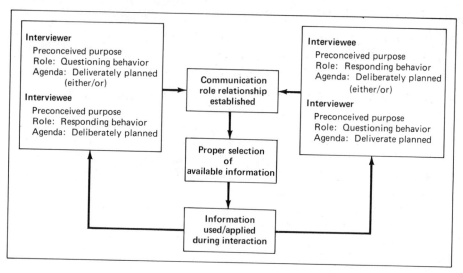

requested some time ago. This supervisor, wishing to pursue her intended goal, provides a short and vague response. This employee interprets this response as merely another "management stall tactic." Then the interpersonal relationship between the interviewer and interviewee becomes guarded. This change in the interpersonal relationship, activated by the communication behavior role, will no doubt affect what information each party offers to the other.

In this situation, the selection process for both the interviewer and the interviewee was affected by the communication role relationship established. The way each party interprets the information cues as the interview progresses will have serious consequences on their choice of what information they give in response to each other.

In another example, an employer is interviewing an applicant for a job opening in a middle-management position of a large organization. The interview gets underway and the employer starts with responding behavior roles by discussing the great opportunity one could have by working with his organization. The nervous applicant is confused by the responding behavior and unsure of what kind of communication is expected. He selects from the available information presented by the employer and concludes that he is being given stock propaganda from an exaggerated and biased viewpoint. Once this applicant has processed the information in this way, his responding or questioning will be greatly influenced during the rest of the interview. Under such circumstances, it would be difficult for either party to seek the explicit information desired. The communication behavior roles have also affected the interpersonal relationship in this interview. Communication breakdown is now quite possible and probable.

If both parties establish a mutually understood communication role relationship, the next step of selecting information becomes much easier. Both parties can process the information, selecting what they want to use, provide, or pursue in greater depth.

Based on both parties' interpretations during this stage, the interview will continue with the selected information, and both parties will choose communication behaviors based on their preconceived purpose and agendas. The process continues in this transactional setting with much dynamic potential contained in the communication behavior roles. The significance of the communication behavior roles becomes apparent. There are, however, several other factors in the interview that should also be given serious consideration.

LISTENING: A VITAL SKILL
FOR INTERVIEWING

Effective listening is paramount to a mutually understood role relationship. That listening is vital to communication is very clearly pointed out in many research studies. In most communication models, it is reflected in the feedback function. This listening function is equally important in the interview. As previously mentioned, the roles of interviewer and interviewee both require the use of effective listening skills to seek, provide, and select desired information. Unfortunately, listening skills are not instinctive; they must be learned by means of experience and deliberate awareness. Box 7-1 provides a list of *Do's* and *Don't's* that you may find helpful in your efforts to improve your listening.

BOX 7-1   INTERVIEW LISTENING POINTERS

Do's	Don't's
Do remove all distractions.	Don't dismiss a speaker or topic because it is uninteresting to you.
Do listen for complete ideas as opposed to isolated facts.	Don't evaluate a statement before it is completed.
Do remain objective without allowing bias to distract you.	Don't ignore ideas because you perceive them to be too difficult.
Do listen responsively to the speaker, offering constructive feedback.	Don't be afraid of using critical thinking.
Do strive to keep the communication circular with nonverbal listening cues.	Don't lose contact by daydreaming or planning responses on the speaker's time.

During an interview, an effective listener will use the entire body. The eyes reflect the attitude of the listener. The facial expressions, movements of the head and body, and the physical space between speaker and listener all provide signal cues about information feedback (see Figure 7-2). This feedback is the means by which the speaker measures the effectiveness of the communication during the interview. An effective listener will maintain a brief pause after the speaker has finished before beginning to respond. Furthermore, an effective listener will begin the response with a transitional word, phrase, or thought that will serve as a bridge between what has been spoken and what is about to be spoken. *Now, also, yet, in addition,* and *then* are just a few examples of transition words. *On account of, in summary, by the way,* and *in terms of* are some common transitional phrases. These transitions do not add to the content of the information, but they do *guide* the direction of the content. In some situations, the brief pause alone will serve as a listening transition. Review Chapter 2 for the use of proper listening skills.

PLANNING: A VITAL ACTIVITY FOR INTERVIEWING

Equally important for a clear understanding of the role relationship between interviewer and interviewee is careful planning. This planning includes establishing a purpose and some goals to aim for during the interview. Both parties need to be aware of the purpose and goals.

FIGURE 7-2 As a form of communication, the interview is uniquely dynamic and interactive.

The working agenda—planning what items need to be covered during the interview—should be given some thought. In fact, the purpose, goals, and agenda are all interdependent on one another. It helps to view the purpose as the target and the agenda as the bow and arrow used to hit the target dead center. Aiming for the target is important but not always so easy to do.

SELF-DISCLOSURE: A SHARED ACTIVITY WHEN INTERVIEWING

Another major concern for mutual understanding in the communication role relationship is the function of self-disclosure during an interview. Self-disclosure is one's openness of expression during a transaction. As simple as this sounds, it is not always easy to practice. To maintain openness in our behavior and language can be difficult. We may at times feel threatened or coerced if we provide certain pieces of information. Seldom do we practice complete self-disclosure in our communication. Erving Goffman[3] points out how people quickly learn to play ritualistic games in social settings. These games and behaviors become a part of us and appear in our communication behaviors. We participate in these behaviors as a way of protecting our inner selves. For example, in an appraisal interview, the supervisor may start by asking how the subordinate is "feeling today." The supervisor is expecting a "fine" subordinate. The subordinate may be very upset, but he or she knows that this interview is not the time or the place to give the true answer. So he or she says "fine," and both parties mutually agree to accept the "expected" response. Such an expected response can be the start of communication barriers that may influence the communication role behaviors in a negative way. Self-disclosure is a way of preventing ritualistic games from becoming communication barriers.

In an effort to demonstrate self-disclosure, we can look at the Johari Window (see Figure 7-3) developed by Joseph Luft and Harrington Ingram.[4]

If we apply this model to the interview situation, the interviewer and interviewee's self-disclosure should reflect some change as the interview progresses. In fact, it would look something like Figure 7-4.

If, at the end of the interview, the hidden and unknown areas (III and IV) are smaller, both parties have successfully made progressive efforts at self-disclosure. It is through the expansion of areas I and II that the purpose of the interview can most easily be accomplished. If the interview agenda is carefully structured around the planned purpose, the areas known to others will expand as each step of the agenda is completed. The communication behavior roles will be clear and contribute to accomplishing the purpose.

There is an element of risk in self-disclosure, and there must be mutual trust in order to minimize these fears. Both parties have to analyze the personal risk in relationship to the purpose of the interview and decide if the values merit taking the risk. Obviously, the disclosure should include only information relevant to the interview. Self-disclosure, in an interview, does not mean pouring out all the personal troubles both parties are facing in their personal lives.

INTERPERSONAL RELATIONSHIPS:
A COOPERATIVE FUNCTION
IN THE INTERVIEW

Individuals can assume many interpersonal roles in the dyadic situation of the interview. Eric Berne[5] contends that there are three basic relationships that occur in interpersonal encounters. He refers to them as transactional relationships based on three ego states within the person. He labels them:

> The **parent** role: This provides protection, guiding the individual by making up rules and setting boundaries.

> The **adult** role: This concentrates on gathering objective information, emphasizing the logical side of things rather than the emotional.

> The **child** role: This is composed of positive and negative traits witnessed in small children, such as dependency, rebellion, spontaneity, delights, curiosity, and lack of seriousness.

People communicate with one another in interpersonal settings using these three roles. The interview can take on a variety of role relationships as the inter-

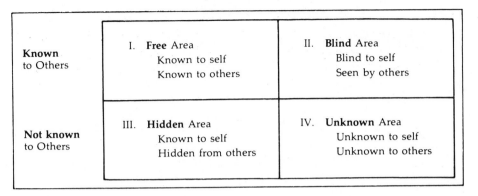

FIGURE 7-3   Johari Window.

viewer and interviewee incorporate these interpersonal roles into their communication behavior. According to Harris's[6] rationale, the complementary or parallel transaction as indicated in Figure 7-5 is the most effective. The first rule of communication in transactional analysis is based on a parallel structure. When the stimulus (interviewer) and response (interviewee) are parallel, the transaction is complementary and should be able to continue indefinitely without interference. If the interviewer and interviewee are relating as adult to adult, child to child, or parent to parent, the communication process will flow smoothly.

Another situation occurs when no parallel relationship exists. For example, in a disciplinary interview, a foreman in communicating with her subordinate worker may find it difficult to establish a parallel relationship with the worker. She may appear in a parent role and relate in this manner to the worker, who becomes angry and feels he is receiving unfair treatment. He sulks and takes on the role of the child during the course of the interview. This establishes a crossed transactonal relationship, one that will definitely interfere with the communication. Figure 7-6 visualizes this crossed transactional relationship between the foreman and her subordinate. In such a situation, you can see how the discussion that centers around a

FIGURE 7-4   Self-disclosure development in the interview.

OPENING OF INTERVIEW		CLOSURE OF INTERVIEW	
I. **Free** Area	II. **Blind** Area	I. **Free** Area	II. **Blind** Area
III. **Hidden** Area	IV. **Unknown** Area	III. **Hidden** Area	IV. **Unknown** Area

ROLE (interviewer)	INTERVIEW ROLE RELATIONSHIP	ROLE (interviewee)
Parent **Adult** **Child**	P ⟷ P A ⟷ A C C	**Parent** **Adult** **Child**

FIGURE 7-5   Complementary or parallel transaction in the interview.

criticism of action and a reprimand could erupt into a negative interpersonal relationship that could break down the communication relationship. The purpose of the interview could be lost, and in the final analysis the interview could be a total failure. The parallel relationship is more workable, and it will function more efficiently in communication behavior.

Careful planning, self-disclosure, interpersonal relationships, and how they influence the communication behavior roles in an interview are significant. When we remember that interviewing is a communication process aimed at seeking or providing information that is based on a preconceived purpose and is open to a unique dynamic relationship, influenced by the behavior roles of the interviewer and the interviewee, we should now understand how it functions.

TYPES OF INTERVIEWS COMMON IN THE BUSINESS ENVIRONMENT

There are four general categories of interviews: information-gathering; problem-solving; evaluative; and persuasive. These general categories are based on the purpose of each interview as well as on the situation for which the interview has been chosen as the appropriate communication tool.

Information-gathering interviews.   Job interviews, counseling interviews, training interviews, and personality or authority interviews are all concerned with gathering information. The parties involved in these situations are either seeking or

FIGURE 7-6   Crossed transactional relationship in the interview.

FOREMAN	DISCIPLINARY INTERVIEW	SUBORDINATE WORKER
Parent **Adult** **Child**	P ⟶ P A A C C	**Parent** **Adult** **Child**

BOX 7-2   QUESTIONS TO DETERMINE INFORMATION-GATHERING

1. What is the purpose of this interview?
2. Why is the information being gathered or disseminated?
3. What is my relationship to the information?
4. How will I be affected by the information-gathering interview?
5. What contribution is expected of me in this situation?
6. What growth and development should derive from this interview?
7. What limitations should be considered regarding this interview?

providing information on specific subjects to specific persons. The questions in Box 7-2 serve as a guide in determining if this is the type of interview to use for a specific situation. These questions will help you to determine your role as interviewer and interviewee as you venture into the information-gathering interview. There is preparation you can do prior to an information-gathering interview. The more time and effort that go into this preparation stage, the greater are the chances for success in such an encounter. Box 7-3 gives an example of this stage.

BOX 7-3   PREPARING FOR THE INFORMATION-GATHERING INTERVIEW:
AN EXAMPLE

1. Define the purpose for the interview in a carefully worded descriptive statement.
   Example: "The purpose for giving this information is to train two employees to operate the new office copy machine."
2. Organize an outlined agenda of the procedure to be followed during the interview session.
   Example:
   a. explain why the new machine was purchased
   b. ask if employees have had experience working with this machine
   c. assure employees of the ease in operating the machine
   d. use machine manual to explain each step of the process
   e. allow time for questions after each step
   f. ask employees to explain process to one another
   g. practice using each step
   h. ask for final questions and comments
   i. include a word of praise for their willingness to learn machine
3. Review the agenda as planned for specifics.
   a. check the time scheduled for the interview
   b. check the location where the interview will occur
   c. check procedure for the number of persons to be involved
   d. consider the abilities of the individuals involved
   e. agenda should meet the specific requirements of the purpose
4. Use the written agenda for working notes during the interview and allow yourself to concentrate on listening.

In addition to following these four steps before the actual interview, there are some other items that should be considered. These items will also help to ensure the success of the interview.

If it is necessary to conduct a series of interviews and the collecting of information is elaborate, it is best to keep the actual note-taking during the interview to a minimum. It may be necessary to schedule the interviews a few moments apart to have time for making notes between the interview sessions. Note-taking can also interfere with proper listening skills; this is another reason for avoiding it.

The job interview is but one type of information gathering. Because of its concern to students, we have chosen to apply it to the dynamic model shown in Figure 7-7. This model shows what to do before, during, and after the interview.

FIGURE 7-7   Selection interview model.

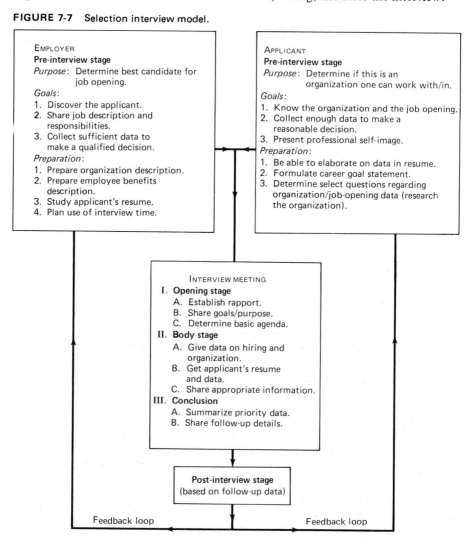

Problem-solving interviews.   These situations include disciplinary interviews, problem-defining interviews, solution-analysis interviews, and mutual-problem interviews. The purpose of these interviews is to resolve conflicts. Often such interviews involve groups of people. For example, a group of hospital administrators about to build a new cardiac unit might wish to tour another hospital facility and meet with its administrators in order to anticipate possible problems in such an endeavor. Such interviews are not always easy to conduct, and they can easily get off target. Careful planning is crucial. The purpose must be carefully thought out, and the agenda should be structured in a way that will achieve the purpose. In such problem solving interviews, definitions are sometimes very important. Often restrictions or boundaries must be established in order to focus the concentration on the problem or solution. If the problem has been defined, then all parties must know about it before going into the interview.

In planning for this kind of interview, we suggest some guide questions that will help you to organize around a purpose statement and an agenda.

The problem-solution interview, even though it is complex in nature, will function smoothly after considering the questions in Box 7-4. Since this is a more complex situation., it would do well for the novice interviewer or interviewee to gain some experience working with information-gathering situations first. Dealing with conflict and search for resolution demands a greater mastery of speaking and listening skills.

BOX 7-4   GUIDELINE QUESTIONS FOR PREPARING PROBLEM-SOLVING INTERVIEWS

1. What kind of search has been done to define the problem?
2. Has the defined or perceived problem been confirmed?
3. Should concentration on the problem receive first concern?
4. If there is more than one problem, has a priority list been made?
5. Should the immediate concern focus on the solution?
6. Is there more than one solution to be considered?
7. Can a priority be determined if multiple solutions are possible?
8. Are there any serious limitations to be considered in working with the problem or solution?

Counselors in some huge businesses would diagram a problem-solving interview in the way shown in the action model in Figure 7-8.

Evaluation interviews.   These situations include such circumstances as job-appraisal interviews, program-assessment interviews, budget-review interviews, promotion interviews, equipment-rating interviews, and exit interviews. The preplanned purpose and the agenda are necessary for successful interviewing in these situation. Speaking and listening skills are important for the communication proc-

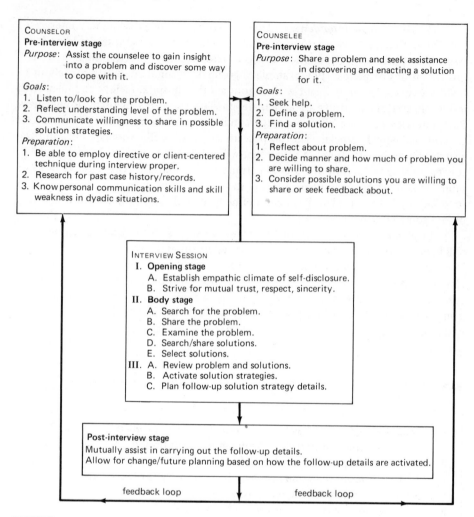

COUNSELOR
Pre-interview stage
Purpose: Assist the counselee to gain insight
into a problem and discover some way
to cope with it.
Goals:
1. Listen to/look for the problem.
2. Reflect understanding level of the problem.
3. Communicate willingness to share in possible
   solution strategies.
Preparation:
1. Be able to employ directive or client-centered
   technique during interview proper.
2. Research for past case history/records.
3. Know personal communication skills and skill
   weakness in dyadic situations.

COUNSELEE
Pre-interview stage
Purpose: Share a problem and seek assistance
in discovering and enacting a solution
for it.
Goals:
1. Seek help.
2. Define a problem.
3. Find a solution.
Preparation:
1. Reflect about problem.
2. Decide manner and how much of problem you
   are willing to share.
3. Consider possible solutions you are willing to
   share or seek feedback about.

INTERVIEW SESSION
  I. **Opening stage**
      A. Establish empathic climate of self-disclosure.
      B. Strive for mutual trust, respect, sincerity.
 II. **Body stage**
      A. Search for the problem.
      B. Share the problem.
      C. Examine the problem.
      D. Search/share solutions.
      E. Select solutions.
III. A. Review problem and solutions.
      B. Activate solution strategies.
      C. Plan follow-up solution strategy details.

Post-interview stage
Mutually assist in carrying out the follow-up details.
Allow for change/future planning based on how the follow-up details are activated.

feedback loop   feedback loop

FIGURE 7-8   Counselor's problem-solving interview model.

ess, but they also take on the added dimension of carrying out the evaluation
process.

Unlike the information-gathering or the problem-solving interview, the evaluation focuses on the evaluative climate in such a situation. When the parties take on
the responsibility of evaluating with that of communicating effectively, objectivity
must be displayed. Furthermore, evaluation requires accountability in how the
information is used during the interview. The information must be reliable and
valid. The emphasis on self-disclosure may become a significant factor as well as
other interpersonal factors when promotion, bonuses, demerits, or the like are
involved. Obviously, listening skills must be functioning at their very best. Validity,
reliability, and accountability will only operate effectively with objective listening.

As in the other interview situations, planning is one of the best ways to ensure success in such communication activity. Box 7-5 gives a list of guideline questions to help you get started in planning a realistic purpose and in designing an agenda that will achieve it.

BOX 7-5   GUIDELINE QUESTIONS FOR PLANNING EVALUATION INTERVIEWS

1. Why is this interview taking place?
2. What specifically is to be evaluated?
3. Who should be involved in this evaluation process?
4. Why should these parties be involved in this process?
5. What evaluation criteria should be used during this interview?
6. How can this set of criteria be used objectively and fairly?
7. Are there any limitations to be considered in this situation?
8. What would be an appropriate way to establish the evaluative climate necessary for such an interview?
9. Are there any legal forms or signatures that will be needed for conducting this interview session?

The responses to these questions will make the task of setting up the interview, as well as creating a clear purpose, realistic. As in other kinds of interviews, taking notes usually interferes with the interview process. In an evaluation, taking notes can be a very threatening activity. Many institutions have standard forms for such interviews. These are for legal protection, but they also serve as excellent notes for a working agenda, preventing the omission of necessity information. These forms also help to keep the interview on target; it is easy to go astray when evaluating details.

Evaluation interviews require a high level of mastery in using specific communication skills. In many business organizations, individuals are specifically trained to conduct these kinds of interviews.

We have chosen to diagram the job-appraisal interview to demonstrate how the dynamic model operates in an evaluative interview (see Figure 7-10).

Persuasive interviews.   This category includes such situations as sales interviews, design-acceptance interviews, severance interviews, and stress-testing interviews. These interviews, like those in all the other categories, require planning and effective use of speaking and listening skills. In the persuasive situation, the function of the communication is viewed from two perspectives: the persuader and the persuadee. Much like the interviewing-role behaviors of questioning and responding, the roles of persuader and persuadee can also fluctuate between the interviewing parties.

The parties usually have conflicting views on the focus of the interview. Perhaps only one is attempting to function as a persuader. For example, a young designer may be trying to persuade his boss that his new design is better than the

FIGURE 7-9   Evaluation interviews that involve job behavior can be difficult if both parties' needs are not met.

one currently in use. In this situation, the boss may sit back and expect the designer to offer enough evidence to persuade her to agree. In another situation, both parties may wish to persuade. An accountant may have one program for record-keeping that is very workable for his job requirements, but when he is called in for an interview with his manager, he discovers that his manager wants him to switch to a new program. During the course of the dialogue both individuals are going to act as persuader and persaudee, each trying to convince the other.

Since such interviews by necessity revolve around opposite or competitive viewpoints, the interpersonal relationship between such parties can interfere with the openness of the communication. Self-disclosure in such situations carries a much higher risk. Severance interviews are good examples of this possible occurrence. The employer knows in advance that she must let the employee go; no matter what is said during the interview, the outcome is predetermined. It may be the employer's purpose to persuade the employee to resign rather than be fired. On the other hand, the employee may feel he is being treated unfairly and see this interview as an opportunity for him to persuade the employer to give him a second change. The parties are at cross purposes; the interpersonal relationship is in jeopardy; and the communication behavior roles are definitely going to affect the interview process in a negative way. Certainly, awareness of these factors will not change the decision, but it could affect the attitudes and behavior of the parties involved, making the interview a positive experience for both. Both could learn from the experience and help one another; the employer could learn how to prevent

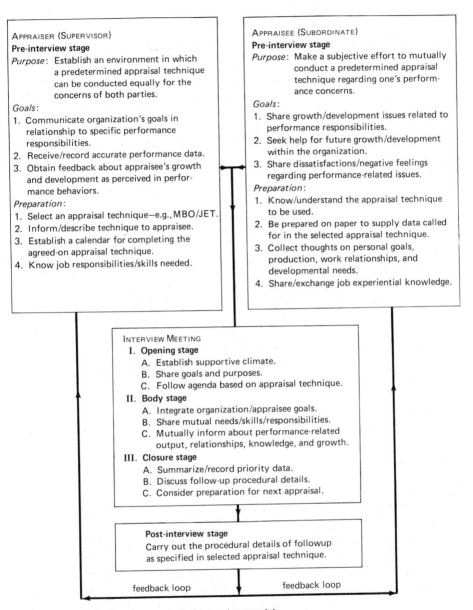

FIGURE 7-10 Performance-appraisal interview model.

such a situation in the future, and the employee could learn something for the next job.

The planning stage for a persuasive interview requires careful consideration of the purpose and agenda (see Box 7-6). A salesperson and customer must have a common understanding of purpose in a sales interview, or there will be no persuasion.

BOX 7-6   GUIDELINE QUESTIONS FOR PLANNING A PERSUASIVE INTERVIEW

1. Who is being persuaded?
2. Why is the persuasion taking place?
3. Will specific information be needed prior to the interview?
4. What will this specific information be?
5. How will persuasive strategies be used during the interview?
6. Will the strategy function within the limitations of the space and time planned for the interview?
7. What type of interpersonal relationship should be expected at the beginning of the interview?

The agenda likewise must have the same careful consideration. In your efforts to prepare for such a persuasive interview, we suggest the following sales interview model to guide your communication actions (see Figure 7-11).

Once these preliminary considerations for interviewing have been thought through, the purpose should be apparent, and drafting a workable agenda should be the next step of preparation.

As you reflect on the four general categories of interviews, the apparent distinguishing factor is the purpose. The agenda, although a more detailed item, is designed around the purpose of the interview. Planning—combined with the effective use of specialized skills—is the key action for successful interviewing. Box 7-7 provides nine simple but essential guidelines to consider for all interviewing.

BOX 7-7   CONSIDERATIONS FOR SUCCESSFUL INTERVIEWING

1. Start the interview on time with a *positive* note.
2. Be continually aware of your use of communication skills.
3. Be sensitive to the interpersonal relationships present when the interview begins.
4. Freely discuss the purpose of the interview at the beginning.
5. Make the agenda available to the other parties in advance.
6. Strive to use self-disclosure with pertinent information.
7. Be sensitive to nonverbal cues such as head nodding, body posture, gestures, and facial expression.
8. Summarize all of the important information covered during the interview.
9. End the interview on an interpersonal or conversational note.

QUESTIONS AND RESPONSE SKILLS
FOR INTERVIEWING

The use of the questions and responses is central to successful, effective performance in interviews. This particular skill requires experience and practice in order to be performed with proficiency. As you recall, we defined the interviewer as the

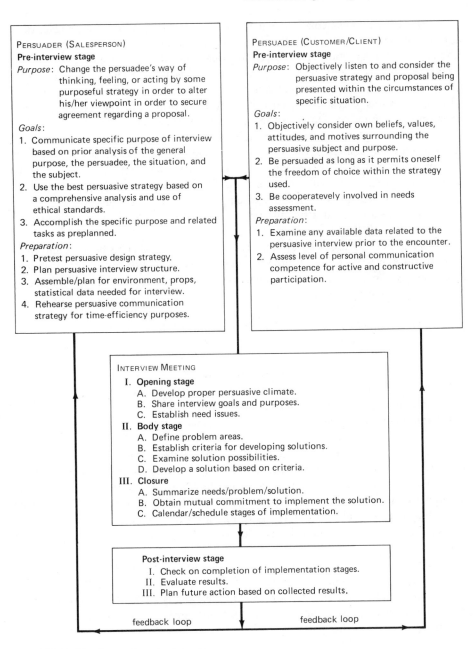

PERSUADER (SALESPERSON)

Pre-interview stage

Purpose: Change the persuadee's way of thinking, feeling, or acting by some purposeful strategy in order to alter his/her viewpoint in order to secure agreement regarding a proposal.

Goals:

1. Communicate specific purpose of interview based on prior analysis of the general purpose, the persuadee, the situation, and the subject.
2. Use the best persuasive strategy based on a comprehensive analysis and use of ethical standards.
3. Accomplish the specific purpose and related tasks as preplanned.

Preparation:

1. Pretest persuasive design strategy.
2. Plan persuasive interview structure.
3. Assemble/plan for environment, props, statistical data needed for interview.
4. Rehearse persuasive communication strategy for time-efficiency purposes.

PERSUADEE (CUSTOMER/CLIENT)

Pre-interview stage

Purpose: Objectively listen to and consider the persuasive strategy and proposal being presented within the circumstances of specific situation.

Goals:

1. Objectively consider own beliefs, values, attitudes, and motives surrounding the persuasive subject and purpose.
2. Be persuaded as long as it permits oneself the freedom of choice within the strategy used.
3. Be cooperatevely involved in needs assessment.

Preparation:

1. Examine any available data related to the persuasive interview prior to the encounter.
2. Assess level of personal communication competence for active and constructive participation.

INTERVIEW MEETING

I. **Opening stage**
   A. Develop proper persuasive climate.
   B. Share interview goals and purposes.
   C. Establish need issues.

II. **Body stage**
   A. Define problem areas.
   B. Establish criteria for developing solutions.
   C. Examine solution possibilities.
   D. Develop a solution based on criteria.

III. **Closure**
   A. Summarize needs/problem/solution.
   B. Obtain mutual commitment to implement the solution.
   C. Calendar/schedule stages of implementation.

Post-interview stage
   I. Check on completion of implementation stages.
   II. Evaluate results.
   III. Plan future action based on collected results.

feedback loop   feedback loop

FIGURE 7-11 Persuasive sales interview.

party who uses questioning behaviors and the interviewee as the party who uses responding behaviors. Therefore, the obvious focus in the interview situation is on efficient uses of questioning.

Questioning behavior.   From the viewpoint of the interviewer's role, there are four basic categories of questions: the direct question, the open-ended question, the clarification question and the probing question. All four categories are used for seeking information, but the distinctive feature of each is the reason for choosing it. The interviewer must realize that questions have two levels of communication. The first and obvious level is the specific request for information. The second level provides information for the interviewee about the focus of the interview.

Asking a question establishes the basis of the communication behavior role. How a question is phrased, the tone of voice, and the emphasis on specific words in the question can all convey second-level meaning to the listener. For example, an interview can start off with the question, "Well, how are you feeling about your job today?" If the questioner chose to emphasize "how," the question would take on a certain meaning; but if the questioner chose to emphasize "today," that would imply a quite a different meaning.

Using questioning skills effectively requires the speaker to be alert and to be able to use the voice properly for the intended meaning. For this reason, some job interviewers for large business organizations prefer not to conduct early morning interviews if they can avoid it.

The direct question.   The direct question has four specific functions in an interview:

1.   to collect exact, detailed information
2.   to let the interviewee know the type of information that is being sought
3.   to eliminate vagueness or misunderstanding
4.   to quickly direct the interview toward a specific goal

The direct question is explicit and can save a great deal of time when necessary. If the interview gets off target, this is one effective way to turn it back to the desired direction. The direct question should be used with caution, however, since a series of direct questions can appear very threatening to the interviewee. This individual may feel as if he or she is being "grilled," and this may put the interviewee on the defensive and influence the atmosphere of the interview in a negative way.

The most serious drawback to extensive use of the direct question is the limitation that it puts on the responses of the interviewee. These questions call for exact, but usually short, responses. The interviewee is given little opportunity to express personal opinions; and this, in turn, prevents the interviewer from really getting to know the other party.

The open-ended question.   This question does not call for an exact response. It provides more freedom of response and imposes fewer limitations on the kind of information. This type of questioning encourages personal opinion, which reflects personal attitude—a factor that may be very important to the interviewer. If the interviewer is more concerned about the attitude surrounding the response rather than the correctness of the response, the open-ended question is the better choice. There are several specific instances when open-ended questions should be used:

1. to give the interviewee more control of the content in the communication exchange
2. to obtain selected information without creating a defensive atmosphere
3. to encourage a relaxed atmosphere for expressing personal opinion
4. to open up the focus of the interview to include additional subject areas
5. to obtain the attitudes rather than objective responses of the interviewee
6. to prevent the interviewer from indicating any personal bias in the wording of the questions

Like the direct question, the open-ended question has its drawbacks. Responses to this type of question take up more time, and often time is a serious limitation to begin with. Then, too, it can easily get an interview off target. Both parties can get off on a tangent and quickly lose sight of their goal. The interviewer, when using this line of questioning, must have very efficient listening skills in order to select the important issues from the open response.

The clarification question.   This line of questioning is designed to obtain detailed or extended information. Frequently a question is misunderstood for some reason and must be reworded, or similar type questions must be asked. If an interviewer finds it necessary to use a lot of clarification questions, this may be an indication that his or her line of questioning needs to be examined.

There are some specific reasons for using the clarification questions, such as:

1. to clear up any confusion created by a poorly structured question
2. to obtain a detailed explanation of an interviewee's response
3. to seek a definition for some term or phrase used by the interviewee
4. to imply to the interviewee an interest in some pieces of information supplied by him or her

The clarification question can also get the interview off target if overused. It can be a time-consuming method of questioning, as it requires time for the interviwee to rethink the previous response. If the response is slow in coming, there is a tendency for the questioner to cut off the response, and this is a negative behavior. If this occurs several times during the course of a single interview, it can cause hostile feelings and interfere with the role relationship between the parties.

The probing question.   This type of question is used to obtain additional information to a previous question that has been asked. All interviewers have a need to probe during any interview. The questioner is telling the other party that he or she wants to pursue a topic or issue more in depth.

There are some specific reasons for using probing questions in an interview:

1. to seek more detail about some information that has already been provided
2. to confirm a belief or feeling that one develops about the other person during the course of the interview
3. to substantiate to the other party that this is indeed what he or she has stated during the interaction of the interview
4. to demonstrate to the other party a feeling of concern and interest

Probing questions can be misused during any interview. If the probing gets too personal or moves both parties away from the original purpose for conducting the interview, then such questions are not productive. Probing questions, if used too frequently within one interview, can intimidate the other person, who may then feel awkward and less cooperative about the total, and essential, communication interaction.

RESPONDING BEHAVIOR

Responding behavior, the function of the interviewee, also requires a certain level of mastery. When the questions are directed to the interviewee, he or she has several techniques available for handling the situation, and several type of responses.

The three ways in which responses can be used are to give complete, partial, or biased answers. The complete response, although accurate, may be time-consuming. Certainly, more time to reflect is needed for the interviewee to organize such a response. Sometimes, if the pause to organize an answer is long, an interviewer may interpret this as a "stall tactic." A complete answer does provide exact and detailed data, but the interviewee must determine if this is what the interviewer is actually seeking. Obviously, the best safeguard for dealing with complete responses is to anticipate them before the interview and have some prepared information to rely on. For example, individuals are frequently asked in an interview to discuss their career goals or ambitions. This is an open-ended question, and an interviewee who has not given this subject some thought prior to the interview may have a difficult time composing a response.

The partial answer is, of course, incomplete in the real sense of the word. There are situations in which a complete response is unnecessary. Some of the information can be assumed by both parties. But there is, again, the danger of misunderstanding, or of vague or poorly structured responses.

The biased response reflects an opinion. This is not automatically a negative response pattern. Frequently, the interviewer is searching for an opinion, and if so, the interviewee should respond accordingly. Sensible judgment is obviously necessary, since not all questions call for an opinion-based response. The open-ended questions are the ones that usually call for the biased response, while the others usually do not.

The interviewee has a choice of responding techniques, according to the nature of the interview. The interviewee can respond to a question by asking a question. If the interviewer's question is unclear, this is a good technique to use rather than take the chance on giving a poor response. Another technique is to respond but to qualify the answer, allowing the freedom to alter the response when applied to specific instances. Another technique is to respond by telling a story, describing an analogy (comparing two similar circumstances) or creating a specific example.

In the final analysis, the use of questions and responses is the core of communication in an interview. Mastery of this skill distinguishes the productive interview from the one that is ineffective. The novice communicator should practice working with question and response techniques as a means of becoming an effective interviewer and interviewee.

BASIC PROCEDURE FOR CONDUCTING THE ACTUAL INTERVIEW

You have learned that there is a wide variety of interviews. Even though you have become aware of the differences, some factors are common to all interview situations. These similarities allow us to design a procedure that you can follow when you are preparing for such a communication activity. A clearly defined purpose and agenda is one common ingredient to all interviews.

After you have a statement of purpose and a basic agenda sketched out for a particular interview, the procedure outlines in Box 7-8 will help you to make the

---

BOX 7-8   PROCEDURE FOR CONDUCTING AN INTERVIEW

1. Prepare the physical environment prior to the interview.
   a.   make the setting pleasant and comfortable
   b.   make the setting workable for the particular type of interview
2. Establish the atmosphere at the opening of the interview.
   a.   plan a greeting that is friendly and warm
   b.   establish a positive mood in a businesslike fashion
3. Clarify the purpose of the interview.
   a.   discuss the statement of purpose
   b.   define any terms or limitations to the content of the interview
   c.   briefly mention any constraints, such as time or possible interruptions
4. Outline the agenda and relate it to the target of the interview.
   a.   use only as much detail as the situation requires
   b.   clearly indicate how you think the agenda should operate
5. Activate the agenda.
   a.   maintain a positive motivation for the participant(s)
   b.   periodically refer to the interview target and do minisummaries

6. Summarize all of the major issues of the interview.
7. Conduct a final closure.
   a. plan for a follow-up if it is called for
   b. thank the contributors

final preparations for a successful interview. If you find that some variation to this procedure is necessary, the guideline questions provided for the four interview categories should assist you in making this adjustment. After reviewing some of the key issues presented, you should be ready to practice the interview skills discussed in this chapter.

A REVIEW OF KEY ISSUES

The interview is a communication process used to seek information based on a preconceived purpose, in a specific dynamic relationship influenced by the roles of the interviewer and interviewee. This activity is a part of our professional work, and it can play a significant part in our career.

In a few basic guidelines for effective listening skills are necessary in interviewing.

Careful planning of the purpose and agenda of any interview will provide a more efficient interview.

There are four general types of interviews:
1. information-gathering
2. problem-solving
3. evaluative
4. persuasive

These four types are distinguished by the function for which they are intended.

Question and answer skills are at the core of interviewing.

There are three types of answers used in interviewing: the complete response, the partial response, and the biased response.

The basic procedure for conducting an interview is
1. Prepare the physical environment.
2. Prepare the psychological environment.
3. Clarify the target.
4. Outline the agenda and relate it to the target.
5. Activate the agenda.
6. Summarize the key issues of the interview.
7. Provide an appropriate closing.

EXPERIENCING EXPERIENCES

This chapter has presented you with a large number of skills that are specifically designed for interviewing activities. Skills, by definition, require using one's knowledge effectively. In addition to presenting skills, this chapter has also provided a number of sets of guidelines. Guidelines are an indication of suggested policies created for achieving a determined goal. And for you, this chapter goal has been to learn how to conduct successful interviews as a part of your professional activity. You have already learned that experience is the best way to master skills. Therefore, the following activities have been designed to provide some experiences in order for you to practice the skills presented in this chapter. Have fun experiencing, and learn.

ACTIVITY 1

General Type: Information-gathering interview
Specific Type: Job interview
Situation: You are to interview a young woman who is applying for the job of waitress in a small restuaurant that does a heavy business at lunchtime for professional people working in the local area.

Purpose Statement: _____

_____

Agenda: Time Allotted:_____ mins.

Closing:

After the interview has been completed, on the reverse side of your sheet makes a list of the significant data you wish to keep on file regarding this interview.

ACTIVITY 2

General Type: Problem-solving interview
Specific Type: Disciplinary interview
Situation: Joel Brown never wears his safety glasses when he goes around the machinery. Call Joel into the office and deal with this safety issue.

Purpose Statement: _____

_____

Agenda: Time Allotted:_____ mins.

Closing:

EXERCISES

1. After you have completed the paperwork experiences, get a classmate to be the other person and role-play your best-planned interview.

2. After the interview, invite class discussion. Focus on:
    a. the good qualities
    b. the weaknesses
    c. ways to capitalize on the strong qualities
    d. ways to eliminate the weaknesses

3. If you have access to videotaping equipment, tape a simulated interview. Play the tape back and have your classmates present a brief written critique, using the four points listed in the exercise above. Compare the viewpoints.

4. Ask a professional from the community who interviews on a regular basis to speak to you about his or her professional experiences. Plan good questions to ask this person.

5. Arrange to visit a personnel department in a large business organization. Look at facilities, meet the staff, talk about interview skills as they are applied in real situations, and look at the various kinds of interviews this company uses.

6. If you are interested in a particular career, look in the yellow pages and find a professional person doing this type of work. Make an appointment for an interview to obtain as much information as possible about this career.

NOTES

1. Robert Goyer and Michael Sincoff, *Interviewing Methods.* Dubuque, Iowa: Kendall Hunt Pub., 1977.
2. Charles Stewart and William Cash, *Interviewing: Principles and Practices.* Dubuque, Iowa: Wm. C. Brown Co., 1978.
3. Erving Goffman, *Interaction Ritual: Essays in Face to Face Behavior.* Garden City, N.Y.: Anchor Books, 1967.
4. Joseph Luft and Harrington Ingram, *Of Human Action.* Palo Alto, California: National Press Book, 1969.
5. Eric Berne, *Games People Play.* New York: Grove Press, 1967.
6. Thomas Harris, *I'm Okay–You're Okay.* New York: Avon, 1973.

CHAPTER EIGHT

PROBLEM-SOLVING MEETINGS

A great deal of business communication takes place in the problem-solving meeting. In fact, we know that it is not uncommon for the business person to spend a major portion of the day going from one meeting to another. The cooperative venture of working together to create success in business naturally requires meeting together. But if we could peer into the minds and feelings of individuals who have either led a meeting or acted as one of the participants, we would find a great deal of dissatisfaction. The dissatisfaction stems from the fact that time is wasted, ideas are left unsaid, and perhaps even feelings have been hurt because the meeting was not conducted efficiently. Often participants seemed unaware of the need to use effective communication skills in the small group.

To encourage you to use such skills, this chapter focuses attention on the nature and function of a small-group meeting, the role of leadership, and ways to act as a participant. In a subsequent chapter, attention is focused on much larger business meetings and business conferences in which many people work both collectively and in small subgroups to achieve specified goals.

There are many books that deal solely with small-group communication, and each one specifies an ideal range for the size of a small group. According to Vincent DiSalvo, whose definition is consistent with the views of many others, "A small group is defined as three or more individuals who are engaged in face-to-face interaction with one another in such a manner that each person influences and is

143

influenced by each of the other individuals."[1] DiSalvo indicates that the ideal size of a small group is between five and seven members, and the upper limit is about twenty. Admittedly, there are some business meetings in which three persons are just right, but most often this number is too small, while a meeting with twenty people generally accomplishes little unless the group is divided into several smaller groups. A group too small for its task may produce unsatisfactory results, while a group too large often becomes unwieldy and unproductive because some members are neither heard from nor considered.

We know that business persons frequently find themselves frustrated in meetings. Being unsettled, ill-at-ease, perhaps angry, is not uncommon. There are, of course, numerous times when people leave meetings feeling satisfied and certain that a great deal was accomplished, both in terms of their own personal needs and the task goals of the group. To help you understand why a person would leave a small-group session feeling good and satisfied while another would leave feeling quite the opposite, we shall examine the elements of small-group communication for the business person. The major purpose of this chapter is to significantly help you to become an effective communicator in meetings. Because the majority of business meetings are held to solve problems, we shall focus on the problem-solving meeting.

PROBLEM-SOLVING MEETINGS

The problem-solving meeting, one with a specific task and/or set of goals to achieve, is the sort of group studied most frequently by researchers. Although there are important psychological dimensions in the problem-solving group, the emphasis is usually on logical ways to collectively eliminate a problem. From an interpersonal perspective, both relationship and task goals are important, but the group seeks to concentrate on a common problem. For instance, a radio station is staffed by a variety of creative people with a wide range of age and background. The problem that brings them all together is a common love for radio as a medium for communication. When two rating systems reveal that the station is ranked seventh out of nine in the market area, the staff is charged with the responsibility of helping to increase their station's popularity until it becomes one of the top three. Several meetings are called by the general manager to propose a plan to solve the problem. Two members from each department at the station are appointed to the group, and one of the members is elected to serve as chairperson or leader for the group. This sort of group is typical of those formed in the business world.

Certain conditions and patterns of analysis reveal the nature of functions of this type of problem-solving group. We know that the problem-solving group is likely to achieve positive goals if it becomes both dynamic and cohesive. A dynamic group is one in which each participant makes frequent, direct, and constructive contributions. If the group is cohesive, its members have a commitment to rhetorical dialogue. Dialog is communication that requires working together carefully, accurately, and openly to achieve mutual understanding and solve a common problem. A cohesive group encourages cooperative efforts to achieve its ends.

As the group works toward achieving its goals in the meetings, it will confront problems external to the group and those which arise out of working together on the major task. The first kind of problem can be identified as the task problem, while the second is the maintenance problem. The group must strive to deal with these and remain always dynamic and cohesive. The task problems are external to the group. The group at the radio station worked with information that aimed at boosting the station's ratings; and in the process, members behaved in social and emotional ways within the group. Positive and healthy maintenance behavior helps the problem-solving group complete its task.

A system for observing and understanding small-group behavior has been developed by Robert F. Bales (see Figure 8-1). He has, through research, produced a system of categories that provides not only analysis of small-group behavior but suggests ways to participate in a small group.[2] To make a decision and solve a problem, a group must adapt to conditions outside the group. Members must talk and act in ways that can bring about change. In addition, the members of the group express ideas with feeling, so that each member's appropriate personal needs can be understood. This may or may not result in an integrative working unit. In small groups, there are individual needs and group needs; and, ideally, a group should achieve and maintain a balance that can meet both sets of needs. However, in the life of a group, the activity shifts from such a balance as the communicators move back and forth from concern for individual needs to the needs grounded in the group's problem. Essentially, the group strives to spend its time on the task without ignoring the internal problems. To see how adjustments can be made to create a healthy climate within the group and solve the external problem, we can use Bales's categories of small-group behaviors. The categories provide a method for analysis of group communication and the application of principles for effectiveness.

When you understand the behaviors outlined by Bales, you can use them to predict and understand both your behaviors and those of others at the meeting. This insight can help you to contribute productively to the meetings you attend—if you continually work on positive relationship and task goals.

As we examine the problem-solving formats, leadership behavior, and guidelines for participation, the categories become increasingly useful. Effective problem-solving meetings require preparation. The leader develops an agenda before the first meeting and subsequently the group progresses toward the solution of the problem by following this agenda. Participants receive a copy of the agenda at least a day in advance of a scheduled meeting. This encourages the participants to prepare carefully for the meeting

Generally, a problem-solving group has two primary goals. The first is to agree on an appropriate format, and the second is to agree on the answers to the questions found within the scope of the format. Here the term *format* indicates a method of using an outline of topics to be considered by the group. The most useful model of this technique is based upon the reflective thinking pattern (see Box 8-1).

		CATEGORY
Positive Social–Emotional	A	1. *Shows Solidarity*, raises other's status, gives help, rewards, shows affection, acts of pacification:
		2. *Shows Tension Release*, laughs, shows satisfaction, jokes, trying to amuse or entertain, clowning:
		3. *Shows Agreement*, passive acceptance, understands, concurs, unassertive, includes agreement with an observation or course of action:
Task– Positive	B	4. *Gives Suggestion*, direction, suggesting concrete ways of attaining a goal, proposing a solution, indicating where to start:
		5. *Gives Opinion*, evaluation, analysis, expresses feelings, a wish, reasoning, calculating, thinking:
		6. *Gives Information*, orientation, repeats, clarifies, confirms, brings the group up to date:
Task– Negative	C	7. *Asks for Information*, expresses a lack of knowledge, asks for orientation, repetition, confirmation:
		8. *Asks for opinion*, evaluation, analysis, expression of feeling, open-ended questions, attempts to encourage a statement or reaction:
		9. *Asks for Suggestions*, direction, possible ways of action, questions or requests as to how the discussion should proceed:
Negative Social– Emotional	D	10. *Shows Disagreement*, passive rejection, appears skeptical, disagreement over ideas, ignoring the request of another member, any behavior which blocks or restrains the group:
		11. *Shows Tension*, asks for help, withdraws out of the field, restless, emotional, bored, trembling, on edge:
		12. *Shows Antagonism*, deflates other's status, dominates, purposefully ignores directions, attempts to control without other's consent:

a   b   c   d   e   f

Key:

a. Problems of Communication   d. Problems of Decision
b. Problems of Evaluation   e. Problems of Tension Reduction
c. Problems of Control   f. Problems of Reintegration

FIGURE 8-1   Small-group behavior systems. (Robert F. Bales, *Interaction Process Analysis,* 1950. Permission of the University of Chicago Press.)

BOX 8-1   PROBLEM-SOLVING PATTERN

1. Identify the problem and analyze its nature.
2. Establish criteria for solving the problem.
3. Suggest potential solutions and evaluate them in light of the criteria.
4. Select the most attractive solution and determine how to accomplish it.
5. See that the solution is accomplished and be prepared to evaluate its effectiveness.

A more detailed model for the format is outlined below, and both of these patterns for problem-solving have been used extensively with positive results.

DETAILED PROBLEM-SOLVING MODEL

Analysis
I.   What is the nature of the problem?
    A.   What are the facts of the present situation?
        1.   How can the present situation be described?
            a. What is going on?
            b. Who is involved?
            c. What kinds of difficulties exist?
            d. When did the problem develop?
            e. Have we presented enough factual information to make the nature and scope of the problem clear?
    B.   How serious is the problem?
        1.   Is the problem extensive?
        2.   Is a change (solution) urgent?
        3.   Why is the problem especially important now?
    C.   What are the causes of the problem?
        1.   What is the history of the problem?
        2.   What conditions brought it about?
    D.   What forces are at work to change the present situation?
        1.   What solutions have been tried?
            a. How extensive have they been?
            b. How successful have they been?
        2.   Is there need for additional attempts to solve the problem?
        3.   What will the probable results be if no action is taken?
    E.   To what extent does this group agree on a course of action?
        1.   On what matters does the group seem to agree?
        2.   On which ones do members disagree?
        3.   What real controversies need to be worked out?
Criteria
II.   What standards, criteria, and goals must be met by any solution to the problem?
    A.   How do we determine our criteria?
        1.   Ideally, what seem to be the best guidelines for making judgments?
        2.   How extensive are the criteria to be?
        3.   How do we most effectively apply the criteria?
    B.   What ideals must a solution satisfy?

Probable Solutions
III.   What courses of action seem evident and probable?
     A.   Which of the suggested solutions seem most attractive?
        1.   What are the strengths of each?
        2.   What are the weaknesses of each?
     B.   Which of the solutions is most attractive for solving the problem?
        1.   What are the strengths of the solution?
        2.   What are the weaknesses?
     C.   Have any essential elements been overlooked? If so:
        1.   What are good points about them?
        2.   What are bad points about them?
     D.   How can we sum up the chosen solution?
Accomplishing the Aim
IV.   What steps need to be taken to put the chosen solution into effect?
     A.   How can we evaluate the results?
     B.   Are we prepared to modify this solution or select another if necessary?

By following these steps and questions, the group will be able to outline topics and issues to be faced. At first glance the approach might seem cumbersome and complex, but once you use it in a problem-solving meeting, you will see that it can produce maximum results with minimal waste of time and energy. The group must be precise and comprehensive in achieving its task, and in most cases, if it has done its job completely the evaluation of the solution will be positive and the need for an alternative solution will not arise.

If the group does not have a format indicated by the leader or does not choose one, the early stage of the group process can easily become a collection of

FIGURE 8-2   Problem-solving meetings can take place in a wide variety of settings.

random and disorganized views. There are times when the format is less structured, but the leader keeps track of the issues and decisions well enough that ideas are fully expressed, differences on issues are brought out, and a solution is determined. For more formally structured meetings, we advocate the problem-solving pattern of analysis—with this warning: Some meetings begin by using the reflective-thinking pattern but soon abandon it. Stages are taken out of sequence, some are ignored, the members become side-tracked; and as a result, time is wasted and productivity is minimal. Of course, a good leader will recognize the signs of disorder and take steps to prevent it. Other members may also become aware of the process and assume some leadership as well.

In almost all small groups, some members do most of the talking while one or two others say practically nothing. Not speaking much can often be attributed to passivity in the presence of others, a psychological trait not easily changed in people. However, there are those who are silent because they are not prepared to participate in the meeting. Sometimes the seating arrangements in a meeting discourage some members from contributing. And, of course, if several persons in a meeting form a clique or are just dominating communicators, their behavior will discourage others from trying to speak. There is a fourth reason some do not talk. The subject matter of the meeting may be a highly sensitive, controversial, or emotional one, so that an otherwise conversational person feels inhibited and uncomfortable and keeps quiet most of the time.

Often, these behaviors can be overcome if there is a designated or elected leader. This individual can see that the meeting is scheduled in a room and at a time *most suitable for healthy communication.* He or she can be certain an *agenda* is prepared and distributed to members before the meeting and that the room is arranged for maximum communication. Generally, maximum communication occurs when everyone is seated comfortably face to face, in a circle or around a rectangular table. However, meetings are often held in rooms not equipped for small-group business meetings, or members are seated at a long conference table where some persons are not close to the chairperson or leader and tend to feel out of the discussion. As a matter of fact, a leader can do a great deal to aid the productivity of a meeting *or* to discourage it.

THE QUESTION OF LEADERSHIP

Many researchers have studied the question of leadership. Which work best—groups with a clearly appointed or elected leader, or groups that operate without any particular person serving in the role of leader? In business, almost all meetings are so structured that someone unquestionably serves as the leader or chairperson. Certainly there are informal "brainstorming" sessions, in which business persons meet to develop and bounce ideas off one another, and in these instances, a leader may not be necessary. Quite frequently the role of leader falls to the person who holds the highest business position among the members of the group.

We do not intend to suggest that only the "official" leader can provide leadership in a meeting. Everyone who participates in meetings is responsible for showing leadership traits and characteristics at some time during the life of the group. In one organizational meeting, for example, as certain problems and responsibilities came to the group's attention, different members assumed particular leadership in addressing and handling each problem. But even in this situation, one designated leader was instrumental in coordinating the efforts of the group.

The responsibilities and functions of a leader, whether self-appointed, elected, or designated, are many. To help you understand some major functions and responsibilities of leadership, we shall examine a useful series of statements about what a leader can do (see Box 8-2). Each of these statements is followed by examples that illustrate how it works.

BOX 8-2   LEADERSHIP RESPONSIBILITIES

1. A leader can establish a format for the group; he or she may do this with the help of group participants.
2. A leader can "get the group going" in pertinent and productive directions.
3. A leader can assume responsibility for keeping the group "on the track" and focused on group goals.
4. A leader can make clarifying summaries when they seem necessary to group progress.
5. A leader can assume responsibility for keeping group communication from becoming one-sided.
6. A leader can work to relieve the tensions that result from heated controversy in the group.
7. A leader can ask relevant questions to draw information out of participants for group response.
8. A leader can attempt to keep a group alive by ensuring that no group member remains passive.

These statements can help achieve effective leadership. If you understand the aspects of good leadership, you will yourself be able to analyze the behaviors in business meetings.

1. A leader can establish a format for the group; he or she may do this with the help of the participants.

Establishing a format for the group can be especially useful to each person concerned because it provides clarifying procedures for how the meetings are to operate. The following example illustrates how the failure to establish a format worked against the productivity as well as the communication climate for an important group. The company received the resignation of an important division chief, and instead of turning to the personnel division to suggest potential replacements, top management designated the seven supervisors as a search committee to recommend a replacement. Let us see why this was a mistake.

When the group had its first meeting (five men and two women were present), one of the men was elected quickly and informally to lead the subsequent meetings and to coordinate the search activities until the task was complete. He enthusiastically accepted the responsibility, but in the weeks that followed he and the others ran into difficulties because no format for the meetings was established. There were no agreed upon procedures, no regularly scheduled meeting times, and no procedures to make the applicants' credentials available to the committee members before each meeting. As a result, some of the members felt uncomfortable at the meetings; some missed meetings because of poor scheduling. Furthermore, because there was no orderly, expected procedure, the meetings were too long and unproductive. After several weeks, disgruntled members voiced their frustration and anger to the elected chairperson. He resigned his position of leadership and a second supervisor took over. Things then changed dramatically. A format was chosen and adhered to, meetings were scheduled at agreed-on ties with a time limit placed on each meeting, and everyone was given the agenda and other pertinent information to provide a common basis for communication.

2.   A leader can "get the group going" in pertinent and productive directions.

Without dominating the discussion, the leader can make initial and periodic comments at a meeting, which motivate others to participate and keep the group's attention aimed at the problem. Often, members of a group sit frustrated, while the conversation ranges from football to inflation until another member asks what business specifically should be given consideration. It is also not uncommon for the leader of a group to dominate and manage to such an extent that little real interaction can take place. These situations represent the extremes of the continuum, but, nonetheless, the practices are not rare.

If an ideal case, the leader opens a meeting with several highly pertinent comments. If a printed agenda is in the hands of the participants, the leader calls attention to what the group can begin to work on. Once meaningful talk is underway, others are likely to make contributions. And when the contributions move toward solving the problem, the leader keeps the information coming by asking questions when others do not, offering appropriate summaries, and providing a closing (a "wrapping-up summation"). In the overall transaction of business, the leader can be especially useful to the group by working to keep the focus of the meeting on the major task the group faces—keeping "on the track."

3.   A leader can assume responsibility for keeping the group "on the track" and focused on group goals.

A business executive once noted that one of her subordinates had graduated from a local university with a major in communication theory. Therefore, she invited him to serve on a membership committee for a professional organization to which they both belonged. From the start, she indicated to him that she believed he could strengthen the group process by using his expertise as a communication theorist. He could analyze the process and advise the group.

From the beginning, this communication specialist discovered that the group suffered because the designated leader was highly nondirective and either unwilling or unable to assert himself in the group process. Moreover, the other members of the group spent most of the meeting digressing from the major task at hand. The effect was that after four weekly meetings of the membership committee, no actual progress has been made toward determining a plan to recruit new members. The communication theorist then presented the leader and the group with a carefully developed flow chart of comments made in light of the group's agreed-on task. The members of the group acknowledged their unproductive talk and asked him to provide regular guidance as they worked. He became an active co-leader of the group, and the meetings produced a workable membership drive the organization used throughout the year. The big problem in the early meetings was simply that the group had become sidetracked, and the leader did not step in to get them back on the subject of solving the main problem.

Getting on the track and staying there often requires the leader to provide concrete statements about focusing on the task. There are times when the transactions become complex or confused and members of the group become frustrated or take the talk off onto side issues, away from the path the group should be on. The leader must be sensitive to these problems and step in with a clarifying summary.

4. *A leader can make clarifying summaries when they seem necessary to group progress.*

When a meeting gets bogged down and confused, members either cope with the confusion by making additional comments to increase it, or they fall silent. In these situations, one of the best ways to move forward is for the leader to provide a summary.

At a business meeting for a fast-food chain, a group met to determine who was to receive the regional Employee of the Month award. The nominees were drawn from lists of employees submitted by each franchise in the region. The criteria were explained to the committee members by top management, and an argument developed over what these criteria actually measured in an employee's job performance. This argument can be compared to boxers who get wrapped up on the ropes until a referee enters in and pulls them apart. The leader of this meeting summarized her perception of the agrument and continued her analysis until all views were clear to the members and consensus was achieved on the value of the criteria. This leader's work was instrumental to the group's total progress. While providing the internal summaries the leader also helped to keep the comments from becoming one-sided, which brings us to the fifth responsibility of an effective leader.

5.   *A leader can assume responsibility for keeping group communication from being one-sided.*

When the regional Employee of the Month Selection Committee began its meetings, several problems in the group process were encountered and handled through effective leadership. After the group had met several times, it became apparent to the leader that two members of the committee were extremely biased in their view of what constituted outstanding employees and which stores were most likely to have them. The other members of the group did not seem willing to focus attention on accusations of bias, for nothing was said to the two. The leader, however, worked out some direct but tactful statements to make the two aware of the barriers the bias created. Besides offering summaries and transitions, she raised probing questions to help the group avoid being one-sided, and she invited each member to speak.

After all, at one time or another we all have had some particular attitude that has clouded for us the real value in someone else's ideas. The leader must be able to recognize attitudes that create misunderstanding and strong differences, rather than mutual understanding and compromise. She or he can intercede and explain the importance of empathy and objectivity in meeting the task. At a meeting about promotion and tenure in a university history department, one member who had held a graduate research associate position for three years of doctoral study seemed to recognize only the merits of research activities, while a colleague forcefully argued the importance of classroom teaching. The leader had to remind both members that they were being very one-sided.

6.   *A leader can work to relieve the tension that results from heated controversy in the group.*

There is nothing inherently wrong with a heated discussion. It is both normal and healthy for emotional expression to take place. Kept below the surface, these feelings often have the potential to do damage. However, when they erupt into argument, they should be stifled. The leader must be able to intervene with a nonjudgmental comment that serves to relieve the tension and promote the progress of the flow of communication.

The leader must intervene wisely, so that the members expressing strong emotions do not feel as if they are being ridiculed, reprimanded, or repressed. When a pastoral relations committee of a large church met to determine if their minister should be reappointed, the pattern of interchange frequently became explosive. Emotions were displayed in a variety of ways—loud diatribes, sarcastic laughter, tears. Some members of the committee were strongly in favor of the pastor's reappointment while others were strongly against it. The chairperson had the delicate but highly important task of seeing that all the members were allowed to express themselves in healthy ways—healthy for the group and healthy for the individual members involved in the controversy.

This task of relieving tension is perhaps the most sensitive one the leader faces. People need to express strong feelings, or they carry their anger away from the group or they may even quit the group. So the leader must act directly and with fairness and empathy to encourage open confrontation while encouraging the focus on productivity as well. Perhaps an effective way to show this encouragement is by asking questions to draw pertinent information from the embroiled participants.

7.   *A leader can ask relevant questions to draw information from participants for group response.*

For a number of reasons, some group members hesitate to speak up in a business meeting or in other small groups. The reasons may range from general fear of communication to fear arising from a subordinate position in the group. But in any case, most members usually do have some constructive and important ideas, and some will never get into the flow of communication unless they are brought out by a leader's questions.

For the leader to ask relevant questions, he or she must be able to conceptualize and analyze the group process carefully and accurately. Listening is important for every group member but especially for the leader. Asking relevant questions can be contagious—if the leader questions, others are likely to question, also. As long as questions are asked and members are encouraged and supported as contributors in the effort to complete the task, there will be a high level of understanding and productivity.

8.   *A leader can attempt to keep a group alive by ensuring that no group member remains passive.*

At this point in our discussion the eighth responsibility may seem redundant, but it serves to emphasize the importance of having every person contribute to the talk. Furthermore, the key word here is "alive," for meetings often become dull and dreary when several members are not contributing to the dynamic activity in the group. Occasionally a group seems almost lifeless because one or two persons dominate the discussion. This usually happens for one of two reasons: Some people have a dominating personality and cannot keep quiet long enough to encourage others to speak; some people are so interested and well prepared that others lean back and let these members do most of the work.

Rolly was one of the most outstanding students in a course in business communication. During an assignment in which students were simulating a business meeting, he did most of the talking. He was neither abrasive nor overly aggressive in communication, but he was highly motivated, enthusiastic and well prepared. After two meetings were held, the instructor met with Rolly privately and told him he would receive an "A" for the assignment. Then the instructor asked him to refrain from commenting in the group. The next period he came in to class, set his materials in front of him and said nothing. Neither did anyone else, at first, because they were waiting for Rolly to carry them along. But after about five minutes of discomfort, the group leader began by asking others to make contributions toward solving the problem they had been given by management. When Rolly was asked, he simply indicated that he needed time to think and he deferred to others in the group. This was the only meeting that came close to a good and productive business meeting, because everyone was encouraged to add to the group. Let us consider next a different setting, a brewery for a local beer. The brewery wanted to become strong competition for nationally distributed products. The public relations department wanted to schedule some promotional activities in neighborhood shopping centers and sought the advice of a group of managers from other departments. No one seemed able to get a word in because one person, Burt, talked on and on. The leader, a woman from public relations, finally began to ask others to express themselves. She did not want to ignore or anger Burt, so after the meeting she asked him to join her for coffee. She thanked him for his important contributions, but explained she needed that of others as well. He responded favorably, and throughout the series of meetings, the group was alive with a variety of contributions, and members felt enthusiastic about the group and their individual efforts.

If a group becomes dull or dead and the meetings are unproductive, everyone is at fault. But the leader can help create a meeting quite the opposite in nature by following the eight guidelines we have been discussing and by encouraging everyone to participate.

PARTICIPATION—GUIDELINES FOR PRODUCTIVE ACTIVITY

The list of guidelines for effective communication in small groups could be quite long. Let us now examine such a list—a concise group of six guidelines (see Box 8-3). These six guidelines are easy to remember and use; study them carefully and then test each one by observing meetings and by personal participation.

BOX 8-3   GUIDELINES FOR PRODUCTIVE ACTIVITY

1. Genuinely seek to understand and find an answer to the common problem with which the group is faced.
2. Work toward the *same* task goal as the others and work toward healthy *relational* goals in the process.
3. Have little concern about what may be the particular solution as long as it is the best answer the group can find.
4. Maintain objectivity and a realistic detachment from your own proposals.
5. Bring information to the group and offer it freely.
6. Listen to everything stated both verbally and nonverbally, and respond with the group goal in mind.

These guidelines become more meaningful when we examine them in light of examples demonstrating how they affect the success of a group.

1. Genuinely seek to understand and find an answer to the common problem with which the group is faced.

The key word here is perhaps "genuinely," because it is the one word advising the participant to enter into communication with a particular attitude. Some participants in group meetings enter with a moderate interest in working to solve a common problem or have their own hidden agenda of what to gain from a meeting. When a person's attitude is characterized by indifference or strong private motives rather than those of the group as a whole, then her or his contributions are likely to detract from the group discussion or have little value to the realization of group goals. At a meeting called to establish human-relations training groups for a huge metropolitan clothing chain, an executive vice-president suddenly walked in on the three men and two women who were charged with the task. One of these members, Thom, an aggressive and rising executive, was only moderately interested in human-relations training and yet was, at the same time, among those who would profit from such training. During two sessions, his participation in the group was "forced" and infrequent. At the third meeting, when the vice-president appeared, Thom turned into quite a talker. To the others in the group, his new energy seemed false and of little help. He had not sought genuine understanding and, whether silent or speaking, made little or no contribution to their joint effort.

2. Work toward the same task goal as the others and work toward healthy relational goals in the process.

When individuals meet to communicate on a one-to-one basis, in a group, or even when one speaker addresses an audience, there are two types of communication goals: task and relationship goals. The task goal is shared by the participants and aimed at discovering what must be known and done in order to understand and solve a problem. Relationship goals are those that determine what must be done to bring participants closer together as persons relating to one another. Task goals focus on the knowledge of the individual in relation to other information brought into the group experience and on the methods and procedures for using this knowledge effectively. As William Brown puts it, when the communiator's purpose "becomes 'content' or task-centered, he aims at approach or withdrawal behavior from his listener not in relation to himself (or herself), primarily, but in relation to some proposal of his or another. His rhetorical purpose is to effect acceptance or rejection of (1) conceptions as facts, (2) evaluation of them, and (3) policies based upon them."[3] In a word, participants are directing their conscious attempts at analysis and reasoning in order to get the job done. In the process of dealing with tasks to solve a problem, relationship goals are also important.

Relationship goals are those whose aim is to adjust human relations so that healthy communication can be established, and a climate of liking, trust, and acceptance among group members will prevail. If you want to feel good about yourself as a participant and feel good about others in the group setting, you can establish interpersonal goals. These goals help to create positive interpersonal communication in the meetings. By empathizing with others, listening actively as well as talking constructively, and by being sensitive to both the nonverbal as well as the verbal messages of all other communicators in a group, you can grow in human relationships. This growth can contribute to the achievement of the content goals. For example, in an academic setting, a department faculty with diverse interests began a series of meetings to shape new priorities for the operating budget. Two of the members of the nine-person faculty were antagonistic, an attitude they projected both with words and nonverbal expressions. As a result, the other seven members began to feel considerably uncomfortable. The chairperson, sensing that the antagonists did not have positive interpersonal goals, confronted them with his impression during the meeting. A discussion of feelings and interpersonal relationships followed, and healthy goals were chosen. Aiming at these goals as well as the content goals, the group worked effectively in five business meetings to accomplish its task.

3. Have little concern about what may be the particular solution as long as it is the best answer the group can find.

Often communicators enter into group discussion and problem-solving with some notion about what "particular" solution is actually needed. The challenge for this person is: "How can I get the others to see this solution as clearly as I see it?" Or, "I know that others are going to come up with answers I have already considered, but I have given this problem much thought and with cautious persuasive efforts I can influence others to see this solution as I see it." This participant is concerned with her or his particular solution, regardless of whether it actually is best.

Members of a group ideally look at themselves as a group made up of individuals rather than as individuals constrained by a group setting. We know from experience and research in the business and professional world that often two heads are better than one, and three are better than two. A group of five to nine people can be quite effective when it has cohesion, cooperation, and common concentration. For example—in an effort to improve communications in the state's Department of Natural Resources, a team of assistant directors is assembled by the director. She asks them to give her an accurate analysis of the current state of communications as well as a method for creating healthy change in the working environment in the state offices. At the onset of a series of meetings, the assistant directors appear suspicious of one another, and of the task before them and of using the group process for problem solving. In addition, each participant seems highly protective toward her or his own division. For example, Terry believes that communication among the employees of the Division of Planning is as good as can realistically be expected; if a problem exists, it is not experienced at the planning level. As the group works together, the leader begins to acknowledge that something is wrong—members are concerned about particular solutions rather than a best solution! The members agree that a problem exists. A communication barrier has been set up. Until each member develops a shared image of the group, finding the best answer to the common problem seems impossible. The leader introduces

FIGURE 8-3 The active participation of all members ensures effective work toward group goals.

confrontational dialog into the group of individuals and, shortly afterwards, the individuals come to see themselves as one group with a highly important task—to find the *best* solution!

4.   *Maintain objectivity and a realistic detachment from your own proposals.*

Pursuit of the best answer cannot be achieved without objectivity and detachment from personal proposals. Pure objectivity is unattainable, but each participant in a business meeting can be as objectively subjective as possible. As intelligent people, we all probably enjoy the idea that we are usually objective, that we rely on reason and sound judgment. However, each of us is ego-involved with a number of individuals, activities, and commitments in our lives. When we have to communicate with others at a time when we must also deal with objects, events, ideas, or persons affecting our feelings about ourselves, we find it difficult to maintain objectivity.

A communicator's ego-involvement can be a positive factor in the group process if he or she contributes information and perspectives unknown to others in the group. The knowledgeable and the committed participant must share personal views openly with the belief that they may add fiber to the fabric of the answer, rather than that they form the only realistic answer that seems feasible. This attitude requires some "letting go," or a realistic detachment from one's own proposals. Imagine a huge metropolitan church served by six pastors. The Board of Governors for the church compiles a survey to determine if the programs of the church are meeting the needs of the majority of the members. They find, to their surprise, that many members indicate dissatisfaction with the programs and the ways in which they are being carried out. With this information in their hands, the Board decides to analyze the problem in a series of special meetings. Their goal is to develop an overall program made up of carefully selected programs that can meet the apparent needs of the congregation. After an initial meeting, the members of the group realize that some individuals in the group are strongly committed to programs that have received negative criticism in the survey. Moreover, before a careful analysis is complete, some members argue strongly for new proposals. The group seems unproductive and bogged down until the Chairperson of the Board intervenes to describe what is happening. He calls for objectivity toward the proposals of each member. After the problem has been fully analyzed, solutions can be suggested. For maximum value to the group, each individual must maintain objectivity and a realistic detachment both from her or his own proposal and from those the participant finds a strong personal attachment to.

5. *Bring information to the group and offer it freely.*

Susan always brings a great deal of information to the group meetings, while the other five members bring little. She does most of the talking while the others appear to do most of the listening. The group is charged with the problem of creating a training course in decision making, and the leader has become frustrated after several days of observation. Little information, outside of Susan's ideas, is being introduced. Susan, too, has become concerned. She decides not to contribute until others begin to bring information to the meetings and talk as informed participants. The next two meetings are difficult for everyone in the group. Susan really wants to talk but she remains firm in her silence. The others may have wanted to talk, but they have have not brought in information. After a great deal of squirming, some coughing and throat-clearing, the group manages to survive two meetings with Susan silent, and the third meeting is remarkably different. The others are prepared and highly active.

Even when everyone has information to offer the group effort, there are times when information is not given freely. Because of interorganizational competitiveness, fear of taking risks, or similar reasons, individuals working a group hold back ideas and information which could help the group considerably. Sara works for the electric company's public information department. She is a member of a committee to create a speakers' bureau in cooperation with the department of Special Programs and Consumer Services, and she often withholds information she could have contributed. She and her supervisor believe the bureau could have been developed exclusively by the Department of Public Information, and they hope that top management will give them this task when the results of the present group prove unsatisfactory. This sort of petty behavior is not uncommon in the organizational world. However, time, energy, and money can be saved through group communication if everyone in a group brings information to each meeting and offers it freely. The information is to be current and pertinent, requiring careful thought and research before the meetings.

6. *Pay attention to all signals, both verbal and nonverbal, and respond with the group goal in mind.*

Paying attention to all information—verbal and nonverbal—is extremely difficult. In the group process, members find information offered in group interaction more difficult to absorb than information in a speech or in a dyadic experience. Some information is highly pertinent, some language is clear, some expressions seem organized. Often, however, this is not the case. Also, there are times when we all let our minds wander. We are not really listening because we are busy constructing something to say the first time there is an opportunity.

In addition to words, of course, there are the sounds and physical expressions that also give us information. John always puts his hand over his mouth when he begins to talk about an idea that evokes strong feelings in him, and Mary always casts her eyes toward the ceiling when she speaks to Thom, a person she feels afraid of. When Jim listens in disagreement, especially to Barb, he shifts a lot and begins doodling with his pencil. These behaviors reflect something going on within the communicators. The participant in a group must be sensitive to them.

As one listens, observes, and tries to make sense of what is being said, she or he is advised to respond with the group goal in mind. We know it is easy to lose sight of the group goal when one gets caught up in personal needs.

FORMAL PROCEDURES

A small group does not often find it necessary to use parliamentary procedure. However, business persons should be familiar with these rules so they can use them if a meeting requires it. Every professional person's library ought to have a volume on parliamentary rules. Large meetings or conferences, which are characterized by debate and voting on motions and proposals, are almost always conducted according to these regulations.

Henry Ewbank, in speaking of small committees, tells us that the behavior of members is bound more by the usual rules of good etiquette than the rules of Robert's or Jefferson's manual of parliamentary procedure.[4] Certain elements are necessary for small-group meetings. Perhaps most important is the obligation to abide by the will of the majority in decisions affecting the procedures or substantive matters in the meeting. Of equal importance is the obligation of each participant to respect the rights of the others, no matter what is said. Progress can only be made if everyone works together with good judgment and fairness.

When it is time to reach agreement on an issue, the leader must attempt to guide the group to common consent. An effort is made to draw a conclusion before moving on to other business or finding a solution to the problem analyzed. It is not uncommon for disagreements to surface. In the atmosphere of mutual respect, any dissenter should be able to express dissatisfaction. However, the rule of the majority requires the dissenter to abide by a majority vote. Usually, small-group discussion encourages compromise. Sharing insights, experiences, factual information, and feelings encourages all members to adjust their views and positions on issues and the solution often reflects the contributions of every active participant.

In this chapter our focus has been on the problem-solving group that seeks, over several meetings, to define a problem and present a solution to it. We have chosen to focus on this type of meeting because of the tremendous importance these meetings have in the business world. In the next chapter, we shall examine another kind of collective communication, which takes place in business conferences. Here we sought to help you see the nature of problem-solving communication when three to seven people work cooperatively, carefully, and dynamically together. You should remember the kinds of goals to pursue and behavior to demonstrate in order to ensure that meetings will be effective. When ideas we have examine are applied with appropriate care, they can be profitable, both personally and in meeting business objectives.

A REVIEW OF KEY ISSUES

A small group is defined as three or more individuals who are engaged in face-to-face interaction with one another in such a manner that each person influences and is influenced by each of the other individuals.

A problem-solving meeting has a specific task, which is to discover a logical way to collectively eliminate a problem.

Problem-solving groups must be dynamic, cohesive, cooperative, and committed to rhetorical dialog.

Robert Bales's system for observing and understanding small-group behavior is organized in four categories:
1. behaviors that are positive for accomplishing a group task
2. behaviors that attempt to find answers to problems
3. behaviors that ask questions
4. behaviors that are negative for accomplishing the group goal or task

A problem-solving format based on the reflective-thinking pattern has five steps:
1. identification and analysis
2. criteria
3. probable solutions
4. selection of solution and plans for implementation
5. implementation and evaluation

Leadership is vital to effective problem-solving meetings.
1. A leader can establish a format for the group.
2. A leader can get the group going in a productive direction.
3. A leader can assume responsibility for keeping the group on track.
4. A leader can make clarifying summaries when necessary.
5. A leader can prevent group communication from becoming onesided.
6. A leader can relieve tension resulting from heated controversy.
7. A leader can ask relevant questions to involve all members in group participation.
8. A leader can keep the group alive and active.

Participation guidelines are necessary for productive activity.
1. Seek answers to common problems facing the group.
2. Work toward task and relational goals in the process.
3. Concentrate on finding the best group solution rather than a particular one.
4. Maintain objectivity and detachment with your own proposals.
5. Bring information to the group and offer it freely.
6. Pay attention to verbal and nonverbal communication, responding with the group goal in mind.

Small groups do not need complex procedures, but basic parliamentary procedure will usually take care of most group business when focused on majority rule.

EXPERIENCING EXPERIENCES

Working in problem-solving groups is an exciting form of communication. It challenges you to use your listening as well as your speaking skills. Furthermore, it is an excellent way to develop an understanding of interpersonal relationships that develop in such specialized group encounters.

The opportunity for such experiences is not always available. It is not enough simply to pull a group of individuals together and label them a problem-solving group.

With the following activities, we hope to provide you with challenging and exciting problem-solving group encounters. Use these activities as learning experiences, in which you have the chance to make a mistake without negative consequences. This opportunity does not exist in a professional situation, and therefore, novice participants are very reluctant to get involved. Experiences will make you feel comfortable working in such communication activities, so that when the real opportunities come along on the job, you will be confident and ready to participate.

ACTIVITY 1: Lost on the Moon

You are in a space crew originally scheduled to rendezvous with a mother ship on the lighted surface of the moon. Mechanical difficulties, however, have forced your ship to crash land at a spot some 200 miles from the rendezvous point. The rough landing damaged much of the equipment aboard. Since survival depends on reaching the mother ship, the most critical items available must be chosen for the 200 mile trip. Below are listed the 15 items left intact after the landing. Your task is to rank them in terms of their importance to your crew in its attempt to reach the rendezvous point. Place number 1 by the most important item, number 2 by the second most important item and so on through number 15, the least important.

_____ Box of matches
_____ Food concentrate
_____ 50 feet of nylon rope
_____ Parachute silk
_____ Portable heating unit
_____ Two .45 calibre pistols
_____ One case of dehydrated milk
_____ Two 100-pound tanks of oxygen
_____ Stellar map of moon's constellation
_____ Life raft
_____ Magnetic compass
_____ 5 gallons of water
_____ Signal flares
_____ First-aid kit containing injection needles
_____ Solar-powered FM receiver-transmitter

SCORING KEY

_15_ Box of matches has little or no use on moon.

_4_ Food concentrate can supply daily food required.

_6_ 50 feet of nylon rope is useful in help in climbing.

_8_ Parachute silk can shelter against sun's rays.

_13_ Portable heating unit is useful only if party had landed on the moon's dark side.

_11_ Two .45 calibre pistols: self-propulsion devices could be made from them.

_12_ One case dehydrated milk provides nutrition if mixed with water for drinking.

_1_ Two 100-pound tanks of oxygen fill respiration requirement.

_3_ Stellar map of moon's constellation is a principal means of finding directions.

_9_ Life raft and CO_2 bottle for self-propulsion across chasms.

_14_ Magnetic compass: probably no magnetic pole; thus useless.

_2_ 5 gallons of water: replenishes water loss.

_10_ Signal flares: distress call.

_7_ First-aid kit containing injection needles: oral pills or injection medicine valuable.

_5_ Solar-powered FM receiver-transmitter: distress-signal transmitter, possible communication with mother ship.

ACTIVITY 2: Solve the Puzzle

Before class, prepare a set of squares and an instruction sheet for each group of five students. A set consists of five envelopes containing pieces of stiff paper cut into patterns that will form five 6 X 6-inch squares, as shown in the diagram.

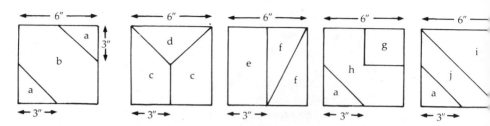

If multiples of three inches are used, several combinations will form one or two squares. Only one combination will form 6 X 6-inch squares. Thus, several individual combinations, but only one total combination, will be possible. Cut the five square into parts *a* through *j* and lightly pencil in the letters.

Then mark the envelopes A through E and distribute the pieces as follows: Envelope, A, pieces *i, h* and *e*; B, pieces *a, a, a* and *c*; C, pieces *a* and *j*; D, pieces *d* and *f*; and E, pieces *g* and *b, f* and *c*. Erase the small letters from the pieces and write instead the envelope letters A thorough E so that the pieces can be easily returned for reuse.

Divide the class into groups of five. All the students need to understand the problem. All the students need to believe that they can help. Instructions must be clear. All the students need to think of the other persons as well as themselves. Describe the experiment as a puzzle that requires cooperation. Read the instructions aloud and give each group a reference copy. Then give the signal to open the envelopes.

The instructions are as follows:

> Each person should have an envelope containing pieces for forming squares. At the signal, the task of the group is to form five squares of equal size. The task is not completed until each person has formed a perfect square and all the squares are of the same size. The rules are as follows: No member may speak. No member may ask for a piece or in any way signal that he or she wants one. Members may give pieces to others. Members may not take pieces. All pieces may not go in the middle.

When all or most of the groups have finished, call time and discuss the experience. Ask such questions as the following: How did you feel when someone held a piece and did not see the solution? What was your reaction when someone finished a square and then sat back without seeing whether his or her solution prevented others from solving the problem? What were your feelings if you finished your square and then began to realize that you would have to break it up and give away a piece? How did you feel about the person who was slow at seeing the solution? If you were that person, how did you feel? Was there a climate that helped or hindered?

If students have helped to monitor, they may have observations to share. In summarizing the discussion, you may wish to review behaviors listed at the beginning. You may also want to ask whether or not the game relates to the way the class works from day to day.

NOTES

1. Vincent DiSalvo, "Small Group Behavior," in John J. Makay, ed., *Exploration in Speech Communication.* Columbus, Ohio: Charles E. Merrill, 1973, p. 111.
2. Robert F. Bales, *Interaction Process Analysis.* Chicago: University of Chicago Press, 1950, p. 9.
3. John J. Makay and William R. Brown, *The Rhetorical Dialogue: Contemporary Concepts and Cases.* Dubuque, Iowa: Wm. C. Brown Co., Publishers, 1972, p. 85.
4. Henry L. Ewbank, *Meeting Management.* Dubuque, Iowa: Wm. C. Brown Co., Publishers, 1968, p. 43.

CHAPTER NINE
COMMUNICATION IN THE CONFERENCE

The business conference is a valuable means of stimulating and consolidating motivation in the individual. The participation of the individual and the interaction with others in a conference setting can provide productive information as well as the creative environment to foster it.

The business conference is a frequently used communication technique. For many organizations, it is the communication tool considered most ideal to an organization in operation. It is not uncommon for some business professionals to have five or six conferences per week. This indicates the significance of the business conference in the professional world.

In this chapter, we will focus on the environment of the conference, its values, purposes, and styles. We will look at perception, power, and conflict, studying their relationship with communiation as it is used in the conference. And finally, we will look at various methods for controlling conflict in a constructive manner in the business conference.

VALUE OF THE CONFERENCE
IN BUSINESS COMMUNICATION

The conference is a very valuable working tool for maintaining open communications. One of its most valuable assets is capability it offers for establishing the appropriate environment for human interaction in order to exchange and create ideas.

The conference format is designed to permit all employees within an organization at all levels to participate in planning, discussing, and deciding on organizational policies, values, programs, services, and products. Participatory management, a rather new concept in business organizations, has been found to be an exciting method of gaining positive results. The conference is the ideal communication tool for incorporating this concept, as well as several others, into the business environment.

The conference is a group activity that focuses on collective thinking and decision-making rather than on the expertise of the individual. The percentage of error that comes from personal bias, lost perspective, or overinvolvement can be significantly reduced by group communication. Group achievement is now endorsed by most business organizations, and often overshadows the limited work of the individual. Good conferences encourage the growth of new ideas through team work, cooperation, and healthy competition. Group energy focuses upon setting goals, planning work, and accomplishing self-rewarding achievement.

For many organizations, the conference has become a vital tool for preventing stagnation and atrophy in all levels of business, which must be able to change constantly in a highly competitive market.

PURPOSES FOR THE CONFERENCE IN BUSINESS COMMUNICATION

There are several types of conference, each with a different purpose. Conferences can be structured to meet any problem or urgent demand occurring in an organiza-

FIGURE 9-1   Business conference formats can range from formal to informal settings.

tion. In Chapter 8 we discussed the problem-solving meeting. This is one kind of conference commonly used by many organizations.

In addition to the problem-solving conference, there is the **decision-making conference**. This is designed for those situations in which a vote must be taken or a choice must be made between selected issues. Usually there is an urgent reason for making the choice—a monetary constraint, a service commitment, a recent program development, a product modification, or possibly a maintenance commitment, all involving a time factor. Such a decision may be short-term, even temporary, but usually it demands immediate attention from a select number of individuals. The decision-making conference is used in such circumstances.

The policy-making conference in some ways is similar to the decision-making conference, but the policy decision usually affects an entire organizational structure. It can affect the employees, the machinery, or the service operations. Policies often have long-term effects and they are thought of as relatively permanent issues. Frequently, their content reflects attitudes concerning the issues, rather than the issues themselves.

Information-sharing conferences are concerned with one or two things: seeking information or providing information to a specific group of individuals. In this case, information is central to the effort, but the focus is on the choice of participants and their relationship to the data that is being sought or provided.

The training conference, a rather new concept, is considered one of the better ways to instruct certain individuals in new methods and data. It is an excellent way to introduce new employees to their work environment and to retain old employees in new job procedures. The training conference provides information, but it also builds positive attitudes about the working situation, a new product, or changes in the organizational structure of the business. Such a conference stresses the importance of working together in groups in order to achieve individual as well as group goals.

Appraisal/evaluation conferences seek to use the working experiences of individuals to better the operations and the environment in an organization. Respect for the individual and praise for individual achievement can be conveyed and used as motivation to maintain the high quality of work in the group. The appraisal/evaluation conference serves such a purpose most effectively.

Counseling conferences provide assistance for specific individuals through the interaction of a group. The sharing, caring, and security that can grow out of such conferences have long-range positive effects on organizational operations.

OPERATIONAL CONFERENCE FORMATS
IN BUSINESS COMMUNICATION

The format of a conference is chosen in accordance with the predetermined need for the conference.

The **buzz session** or **brainstorming session** is a very informal conference. Since it has little structure and is flexible enough to accommodate any number of conferees, it can function well in a variety of situations. Its greatest strength is that it can generate group energy and a large number of ideas in a short period of time. This format is often used as a warm-up session to another conference.

The **committee conference** or **task force** format specializes in serving a large organizational structure. Heavy workloads and limited time schedules are a realistic part of the business environment. Establishing a committee or task force can reduce workloads, unnecessary repetition of work, and misuse of time. A committee grouping usually involves a small number of individuals working together. This permits a great deal of input for each individual serving on the committee. This small committee conference eliminates duplication of work (frequently referred to as "re-invention of the wheel"), an expensive activity that can easily take place in complex organizations.

The **ad-hoc charge** usually grows out of some larger committee. In this situation, a small subcommittee of individuals is assigned to take on a highly specialized task that is temporary in nature. Once such a grouping has accomplished its purpose, it is disbanded.

The **production** or **performance action** is a specialized operation whose focus is on the task: creating a program, developing a process, designing a service, or redeveloping a product. Its format is functional and usually demanding. Conferees come together to interact using their independent skills, resources, and knowledge gained through previous work experience. The task is deliberately operationalized through complex group interaction. The value of the production output is based on the sum total input of the involved individuals interacting with one another.

The **convention** is a complex format using any or all of the above formats over a specific period of time. These select groups come together to share information based on a predetermined theme or common issues. The convention is designed to use some creative combinations of the conference styles outlined above. It has an underlying power structure that determines the specific format for recording and reporting independent group interactions. The aim is to have a record of all the ideas generated as well as a record of all of the group activities. Convention conferences require extensive preliminary planning, and although this planning can be expensive and time consuming, it will directly affect the success of the meeting. The convention has long been recognized as a major part of any professional environment.

THE CONFERENCE
AS A COMMUNICATION ACTIVITY

In Chapter 8 we learned that problem-solving meetings, if they are to function successfully, require awareness on the part of the participants. Each individual has basic responsibilities as an active participant. The success in solving the problem depends largely on how each participant carries out those responsibilities. The conference, like the problem-solving meeting, also requires awareness on the part of its members.

We define the conference as a group of individuals who come together to interchange ideas that are focused on a specific purpose and task. As in all the groups we have studied, the focus is on the productivity of the total rather than the abilities of any one individual. There are basic communication skills that all conferees must employ in order to work collectively and produce efficiently. These skills are not difficult to master. If they were, conferences would not occur so frequently and so successfully in the business environment.

Conferences take time and cost money. In one business organization, all employees at middle-management levels were asked to keep a communication diary for the period of one week. This study involved 134 individuals. They were instructed to record any meeting of three or more people in which they were involved. The total number of meetings at the end of the five-day working period was 819. This averages out to over six meetings per individual. These employees had been asked to record the conference time for each session. The average session was 27.5 minutes in length; all together, these employees had spent 22, 252.5 minutes in conference. If we were to figure how much money was spent in salaries for these employees for this amount of working time, we would discover the cost of conference time for this organization. At the time of this writing, the company was still trying to determine whether the time and money spent on conference activity was worthwhile.

This is but one example. If you were to examine any organization, you would be surprised at the total amount of time scheduled for various types of conferences with all levels of employees. Managers and administrators have positive attitudes about the effectiveness of conference communication; again, this is reflected in the popularity of this kind of meeting. Today, young people entering a career in business are expected to be able to communicate effectively in conference.

Group communication has some distinctive features that participants must be aware of in order to contribute productively to a conference. Factors such as conflict, power, and perception are a very real part of the conference environment. These factors will be discussed later in the chapter. In addition to these factors, the participants must also have an understanding of how the conference operates. It is a process that consists of specific steps. Once a conferee has some idea about the elements and process of the conference, productive participation is a realistic expectation.

THE CONFERENCE PROCESS: A MODEL

In order to clarify the steps in the process of a conference, we have designed a model of the communication flow and the behaviors incorporated within this communication tool. The model shown in Figure 9-2 has five basic steps and one alternate step that is often needed in many conference settings.

Preplanning preliminaries.   Preplanning preliminaries are the procedures that should be completed prior to the conference event. These procedures, properly

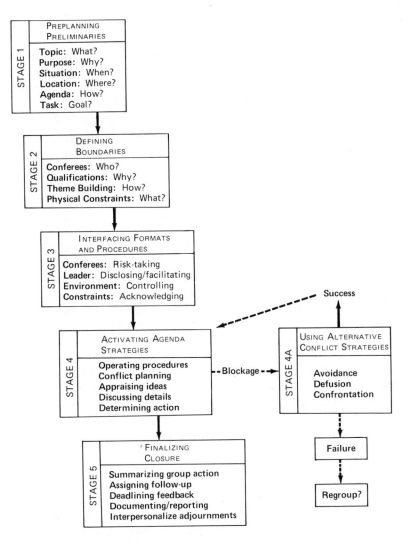

FIGURE 9-2   The conference communication process.

planned, ensure that the process will start productively. The topic should be clearly established. The purpose statement should be constructed so that it clearly describes the intent of the conference. The task should be determined as clearly as possible so that all conferees have a goal to guide their participation. The location should be considered in advance because frequently this will have a significant effect on the purpose, task, and topic. It may be necessary to have the agenda planned in advance.

The operational style chosen and the general purpose intended for the conference are really the factors that determine how much of this planning should be done prior to the conference itself. Obviously, in a production conference the agenda would not be rigidly planned, since this is something the conferees will do as a group in the initial stages of the meeting.

Agenda planning prior to the conference can ensure that productive results will come from the group interaction. The agenda can give individual conferees an indication of what is expected of them. On the other hand, some people argue that rigid agenda planning stifles individual and group creativity. It is true that when individuals meet and work collectively, things often happen unexpectedly—an unexplainable surge of creativity energy is produced.

The benefit of planning basic considerations in advance is merely a way of preparing the participants for group communication. If the planning helps each conferee to get prepared for the conference encounter, it has served its major purpose. The agenda can be changed at the onset of the conference if the participants feel it is necessary.

Defining boundaries.   The next step in the process is to define boundaries. This can be done, in part, prior to the conference; but usually this is one of the first items of business when the participants come together. Who are the conferees? What are their qualifications or purposes as participants? Each conferee should know this information about all of the other participants. This information can significantly affect the communication strategies employed during the interaction. Certainly, the answers to these questions could have an important impact on the topic, purpose, task, location, situation, and agenda. The conferees will want to consider the theme-building aspect of this step immediately and constantly refer to it during the duration of the conference. Each conferee's contribution to theme-building is often the very thing that gets the group energy started. And this, in turn, triggers a positive productivity.

If there are physical constraints—a strict time limit, for example—conferees must be aware of them. Limited funds or restricted use of a conference facility are considerations that cannot be overlooked. Often the conference brings together a group of experts who have other commitments. This will limit their contributions. All such possible constraints should be considered as part of defining boundaries. Should any one of these constraints appear in mid-conference, it could have a significant negative effect on the whole group's productivity. This is not an infrequent occurrence in some organizational structures. One or two of the conferees find they must leave before the meeting is over, and if the other conferees have not been informed of this, the meeting can be disrupted.

Interfacing formats and procedures.   Conferees frequently leave a conference feeling dissatisfied with its results as well as its operation. They cannot point to any single item or aspect of the communication interaction that was faulty, but the atmosphere of the conference was nonproductive. And in fact, the conference was not a success. This occurs when some of the elements involved in the interfacing of formats or procedures are overlooked or not given proper consideration prior to the conference.

The elements that operate in conferences are not considered together (interfaced) clearly beforehand. Excluding this factor often creates dissatisfaction and incompleteness.

Let us consider the factor of *risk-taking.* There are several sources of risks. In the business environment, a conference means that employees work together for a common, agreed-on goal. This can be a threatening situation. Individuals are expected to voice personal and professional opinions that are going to be compared with those of others, in public, in the presence of all conference members. Opinions can look poorly thought out or ignorant; they can offend, anger, or directly conflict with the personal and professional opinions of other participants.

The conference leader or moderator can also present a risk to the other conferees. In any business organization, it is common for a foreman, supervisor, or manager to lead a conference of his or her subordinates, and in this situation there is a realistic legislative power facing every individual in the group. To ignore such elements is wrong and can defeat the positive principles of conference communication. The conference leader must be open about these matters and disclose to the group his or her position and power as it will operate during and possibly after the conference. Often leaders will find that they must also take risks in such a setting, because they must be willing at times to give up their power role to become functional and productive members of the conference.

The *environment or setting* of the conference must be established. Certainly the environment must accommodate the conference task. Can the conferees function with the topic, purpose, situation, agenda, and task in the given environment? If the environment does not create an atmosphere of openness, conferees may feel the risk is too great to get involved. Employees should be sufficiently removed

FIGURE 9-3 Conferees have individual responsibilities to contribute and participate in meetings.

physically and emotionally from their work stations to be free to participate effectively in a conference. It is a common practice for large organizations to take their employees completely away from the work site to a retreat or lodge in order to obtain an open environment. If this can be achieved, the employee will participate more productively as a conferee (see Figure 9-3).

Internal constraints have to be considered at this stage. If two or more conferees do not get along or are known to be unable to work together effectively, this constraint will carry over into the conference activities. Constant interruptions from phone calls, messages, undue noise, and the like are all constraints that can have a negative effect on the conference activity. Vested personal or departmental interests can interfere with how the conferees interface in such group work. Sometimes it becomes necessary for the conferees to deal openly and freely with such constraints. They need to assess them and determine if they are serious enough to interfere with the functioning of the group.

Activating agenda strategies.   The next step is activating the group strategies. The task at this point might be to seek or provide information, or accomplish whatever operational purpose has been determined, according to the conference style that has been chosen. Whether the conferees are sharing information, producing ideas, carrying out a specific task assigned, or convening to learn together, some type of conflict is likely to appear. This conflict may manifest itself in the form of simple confusion among the conferees or it may lead to a direct clash of ideas, beliefs, values, or facts. This conflict is healthy, normal, and should be viewed as positive since it can only come about when interaction is taking place. It is, in fact, an excellent test for the presence of active communication.

Operating procedures for each meeting should be planned in advance. This is usually done in the form of agenda planning. If the agenda is decided in advance and all the conferees know it, the group communication will operate at a more productive level. This way, each individual can be responsible for certain items on the agenda and, with advance preparation, can bring the related details of those items before the group.

When appraising or evaluation ideas, the group can get very unruly. The group can spend 75 percent of the conference time on two agenda items and have only 25 percent of the time left for seven more remaining items. To avoid this problem of poorly assigned time for each item on the agenda, it is best to publish the discussion time for each item. If the group wishes to change it, this can be done easy enough, but at least this time allotment will ensure that the group's work gets done.

Determining action on agenda items must be deliberate and direct. Each group member must know how the item is being handled if the overall meeting is to produce results. Publicly noting the determined action keeps the whole group posted and helps to maintain a productive flow in the group's communication.

Figure 9-4 displays an agenda format designed to keep the group interaction ongoing and productive in most conference situations. The format will serve as an agenda guide for the conferees as well as a method of recording group action. Each

_____ MINUTES to File   MEETING: _____ DATE:_____

_____ FOLLOW-UP Report On   ATTENDEES: _____

REPORTER _____   _____

#	Agenda Item	Issues Discussed/by Whom	Assigned Follow-Up and/or Report of Action

FIGURE 9-4   Multiple active agenda format.

conferee can take his or her own minutes or notes of the proceedings. The conference leader can take the agenda minutes from the meeting and rewrite them with minimum effort as a follow-up report of the conference. This same form then becomes each participant's file copy for the actual conference. In fact, it can also serve as the basis of the next agenda if the group is to meet again.

Using alternative conflict strategies.   In some conferences, conflict marks the moment when blockage occurs. The conflict is complex and involved. It requires alternative strategies. The conferees must decide how they are going to deal with the conflict constructively. They have three basic alternatives: avoidance, defusion, or mediation. These will be discussed in depth later in this chapter. If the alternative strategies do not work and result in failure, then it may be necessary for the conferees to regroup or reconvene at a late time. If the alternative strategy does work, then the conference can move back to its the operational agenda.

Finalizing closure.   This last step in the conference communication is very important, and if not included as a part of the process, the productivity of the group's interaction may never materialize. When this final part of the process is ignored or carelessly dealt with, the common remarks regarding the conference are "It was a waste of my time!" and "What did we really accomplish in there?"

In this step it is important to summarize all the action and information that have occurred to this point. Once the events have been reviewed and the sequential process has been satisfactorily established for each conferee, the group can go on to work assignments and share the follow-up. The conferees should be assigned tasks on the basis of their ability, work schedule, access to resources, and previous personal experience. Deadlines for feedback are very important and should be established when follow-up tasks are assigned.

Any conference needs some type of documentation for future reference. In business organizations that use conference as a major communication tool, documentation is a vital issue. Often there are legal demands for documenting the conference productivity. This can be done in the form of notes, minutes, tapes, report forms, letters, news releases, telephone conversations, or oral reports. Written documentation is the most efficient, and with computer and microfilm, storage and access are not major problems.

The last phase of finalizing closure is the interpersonal. A conference can be closed with many kinds of social amenities, from a simple handshake to an elaborate dinner. Even in the most formal of business conferences, there is always a place for courtesy and personal recognition of conferees who have worked cooperatively and effectively.

This conference communication model has been deliberately designed to be flexible. We believe each conference is unique—no two conferences operate identically, nor can any conference be exactly duplicated. There are too many situational factors involved in this type of a communication activity.

Now that we have examined the entire conference process, we will look at the role of conferees in the conference setting.

RESPONSIBILITIES OF THE CONFEREES

Verbal and nonverbal communication is the common activity shared by conferees; both require the use of a variety of skills. Efficient communication also requires conferees to be well informed.

Perception.   Perception is one important element of verbal and nonverbal communication. We define perception as the process by which we take in and interpret the information supplied by our senses—sight, smell, taste, hearing, and touch. This information allows us to give meaning to our environment. Perception operates in four stages.

1. selecting specific information
2. identifying the selected information
3. organizing the identified information
4. and then interpreting the organized information[1]

Obviously, all people do not perceive the world in the same way. Our perception is influenced by our attitudes, feelings, personal experiences, and environment. Perception is a very personalized function, and it is reflected in our communication with others, no less in the specific setting of a conference than in any other interaction.

Perception is influenced by the physical condition of our sense organs. We need only remove a pair of glasses to realize this. Physical proximity affects perception. Mood and physical factors—from headaches to excitement over bonuses—influence perception, as do conditions such as hunger or poverty. Any of these factors affects perception and communication daily; and they can easily influnce conference communication.

Power.   In addition to perception, there are power relationships that affect conference communication. We define power as the perceived influence that exists among individuals in a conference setting. Power is viewed by conferees as an element possessed by some participants, but not possessed by all. It is frequently referred to as "the ace in the hole." It is very easy for conflict to develop around a power relationship or power role.

Power can be displayed in a variety of ways in the conference environment. **Reward power** is such an example. One conferee has the power to bestow a reward to certain participants, and this creates visible conflict. For example, one conferee may be a departmental supervisor, and it is part of her job to appraise employees for annual bonuses. Her power could easily dominate a conference that consists of her departmental subordinates.

Coercive power is another type that can negatively affect the productiveness of a conference. For example, if one of the conferees is responsible for budget and financial operations, he could easily coerce his fellow conferees into agreeing on an issue by merely hinting at "tightening the purse strings" on some other financial projects totally unrelated to the present issues. In business environments, a great deal of "back scratching" takes place to avoid coercive power factors.

Legitimate power often exists in the conference setting. If one of the conferees is a supervisor for some or all of the other conferees, this fact cannot be denied. In some situations, one conferee is charged with legitimate power to take final responsibility for the productivity of the conference. Such a power factor must be reckoned with, and if not properly used, it can destroy or seriously interfere with the interfacing of conferees.

Ownership power can easily exist in a conference. One individual presents an idea and then promptly claims ownership. We like to feel that the project, idea, or program is "our baby," implying a hands-off policy that makes it difficult for other conferees to work collectively with it. In organizations that have separate operating departments, group or departmental ownership frequently exists. As college students you may have witnessed this as you moved from one academic department to another for your various courses. Ownership power has a tendency to create negative feelings in conference settings.

Expert power often shows up in a conference, and it can also have negative consequences on the conference communication. One conferee may consider himself a specialist in a particular area and see himself as the final authority. Or several conferees may see one individual as the "resident expert." If several perceive one conferee as the expert, they may hold back their contributions, reject their own unspoken ideas, or sit back, rather than interact with the rest of the group. In any of these situations, the productivity of the conference is negatively affected.

Positive suggestions for conferees.　In addition to understanding the responsibilities of perception and power in conference communication, conferees should consider some positive suggestions:

Each conferee should take his or her role seriously and go into a conference with a positive attitude. This attitude is reflected in the effort each conferee displays in the use of effective speaking and listening skills. There must be willingness to use these skills objectively and communally.

Conferees must be willing to invest time, effort, and personal commitment to the conference task, purpose, and agenda without fear of failure. The fear of how one will be perceived by peers, superiors, and subordinates can easily stifle the free flow and open communication of ideas.

Conferees should put group needs above personal needs. Not sharing ideas in a conference situation for fear of not receiving due recognition takes away from the intrinsic value of conferring. The "good old suggestion box" cannot provide the employee with the feedback and unbiased peer appraisal that can come when the idea is presented in a conference setting.

Conferees must be willing to take risks. This is a part of the interaction process as discussed in the model. Going into a conference realizing this and practicing it can lead participants to make a significant positive contribution toward the success of any conference.

When one participant functions in a leadership role, this conferee has added responsibilities. They were carefully listed in Box 8-2, and you may now review the eight guidelines briefly.

CONFLICT: A BASIC PART
OF CONFERENCE COMMUNICATION

We define conflict as recognition of the differences among individuals and groups. It becomes a problem only when opponents neutralize, damage, or eliminate one another's contributions. Fred Jandt has pointed out that conflict cannot exist without verbal and nonverbal communication because humans define their relationships through these channels.[2] Conflict is a perceived relationship displayed in human communication behavior.

Working with conflict in a conference setting has a number of positive values. The most important one is that conflict encourages individuality. Conflict also encourages creativity and stimulates curiosity in the group as well as the individual. Conflict has the capacity of teaching conferees as they interact, and it can test their contributions as each is forced to "look at the other side of the coin." Such testing situations generate "What if?" questions. Conflict also supports cohesiveness in certain situations. It can establish factions within a conference; a number of conferees will come to the support of one specific idea or concept that develops in a conflict. Conflict can also define power roles and relationships that may have existed unnoticed by some participants, who perceived a problem but could not define it. The last value of conflict is the challenge. In business environments this is very important. It is a recognized fact that many individuals thrive on the challenges their jobs afford them. Challenge expressed in positive competition is healthy, creative, and excitingly innovative. Competition is the very basis of the free enterprise system.

At one time, the general attitude toward conflict was that it was something to be avoided. It was considered poor taste and self-defeating to be argumentative. These attitudes have changed drastically since the conflicts of the 1960s. Conflict is now viewed as valuable and useful in communication, especially in such circumstances as a conference. To use this valuable aspect of conflict, conferees must understand how it operates.

Conflict functions on many different levels and with varying degrees of success, depending on the circumstances and the situation. There are factors to consider when conflict is used on the intrapersonal or interpersonal level, but our concern in this chapter is conflict as it is used in group situations.

Intragroup conflict. We have learned that the business conference focuses around a task, and this task is defined in relationship to the subject, the purpose, the situation, the location, and the agenda. If conflict exists at this first step in the process, it must be worked with openly, or the process will break down. If conferees have conflict over tasks or purposes before they go into the process, the conference will not be highly productive. An obvious example of this is the conference involving individuals representing both labor and management. These conferees would more than likely have very different views regarding the task and purpose of a conference situation.

If defining boundaries offers possible benefits or rewards to certain conferees, a rather hostile situation can quickly develop. This type of conflict would interfere with the conference process and could easily prevent it from moving forward. For example, conferences dealing with purchasing new equipment, reducing work loads, restructuring budgets, or revising work schedules involve reward for some and losses for others. Such conflicts cannot be ignored if they enter into the conference setting.

Once conferees are interfacing with one another, they may perceive their operating strategies from different viewpoints. This conflict situation can seriously interfere with the intragroup productivity. Some conferees may be attempting to evaluate a program while at the same time, others may see the program as a problem and therefore focus on its solution. They perceive different working roles and approaches to achieving their agreed-on conference purpose and task. Working roles create conflict when power relationships develop and some conferees change their roles to accommodate the power relationship. For example, a conference is held to investigate additional employee benefits that are being considered. Some of the conferees perceive the proposed benefits as a means of increasing their power in the structure of the organization. Because of the perceived vested interest, their roles change within the group, their operational style changes, and these factors can interfere with the conference process. Frequently, a supervisor calls a conference but decides to have one of the subordinates serve as conference leader, hoping to encourage conferees to participate because they feel less fear working with a peer leader. Unfortunately, when that supervisor sits in on the conference, it naturally creates a conflict for the group in working with the appointed conference leader. They are not able to ignore the presence of the "regular" leader.

Intergroup conflict.   When a conference divides into factions and conflict brings out two or three distinct subgroups, effective action can dwindle quickly. Integroup conflict occurs more frequently in large organizations, where a number of groups are brought together, than in smaller, more homogeneous groups. In circumstances such as this, each group has its own goals, and very likely, its own operational style. Each group will be biased because each is sure "its way of doing things" will work since it has worked in the past. Accountants have their way of working in conferences, while salespersons and draftspersons have their own group preferences. Conflicts grow out of such feelings and attitudes. Furthermore, these situational conflicts can easily give rise to power relationships within the conference, making the conflicts more complex and harder to work with.

Intergroup conferences need to establish a superordinate goal that all of the groups can accept. They also need to establish a superordinate task that can function as a guide and measurement for their productivity. As the conflict emerges, the conference communication can quickly deteriorate. If this happens, the interaction of the group can come to a standstill, destroying the conference process. For this reason, intergroup conflict must be worked with as it emerges, or time and very possibly money will be wasted by all parties involved. A superordinate goal and task can serve both as a barometer for the conference processes and as a control to intergroup conflict.

MANAGING GROUP CONFLICT CONSTRUCTIVELY

Working constructively with conflict requires some basic assumptions on the part of all conferees:

1. All conferees must have respect for each individual and his or her contribution to the conference.

2. Open communication must be accepted by all conferees so that each is able to understand all contributions, feel that he or she has contributed something of value, and believe that equal opportunity was provided to everyone.
3. All conferees must understand and agree on the conference subject and task.[3]

In order for you to understand clearly that conflict functions on different levels and that the level of conflict often determines how to deal with it constructively, we have provided you with the model shown in Figure 9-5. We view conflict on a continuum according to its use and prevalence within the conference setting. If the intensity of the conflict is not high, the approach should be a low-activity one. But if the conflict is highly intense, then a high-activity approach must be considered (see Figure 9-5).

Avoidance.   Avoidance is a low-intensity, low-activity approach to conflict. In this situation the parties often ignore the fact that conflict really exists. They patch things together quickly to reflect that something was "accomplished." This may solve the conflict, or it may be a temporary resolution, the conflict reappearing later in the conference.

Some conferees unwillingly accept the opponent's view in order to avoid argument and waste of time. The conflict may again arise later in the conference. When a resolution is forced in order to avoid losing a reward or additional power, it can work temporarily. and in this case, too, the conflict more than likely will reappear later as the conference proceeds.

The avoidance of conflict in an ownership situation may be necessary. Some conferees are willing to resolve the conflict because they accept the other party's ownership of an idea, making the assumption that the "owner" possesses some valuable information they may not. As with the other conflicts quieted by avoidance, as the conference proceeds the conferees may become aware that their previous assumption was false, and the conflict will reappear.

Defusion.   Defusion is another way to approach conflict, and as you can see on the model, it is somewhere in the middle of the continuum of activity and intensity. We can compare it to a bomb. The conflict could set off any number of negative reactions, but if it can be defused, the conference can get on with its task and purpose. In such a situation, one side of the conflict does not appear to be worth arguing when compared to other issues that need attention. Therefore, for the sake of time and value, the conflict is defused by a less than satisfactory compromise, and the conference proceeds to other issues. In organizations that hold many conferences with extremely heavy agendas or complex tasks, defusing conflict is an expedient strategy.

Confrontation.   Highest on the continuum in activity and intensity is the conflict strategy of confrontation. There are three specific, commonly used techniques of confrontation strategy: the power technique, the negotiation technique, and the mediation technique. If these fail, a fourth technique, arbitration, may become necessary.

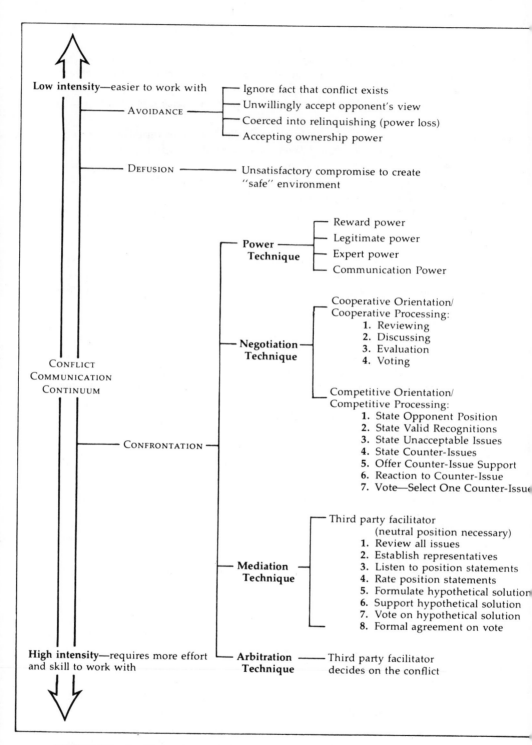

FIGURE 9-5 Conflict as a conference communication strategy.

The power technique functions well when opponents take the time to analyze the power sources. They define them and then they attempt to define the power relationships. They carefully examine both the causes or reasons for the power and the value of the effects of this power on the conflict. To use this approach requires a great deal of risk-taking on the part of the conferees. Opponents have to take the time to look at the total picture and speculate on future considerations. Opponents must decide that the resolution of the conflict is of greater importance to the conference than maintaining or relinquishing the power and power relationship associated with it.

In business environments where the same people meet for regularly scheduled conferences, the power technique can often work rather successfully as a confrontation strategy, because conferees work together and get to know one another in conference situations. These conferees find it easier to take risks and be open with one another in routinely scheduled conferences.

The **negotiation technique** is the second type of confrontation strategy. There are two basic ways to negotiate conflict: cooperative processing or competitive processing. The processing procedure for either alternative is based on the manner in which the conference has dealt with the initiating preliminaries and the defining of boundaries. If the orientation was cooperative, then cooperative processing would be the best choice; if the conference orientation preliminaries were more competitive, then a competitive processing should be used.

The **cooperative processing** follows four basic steps. The issue of conflict is taken through four steps by all of the conferees. The first step consists of doing a complete and exhaustive review of the issue. If the issue involves a number of factors, each one is defined.

The second step is an open discussion of the complete issue, taking into consideration all factors involved in it. All conferees should be allowed full and free expression.

The third step is to evaluate the issue, using the information revealed in the discussion. Sometimes this step is difficult because unbiased evaluation is sometimes awkward to achieve in a conflict situation.

The fourth step is to hold a vote on the issue. With all of the conferees voting in view of the exhaustive discussion and evaluation, the conflict will be resolved by cooperative action.

The cooperative process can be time-consuming when negotiating conflict, but if it is used in an organized fashion, it will very likely succeed. Conferees who are accustomed to working in highly structured situations will not find it a difficult process. In fact, the environment of most organizations encourages cooperative processing.

Competitive processing based on competitive conference orientation is the other form of negotiating that can be used as a conflict strategy. This type of processing grows out of the fact that during the orientation phase of the conference, the conferees were competing through argument or debate. It is assumed that an argumentative atmosphere prevails, and that the conferees are functioning productively within it. In some organizations, this kind of atmosphere exists and employees are quite accustomed to operating with it. This competitive atmosphere may be used to develop products, services, or new programs. Sometimes employees are encouraged to use it to brainstorm, to create quickly, or to speculate on what might be. If the conferees are comfortable in such an atmosphere, they can successfully resolve conflict.

The competitive process follows an argument pattern using seven steps. The first step is to have opponents state their positions on the conflict. This defines viewpoints and clarifies the conflict in the minds of all participants. (2) The second step is for opponents to state any valid objections they perceive regarding any factors surrounding the conflict. This is done to factor out the areas of agreement and move directly to the "heart" of the conflict. (3) The third step is for opponent conferees to clearly state the unacceptable factors they perceive surrounding the conflict. (4) Each opponent proceeds to provide a counterissue and offer evidence to support it. (5) The opponent conferees will consider the counterissue and the counterissue support. (6) The next step is to voice reactions to the counterissue and its support. (7) The last step is to call for a vote to decide which counterissues will be most acceptable to the entire group of conferees. When opposing issues are placed directly against one another, it is easier for the conferees to decide how to resolve the conflict.

Mediation technique is used when the conflict is of high intensity and a sophisticated technique is necessary to resolve it. Mediation is the involvement of a third, neutral party to resolve the conflict. The third-party facilitator may come from the group or, more likely, from outside the conference. The process used in mediation has eight steps. (1) All issues of the conflict are presented before the total group of conferees and the mediator. (2) After the conflict has been reviewed and clearly defined, representatives are established for opposing sides. The representatives can be selected in a number of ways: first, by having each faction select its own representative; second, by having the mediator choose a representative for each side; or third, by having all conferees vote for both factions' representation. (3) Representatives present statements of position to all conferees and the mediator. (4) At this time, the representatives and/or their entire faction should decide on the priority of the position statements. (5) From this list, each faction or its representative should formulate a hypothetical solution to the conflict. (6) After forming the hypothetical solution, each representative supports his or her solution with evidence. (7) The mediator then calls for a vote on the part of all the conferees to select the better hypothetical solution. (8) The final step is to recognize the vote by having the mediator call for some type of formal acceptance.

If mediation does not work, and the conflict is still unresolved, there is **binding arbitration.** This is very time-consuming and expensive. The arbitrator, like the mediator, is a third party neutral to the conflict. This individual makes the decision after careful consideration of the circumstances surrounding the conflict.

When we consider all the alternative strategies available for working constructively with conflict, the value of conflict becomes apparent. Conflict has a lot to contribute to any conference, and since a number of resolutions are available, it does not have to be feared. Conferees can select one strategy to work with the conflict, and if it does not work, there are the other alternatives to use. The strategies all stimulate the conferees to think and consider alternate views when facing conflict. These strategies will generate productive communication of ideas, a process that is basic to any conference.

CONFEREES INTERFACING
WITHIN A CONFERENCE

The interpersonal relationships of the conferees working with one another cannot be overlooked. There are three basic roles that reflect the relationships conferees must work with in conference communication: the peer, the subordinate, and the superior.

The peer.   Peers must be aware of the differences and similarities they face at the conference table. Understanding one another is often difficult when attempting to remove prejudice. Peers, even though aware that they are equals in organizational structure, still see each other in roles and power relationships. The perception of these roles and relationships may or may not be accurate, but they should never interfere with the conference process.

Peers must work with various personalities and a wide variety of operational styles. Most have their own method for getting work done and this is based on individual work pace and rhythm. Awareness of these differences and respect for them permit conference communication relationships to function more productively. Peers in conference do not have to like one another to work together when striving to achieve a specified purpose and task. Friends do not automatically work well together because they are friends. In the conference setting, peers must level with one another by being specific in their communication. Being vague for the sake of being "nice" only confuses issues and encourages misunderstanding. Timing and tact are a part of relating concise communication as well as reflecting positive attitudes. The positive attitudes are important to peer relationships because they do relate to the productiveness of a conference. At times, peers may find it difficult to admit error in a conference because they feel it will reflect personal weakness. Trust is necessary, and peers should realize that not only are errors human, they are also a sign of positive learning.

The subordinate.   When the conferee is working with his or her subordinates, it is rarely difficult to remember where power resides in the conference setting. It is not necessary to advertise it. The productiveness of the conference should come from the skills, talents, and experiences of the conferees. Using power or advertising it will not make subordinates feel comfortable or willing to contribute. They will feel fear and sense the need to be protective of their job or guarded in displaying their abilities of wary of losing their credibility.

Subordinates should be made to feel that their contributions are important and necessary. They should be made to feel free to participate and urged to contribute because they have something significant to offer. This kind of an approach with the subordinate is "getting off on the right foot" in the conference situation.

The superior.   Superiors have specific powers and power realtionships that derive from their position in the business's organizational structure. In such situations, the power cannot be denied or overlooked—it is real. But it does not have to be emphasized. The less power is emphasized, the less threatening is the atmosphere of the conference.

There may very easily be divergent viewpoints at each step of the conference process. The peer, the subordinate, and the superior may see the conference topic, purpose, situation, location, task, and agenda in very different lights. This needs to be considered in the initial stages and certainly in establishing boundaries. Interfacing the formats and procedures of the conference and working with the strategies are also going to reflect these differences. If all the conferees are aware of this, the chances are slim that conflict will remain unresolved.

And finally, all these differences will be reflected in the closing. Time schedules, work loads, and available resources are going to vary considerably among superior, peer, and subordinate. These things will affect assigning follow-up work and meeting feedback deadlines, as well as choosing the methods for documenting the conference activity.

A FINAL THOUGHT

The conference is one of the most valuable tools available for conducting business communications. Conference communication can achieve the designed purposes and tasks in a wide variety of operational styles. Conferees can use perception, power, and conflict in their communication strategies as a means of generating new ideas. The business conference is a practical and efficient activity, and it is also an exciting activity that affords ample opportunity for achieving a great deal of personal satisfaction.

A REVIEW OF KEY ISSUES

A conference performs several important functions.
1.   It is a practical working tool.
2.   It permits all levels of employees to participate.
3.   It encourages individual and group creativity.

4. It uses power, perception, and conflict functions.
5. It encourages growth and development.

The types of conferences are
1. problem solving
2. decision making
3. policy making
4. information sharing
5. training
6. appraisal/evaluation
7. counseling

The conference has a variety of operational styles:
1. buzz session/brainstorming session
2. committee/task force
3. ad hoc charge
4. production/performance action
5. convention

The conference process as a model has six steps:
1. preplanning preliminaries
2. defining boundaries
3. interfacing formats/procedures
4. activating agenda strategies
5. using alternative conflict strategies
6. finalizing closure

Responsibilities of conferees focus on such factors as
    Perception
    Power types
    —reward
    —coercive
    —legitimate
    —ownership
    —expert
    Positive suggestions for conferees

Conflict: A basic part of conference communication should be in
    Positive values
    Intragroup conflict
    Intergroup conflict

Management group conflict can be accomplished by the following strategies:
    Avoidance strategy
    Defusion strategy
    Confrontation strategy, which provides four basic techniques:
    —Power technique
    —Negotation technique, which can take one of two approaches:
    —Cooperative processing
    —Competitive processing
    —Mediation technique
    —Arbitration technique

Conferees interact as:
    —Peer
    —Subordinate
    —Superior

EXPERIENCING EXPERIENCES

Being a participant in a conference may appear to be a rather simple activity since others are also involved in this communication. There is the old adage that there is "safety in numbers." The focus of the conference activity is group inter-action, each individual pulling his or her fair share of the weight. In many ways, this communication tool is more challenging to use because it does require people to relate to one another in order to promote positive communication results.

Along with understanding the many communication principles and con-ference operational styles, there is a definite need for practicing the skills. There is a need to experience the skills in working situations with other individuals in order to have an opportunity to practice. There is also an equal need to experience a variety of situations calling for these skills and principles, since all conferences are different in plan and process. The more opportunity to practice, the more skilled you will become at analysis and selecting the proper strategies for getting the job done. The football player has a lot of information to learn and skills to master, and constant daily practice is what makes the player successful. The same is also true of the conference participant.

ACTIVITY 1: Orientation of the New Employee

Notice: There will be a conference tomorrow to discuss what kind of orienta-tion program Speech Com Corporation should have for new employees. This conference will involve all supervisors from Personnel, Sales, Public Relations, Marketing, Accounting, Purchasing, and Organizational Development. Your task is to design a practical but inexpensive orientation program for all new employees.

Directions: All class members take roles and responsibilities. Give yourselves no more than three class periods to accomplish this task. Select three classmates who should not participate in the conference role play. They are to be process recorders with specific responsibilities:

Processor 1:   Keep a running record of the business agenda
Processor 2:   Keep a conferee communication log
Processor 3:   Keep a conflict strategy chart

At the end of the third day, the three processors get together and compare notes. On the fourth day, they sould give a combined oral report to the class of what really happened during the three days of role playing.

The processor forms on the following pages should be used.

Agenda Item	Brief Description	Action Taken	Follow-up Suggested	Follow-Up Done
Plan agenda	10 minute deciding to set up fair agenda	all agreed to breaking down into four groups	15 minute submeetings	3 minute report back to main group

Processor 1: business agenda log.

Conferee	Contributes New Ideas	Adds to Some Other Idea	Introduces Conflict	Asks A Question	Answers A Question	Volunteers To Do Work	Displays Power
John Smith	/ / /	++++ /	/ /	/ / / /	/	++++ /	/ /

Processor 2: conferee communication log.

Conferee	Avoidance Strategy	Defusion Strategy	Confrontation Strategies				
			Power	Neg.-Coop	Neg.-Com.	Mediation	Arbitration
Jane Field	accepting ownership of John's idea		Reward for slide program		on 1/2 testing idea of Sally's	Representing lost conflict for slide program	

Processor 3: conflict strategy chart.

NOTES

1. Beverly Wakefield, *Perception and Communication.* Speech Communication Association, 1976, p. 5.
2. Fred E. Jandt, ed., *Conflict Resolution Through Communication.* New York: Harper & Row, 1973, p. 2.
3. Robert Doolittle, *Orientation to Communication and Conflict.* Palo Alto, Calif.: Science Research Associates, 1976, pp. 29-31.

CHAPTER TEN

WRITING TO COMMUNICATE IN BUSINESS

"Employees have learned that writing is one of the most important job skills." This statement is from a top executive in a large corporate textile business, and this person is echoing what has been said by many other employers for the last twenty-five years. The greater the job responsibility, the more important writing skills are. The chance for advancement rests on the person's level of writing skills. Unfortunately, most students fail to realize this while still in school. Too late, the truth confronts them—when they are on the job and attempting to write—that conceiving brilliant and exciting new ideas is not enough. If they cannot communicate these ideas to others in writing, they are of little value.

Weak writing can create misunderstanding. Misunderstandings often cost a lot of money and time. It is often difficult to find the source of a misunderstanding when it is spoken, but when it is written, the evidence is on the paper.

Weak writing can also create an unfavorable impression. Writing communicates on several levels, as oral communication does. The content of the message is either clear or unclear, but the secondary information, the message conveyed about the writer, is open to a variety of interpretations.

Employers are looking for people who can write clearly with efficient organization. They want writers who can compose written messages with speed and accuracy. They are looking for employees who can use language effectively with courtesy and tact.

WRITING IN BUSINESS: A RATIONALE

Written communication has distinct advantages over oral communication. These advantages are important in business professions. The first advantage is its precision. A letter, contract, office memo, or formally written report is constructed with carefully chosen words, sentences, and paragraphs. Specific terms can be used for legal or contractual purposes, and the transaction can be documented on paper, letterhead stationary, or contract forms. A date can be affixed to the message to establish sequence, chronology, or ranking significance.

The second advantage is efficiency. Written communication can be filed, mailed, reproduced in exact copy, transcribed, edited, or redesigned. There are inexpensive and easy operational copy machines as well as sophisticated methods for mailing or filing messages—an obvious necessity in all business organizations.

The third advantage of written communication is the personal convenience that it offers to everyone who wishes to use it. Written communication can be composed in any location at the writer's convenience. Such a communication can be worked on, interrupted, and resumed at the writer's will.

The fourth advantage for written communication is the possibility of an exact "replay" of the message. Oral communication cannot provide this, as we discover, when we try to repeat the exact words of another. We quickly realize that even an exact repetition of words cannot duplicate spoken communication.

WRITTEN COMMUNICATION: A MODEL

Several chapters presented you with models for different forms of oral communication. In this chapter we are going to present a model for written communication to demonstrate it as a process (see Figure 10-1). In this model the writer/sender composes a written message using one of many possible mediums. Box 10-1 lists many of the commonly used written media. The composed message is forwarded to the receivers, who are the reader/audience. The reader/audience analyzes the message and reacts in a written or nonwritten mode. At this point feedback occurs, the reader becomes the sender and communicates feedback. It is either verbal or nonverbal (e.g., over the telephone, or by no response at all) or a prepared written message, often taking the form of the original message, using one of the media in Box 10-1. When the feedback response is presented to the original writer/sender, the written communication continues through reprtition of the steps involved or stops.

Unlike this process in speech, one can easily follow its steps when they are in writing. If miscommunication takes place, it becomes less difficult to locate where in the process this has occurred. This fact places a greater emphasis on the role responsibilities involved in written communication. What simply may first appear as an additional problem in written communication turns out to be a "built-in" advantage for using written communication. It provides sources whereby

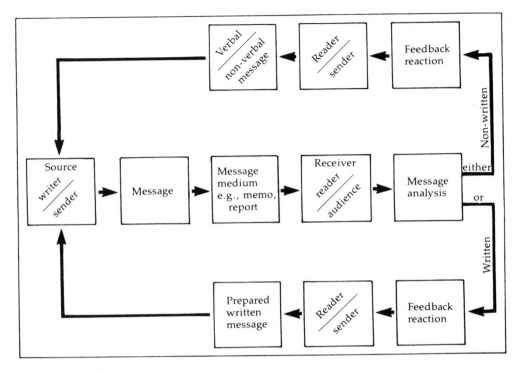

FIGURE 10-1   Written communication model.

organizations can monitor the quality of communications as well as document error.

STYLE: A PERSPECTIVE

Most people think they need to display a particular style when writing. The idea of needing a special style frightens many people making them uncomfortable when using written communication.

Style is the conscious and unconscious choices the writer makes from the options offered in the language he or she uses.[1] Characteristics associated with style are distinctiveness, originality, conformity, and creativity. These qualities are considered difficult to incorporate into one's writing. Style in terms of written communication involves some very specific factors when using written language. Such factors are the length and the complexity of sentences, the possible variations in word order, and the choice of words used for a specific message.

Style serves basic functions for the writer. It can function to communicate the writer's specifically planned purpose for sending the message. Second, style can convey the pattern of the writer's thinking. Third, it helps to establish a specific quality of language the writer wants to convey. Fourth it can be used to create

BOX 10-1   COMMON FORMS OF WRITTEN MESSAGES

Abstracts	Educational literature	Position papers
Administrative orders	Employee publications	Posters
Advertisements	Equipment bids	Press releases
Agenda	Equipment operating	Procedures
Agreements	procedures	Programs
Announcements	Estimates	Proposals
Annual reports	Fact sheets	Prospectuses
Applications	Financial analyses	Questionnaires
Arbitration findings	Fliers	Quotation bids
Attitude surveys	Good-will literature	Radio and television
Bill enclosures	Handbills	commericals
Billboards	Handbooks	Reading-rack literature
Blueprints	Handouts	Recommendations
Booklets	House organs	Recruitment literature
Bulletins	Inquiries	References
Business articles	Interview formats	Replies to inquiries
Business and financial	Instructions	Reports
news	Introductions	Requisitions
Catalogs	Invitations	Research studies
Certificates	Job appraisals	Resolutions
Charts	Job descriptions	Resumes
Circulars	Journal publications	Sales presentations
Citations	Laws and bylaws	Schedules
Claims	Leaflets	Signs
Collection notices	Legal briefs	Specifications
Commemorative	Letters	Speeches
literature	Magazine layouts	Stockholder
Complaints	Manuals	communications
Conference briefs	Market surveys	Suggestions
Consulting proposals	Memorandums	Summaries
Contracts	Minutes	Surveys
Coupons	Order and order	Tags and labels
Credit forms and	forms	Technical papers
letters	Organizational devel-	Telegrams
Data sheets	opment procedures	Training aids
Direct-mail advertising	Package copy	Training programs
Directives	Performance appraisals	Wills
Directories	Plans	Warranty certificates
Dividend notices	Policy statements	Waivers

a particular mood in a reader's mind. And last, it is a way to establish specific meaning that would be lost if the message were quickly summarized, paraphrased, or presented in outline form.

Style also serves important functions for the reader. It provides the basis for the immediate impressions, frequently referred to as "gut reactions." Style indicates to the reader what kind of response the writer expects.

In a highly structured organization, writing style may be dictated by formal policy or tradition through years of usage. Whatever the style, whether organizationally established or left to the individual to develop, clarity should be the primary consideration.

WRITING FOR CLARITY:
SOME SUGGESTIONS

In an effort to maintain clarity, any writer should ask himself some preliminary questions before putting pen to paper.

Who will read this written communication? Is the message intended for one individual or a group of readers? What are their intellectual capabilities? Are there any situational factors that must be considered concerning these readers, such as reading level, time availability, or topics that might be considered personal rather than public matters?

What should the written message enable the reader to do? Are there any specific actions the reader will be expected to take once he or she has read the message? If so, it should be specifically indicated in the message.

What must I do to make my message comprehensible to the reader(s)? This last question forces the writer to select a structure before ever putting any words on paper.

Clarifying through the use of "visual" images. People commonly think in visual images. This information is valuable to writers. Readers understand ideas by forming mental images, even when thinking or reading about abstract information. Writing can create such images directly, or it can be so composed that the reader will have to translate the message into mental images. For example, the sentence: "Successful businessmen smoke expensive cigars" establishes a definite image in the reader's mind. On the other hand, "It was announced by the tobacco industry that sales of the better grades of tobacco have significantly increased among customers who are well established in the business world," requires the reader to translate the statement into some type of mental image.

In short, writing that communicates direct images is clear and easier to comprehend. It is less open to misinterpretation. If readers create only their own images, the greater will be the opportunity for miscommunication. Writers, by creating definite images, can avoid part of this "translation" problem for their readers. The more of these definite images used, the less chance of misinterpretation on the part of the reader.

Clarifying by organizing from the general to the specific. Writers create clarity of style in their approach to the organization of the content. A writer has two options: one is to begin with the general overview and then to focus on specifics. The other is to start with specific ideas and move to a general overview. Unfortunately, many writers choose the latter approach. This approach, although it may feel right to the writer or seem to deal immediately with the "heart of the matter," often ends by confusing the reader.

The reader often reacts to this specific-to-general approach "where is this person coming from?" When the reader is faced with such a message, the reactions are not always positive: "What is he after?" or "What is she really trying to say?" For example, an irate employee is writing up a grievance about a shop problem. But the message begins with some of the bad effects that have come about due to the problem. It would be much better to begin the written message by giving a brief history of the problem, and then present the negative effects. Certainly this approach would make it easier for the reader to understand the content and purpose of the message.

All too often the writer assumes that the situation, the circumstances, or the factual information is apparent to the reader, when in reality this is not so.

Clarifying by minimizing grammatical errors.   For some time, grammar has been a sore point for student and teacher alike. Contrary to the beliefs of many educators, most people learn grammar by listening to others and then imitating what they have heard. We tend to learn English syntax from oral communication usage. Oral grammar is simple and reflects in short sentences. Written grammar is more complex. The more complex the writing style, the greater the chance for grammatical error. The simpler and more forthright the writing style, the lower the percentage of error. Such errors, at best, distract the reader. At worst, they can negate much of the writer's credibility and knowledge.

Clarifying by removal of unnecessary words.   The most common criticism on themes in writing courses is "wordy." We know what that means, but we don't always understand what to do about it. Long, awkwardly constructed sentences are part of this "wordy" syndrome. Written communication can very easily get caught up in this syndrome. This problem is created by an overuse of *utility-connector* words, which are the little words writers use to fill in the sentence. Many believe these words clarify the message, but in reality, they muddle up the message. This makes it more difficult for the reader to find the theme of the communication. Utility-connection words are articles, prepositions, conjunctions, relative pronouns, etc. For example, one supervisor wrote this note to his departmental subordinates: "It is necessary that a reevaluation of the new program be conducted." He could have said, "We have to reevaluate the program." "It," "is," "that," "a," "of," "the," "be conducted" are all utility-connector words for the writer of this sentence, but they are not necessary for the reader. They get in the way and add clutter for the reader. In the time-conscious business world, this writing clutter is a serious hazard to communication. When it is consciously eliminated, the communication style becomes significantly clearer.

Clarifying through persona.   There is an interpersonal message in most written communication. We call it the *persona* and it can take on one of three implications. The first is the impersonal persona. For example, "The evaluation has been accepted." This persona is used very frequently in business writing and government documents. The second persona is referred to as the organizational plural: "We are looking forward to your visit and your presentation." The third persona is the personal one, and it is most direct: "I am pleased to announce that you design has been approved." When a writer attempts to use the impersonal or organizational plural personas, the writing can easily lose clarity. The personal persona is the most direct, and immediately informs the reader of the authorship. The impersonal persona implies a lack of concern and sincerity, and most readers subconsciously read this into the written message. The organizational plural implies a condescending attitude, which can create negative responses in the reader. The personal persona is forthright and to the point. It allows little opportunity for mistaking authorship of the message.

Some organizations define which persona should be used in their written correspondence, but more do not. A writer should use the personal persona style. It is definite and direct in presenting a message to a reader.

SELECTING WORKABLE VOCABULARY

Writers often struggle to find the right word. Unfortunately, in business writing there is little time to search for the right word. Researchers have found that most writers use a "stock" vocabulary, just as speakers do. It is easy to get in the rut of using the same words. This becomes repetitious and boring. Unlike college students who can keep their *Thesaurus* near the typewriter when the need for that "special word" arises, business professionals must rely on their own reservoirs to provide the right word. Unfortunately, the human mind does not provide the organized variety of vocabulary found in a *Thesaurus*.

Here are some guidelines for vocabulary usage.

Use words denotatively.   Many words have two meanings. The denotative meaning is the definition found in a standard dictionary. This meaning has common acceptance because of the dictionary and the frequent usage of the word with the dictionary definition. Denotative meanings of words can change but only over a period of time. They are "safe" because they offer a writer the security of a definition that readers accept.

Connotative meanings of words do not afford the writer this assurance. Connotative meanings are based on the context in which words are used. These meanings vary from person to person and situation to situation. A word may have a meaning in one part of the country and a completely different meaning in another. Unlike the creative writer, the business writer is not concerned with local color or uniqueness of writing style. His or her concern is efficiency and effectiveness of communication. Therefore, it is better for the business writer to use words denotatively when writing business correspondence.

Use positive and negative words selectively.   Some scholars of language have used the terms "god-words" and "devil-words." This is one way of saying that there are positive and negative words. Both are used in business writing. Business writers must be aware of positive and negative words to understand when to use which type. Positive and negative words plant attitudes in the mind of the reader. Executives often want their written communications to imply a positive attitude, but unconsciously use negative words. The following example clearly makes this point. It appeared in a weekly newsletter for a large business organization.

> Most employees realize that companies which discourage enrichment training are at a competitive disadvantage. High-caliber individuals are difficult to attract and there is quick turnover among those hired. The end result is poor quality and less profit.

The message might have come across more successfully if it had read:

> Most employees realize that companies which *encourage* enrichment training are at a competitive *advantage*. High-caliber individuals are *easy* to attract and *maintain*. The end result is *better* quality and *more* profit.

Avoid prejudice words.   Prejudice words, like positive and negative words, imply an attitude. In this situation, the attitude of the writer is implied to the reader. Often, this is deliberately done, but more frequently the writer is unaware. The business communication that refers to an "impractical plan" implies that the writer has a definite negative attitude. If it is an "impractical scheme," the attitude is painted in bold colors. To say, instead, "The plan lacks . . ." at least permits the reader to accept the writer's attitude more objectively. It is clear and sufficiently precise. An "ordinary" or "run-of-the-mill" product implies poor quality; if the writer's concern is to comment on the price, he or she has chosen the wrong descriptive words. To substitute the word "cheap" compounds the attitude. The term "lower price" is clear and it does not communicate a bias.

To imply ownership of ideas, products, and policies can set up a prejudice. "Miss Kelly's idea" may have been a corporate decision, but tacking on the concept of ownership gives an inaccurate impression. While some readers may not be confused by this type of writing, the efficient business writer avoids such communication. "Such cutthroat writing is definitely un-American in the dog-eat-dog environment of business! Prejudice words communicate; nonprejudice words communicate safely."

Eliminate "in-house" words.   Individual companies usually have a long list of "in-house" words. Acronyms are good examples of in-house words. These are short-cut words that have special meaning in an organization. Such words are developed to save time. They can work well for certain communication, but often they become a source of confusion. New employees coming into the organization will not understand such words and certainly readers outside of the organization will not understand. Specialized journals and trade magazines often use such specialized vocabulary. When readers not familiar with the terms use such a periodical, they can quickly become confused. In written communications, it is best to avoid such words. If they are used, they should be defined when first presented to the reader.

Avoid clichéd phrases. Clichés may appear to be colorful additions to business writing but they do not give the reader precise meanings. A new employee may be "head and shoulders"above the previous employee, but that is not a fair statement on a written appraisal. This employee could be "efficient" and/or "effective" with interpersonal skills, or "skillful" with a piece of equipment, or "sneaky" at manipulating, or "better" or covering up errors, and so forth. "As luck would have it, the new machine arrived today"—could implicate the calendar, the post office, the union truck drivers, or a happy employee recently given a raise. Clichés can set a mood or imply an attitude, but rarely do they provide readers with accurate information.

Selecting vocabulary for business writing does not have to involve a large unity of words, but there should be concern for accuracy. Effectiveness in business writing relies on selecting words and phrases that are vivid and precise.

STRUCTURING WORKABLE SENTENCES

Most beginning writers are frightened by sentence structure. They remember with horror the long sentences they were forced to diagram on the blackboard in front of their classmates. Structuring a sentence is arranging all of its parts. This does not imply that sentences must be long or complex. The purpose of structuring a sentence is to write out ideas that communicate effectively.

When we discuss sentence structure, we shall examine specific items. These items include sentence length, selection of verb tense, subject/verb agreement, and designing readable word order within the sentence. The purpose of controlling for sentence structure is to achieve directness for clarity, parallelism for organization, and conciseness for efficiency. When sentences are constructed correctly, they achieve all three goals. Certainly, these goals are important to business writing.

Sentence length. The average number of words per sentence for the best "readability" is seventeen words.[2] This is not to say that every sentence should have exactly seventeen words. If all sentences had the same number of words, they would prove to be very boring. Furthermore, it does not take seventeen words to express every idea.

Variety in business writing does not have or need the emphasis of literary writing. In creative writing, the variety of sentence length may be a significant part of the writer's style. Business writing is striving for brevity and clarity. Long sentences can disjoint simple ideas. The logical break of the period, space, and then moving on to the first word of the next sentence is a visual way to separate ideas.

The type of sentence used has a great deal to do with the length of the sentence. There are four types of sentences: the simple, the compound, the complex, and the complex-compound. In business writing there is very little need for the compound or complex-compound sentences.

The simple sentence has a subject, verb, object, and minimal modifiers. Because it is compact, the structure will express an idea clearly. This is the purpose of the simple sentence. It organizes well; it is brief.

The complex sentence, which is made up of a dependent and independent clause, will effectively take care of more intricate ideas. This sentence type offers the writer a form that will provide detail well for more complicated ideas. It will help the reader understand the relationship between the main clause and subordinate idea.

Compound and complex-compound sentences take more time to compose. The use of these sentence types requires a greater working knowledge of grammar and syntax. To maintain a high level of competence with these skills requires regular writing usage, more usage than the average person has time for on a day to day job basis.

Verb tenses.   Verb tense confuses many people when they are writing, but few think that much about it when speaking. Except for the simple present and past tenses, English verbs demonstrate distinction of time by various phrase combinations. The simple present is "he asks"; the past, "he asked"; but the past perfect is "had asked"; the present perfect is "has asked" or "has been asking"; the future is "he will ask," "will be asking," or "is going to ask"; and the future perfect is "he will have asked," or "he will have been asking."

English has six verb tenses (present, past, present perfect, past perfect, future, and future perfect). In business writing, the present, past, and future tenses are important. The present perfect, past perfect, and future perfect tenses are rarely used in business communications. They can easily confuse the reader. The fine line of distinction they offer is not necessary in most situations.

The writer should be aware however, that in business writing the verb tense should be consistent within a single communication. Some writers change verb tenses within a letter or memo and do not realize they have done so. This small point can create a great deal of confusion. If a shift in tense is necessary, for example, to compare a present program to a former one, then a change in verb tense is justifiable. Most frequently, verb tense violations occur unnoticed in single long sentences that have two or three verbs.

Subject/verb agreement.   The subject and verb are the central focus of any sentence. For writers, the problem in subject/verb agreement occurs when there are compound (double) subjects within a sentence. If there are two separate subjects connected by "and," the verb should be plural. For example, "Margaret and David have good work records." Likewise, when two subjects are pronouns connected by "and," the verb is plural. Usually this is not a problem for a writer. The problem arises when there are two singular subjects, but a singular verb should be used. This construction is used when:

1. both subjects refer to the same person. Ex.: The president and manager was a single position.
2. the subjects are connected by "or" or by "either/or." Ex.: Either Public Relations or Personnel has made the error.
3. a singular subject is connected to a related noun by a preposition rather than a conjunction. Ex.: That case, as well as the preceding one, was the deciding factor.
4. when a singular subject and a plural subject are connected by "or," the verb agrees with the nearer subject. Ex.: John or his sons were always in attendance.

Some writers have trouble dealing with collective nouns, words that are singular in form but plural in meaning. When the collective is considered a single unit, the verb is singular; when the collective noun refers to individuals within a unit, the verb is plural:

1. The Board of Directors has voted in favor of the plan.
2. The Board of Directors have voted 4 to 1 in favor of the plan.

Subject/verb agreement need not be a problem for writers with these few rules as guides. With some awareness of this issue, most writers develop until correct usage becomes a habit.

Word order.   Word order is the arrangement of words and phrases in a sentence. The basic purpose of this arrangement is to express the idea a way that makes it most apparent to the reader. There is the standard order of subject-verb-object, but many writers wish to vary this order from time to time. The danger in changing word order is obvious. The word order can vary to such a degree that the reader gets lost following the "unique" order. The idea or message of the sentence can be totally lost. Literary writing, again, is more concerned about variety in word order as a means of developing a rhythm and communicating subtle shifts in meaning. Business writing is concerned with getting the idea quickly and clearly to the reader. People are trained from early on to expect subject, verb, and object. When this order is not used, they must shift "thinking-reading gears." In the process of doing this, the idea can get lost within the word-order design.

A writer should vary this order when a particular part of the sentence needs special emphasis. The reason for the word-order change is emphasis, *not* variety. For example, "That contract we signed on January 10, 1978," places the emphasis on the contract rather than the date of the signing. Normally the reader would expect, "We signed that contract on January 10, 1978."

When the standard word order is interrupted, usually the reader's comprehension pattern is also interrupted. Another danger is that the change in word order is misleading to the reader. Modifiers (adjectives, adverbs, and adjective and adverbial phrases) should be close to the word they describe. When separated from the word they modify, these modifiers merely add confusion for the reader as he gets lost in the word order structure.

> The shippers have been able to get labels for the boxes they use from Paper-Core with little opposition until recently.

It would read better as:

> Until recently, the shippers have been able to get labels for the boxes they use with little opposition from PaperCore.

Better still, rephrase the message:

> Until recently, the shippers have encountered little opposition from Paper-Core in obtaining labels from the boxes they use.

Another example:

> The sports writers will look forward to seeing you at the horse show in any event.

Less humorous, but closer to the meaning:

> In any event, the sports writer will look forward to seeing you at the horse show.

Misuse of word order is humorous, but it can also lead to costly mistakes in business communications. Simple word order is direct and communicates effectively to readers.

COMPOSING WORKABLE PARAGRAPHS

A paragraph is a series of sentences grouped into a unit based on the theme of the content. The divisional unit of the paragraph is for the benefit of the reader. It functions equally well as an aid in organizing the writer's thoughts. As a divisional unit, the paragraph is a practical and useful entity as long as it guides the reader to a better understanding of the message.

In writing paragraphs, most individuals face three problems. The first problem is underdevelopment, which is a lack of detail to establish the essence of the content in the mind of the reader. The second problem is just the opposite, some writers attempt to put too much detail into the paragraph and confuse the reader.

And the third problem is a lack of connection. In this situation, the writer fails to relate sentences within a single paragraph, or neglects to connect one paragraph to the next.

It should be the purpose of the paragraph to present a single idea, specifically and clearly with brevity. Just as the sentence focuses on one idea, so should the paragraph. The paragraph, as a larger unit than the sentence, attempts to provide the reader with detail to support a general statement. Therefore, the two basic ingredients of the paragraph are the general statement and the support sentences with the necessary details.

The paragraph opener.

The paragraph opener.   Paragraphs should open with a topic sentence. This is a statement that introduces the subject or theme of the paragraph. Topic sentences are very important to readers since they serve as guides through the essence of the written message.

Topic sentences are most important in a series of paragraphs. A writer should use parallel structure of topic sentences. This is an easy method for relating longer written communications to a reader. Topic sentences are the skeletal structure of a multi-paragraph message. If this pattern is established, it is much easier for the reader to follow the message and comprehend the full meaning from a series of paragraphs.

Paragraph cohesiveness.

Paragraph cohesiveness.   Whether a paragraph achieves its purpose depends on the manner in which a reader is led from one statement to the next. The relationship of one paragraph to the next should be apparent to the reader. Transition phrases provide this cohesiveness when the statements within a single paragraph do tie together, then a writer has a solid pattern to guide the reader.

There are a number of ways a writer can establish this relationship among sentences within a single paragraph:

1. Use the same subject from sentence to sentence or use a similar noun or pronoun as a substitute.
2. Use a key word from the first sentence in the second sentence, such as the object in the first statement as the subject of the second.
3. Use a pronoun when referring to the subject of the previous sentence.
4. Use a conjunction or adverb (e.g., *but, however, and*) to indicate a transition to the next sentence.
5. Use similar parallel structure from sentence to sentence.
6. End paragraph with a transitional statement.

It is very important for the writer to establish cohesiveness within each paragraph. If readers get lost within a paragraph, they will remain lost as they move on to the next paragraph and may very possibly lose the entire message of the written communication.

Continuity from paragraph to paragraph.   Just as the writer must strive for cohesiveness within the single paragraph, so must he or she strive for continuity from one paragraph to the next. A writer has "connectors" available for doing this very task. These connectors are transitional phrases. Much like the construction worker uses framing, a writer uses transitions to achieve continuity within a written message structure.

The transition between two paragraphs usually works best when it appears in the first sentence of the second paragraph rather than in the last line of the preceeding paragraph. These transitional sentences point out two important directions: first, they tell readers where they have been; and second, where they are going. These sentences lead the reader from one idea to the next.

Box 10-2 provides a list of some of the more popular phrases and words that function well in transitional sentences. The joining function or purpose the writer may wish to use is listed first, followed by suggested connectors.

BOX 10-2   CONTINUITY CONNECTORS FOR PARAGRAPH WRITING

Joining Function	Continuity Connector
Addition	and, also, too first, second, third . . . etc. besides, furthermore, moreover one . . . another last, in conclusion
Example	for example to point out for instance to illustrate
Cause and Effect	because, on account of, since therefore for the reason in effect
Comparison	in the same manner in a like manner likewise similarly consequently
Contrast	but, in contrast however on the one hand/on the other hand conversely quite unlike positive/negatively nevertheless

Another way for the writer to maintain continuity from paragraph to paragraph is through the use of parallel structure. By merely repeating the grammatical structure in topic and transitional sentences at the beginning of each paragraph, the reader will quickly see the structure to follow the written message with minimum difficulty.

Opening and closing paragraphs.   An opening paragraph should be treated as a preview of the "coming attractions." This paragraph should forewarn the reader about what will follow. Furthermore, it should give some indication of direction. If the written message is going to contain three major points, then the reader should be told there are three points, and each one should be briefly listed.

The purpose of the opening paragraph is to introduce and eliminate surprise or the unexpected in business writing. The directiveness of the opening paragraph sets up the tone of the message, as well as introducing the specific subject and purpose. The mood is important because it establishes the attitude of the writer and attempts to define the expected attitude of the reader.

The closing paragraph, like the opening one, has a special function. This last paragraph in the written message should summarize what has gone before. All main ideas that have appeared in the written communication should be briefly alluded to in the concluding paragraph.

Furthermore, each closing paragraph should have a concluding sentence to clearly indicate to the reader that the message is completed. If this final closing sentence of the last paragraph is missing, the reader will be left hanging. This is a frequent fault with business communications. The words have ended on the paper, but the message seems incomplete to the reader.

When any written communication is composed in a series of paragraphs, there should be an obvious opening and a closing paragraph.

WRITING TO SEEK AND DISPENSE INFORMATION

Searching for or dispensing information is the major purpose for written business communication. Dispensing information includes such diversified tasks as providing highly complicated technical data to offering suggestions for good places to eat. Likewise, searching for information also covers a wide range of situations, from asking for complex procedural formats to seeking personal advice about how to dress for a special presentation.

Since there is such a wide diversity of information-dispensing and information-searching tasks, a writer must be able to assess the specific purpose of the communication, select the proper written format, and structure the written message around that format. This requires critical analysis, and certainly some practical experience. The business writer must know when to use a business-letter format and when to use an interoffice memo. Sometimes the situation calls for a formally designed report. No matter what format is chosen, the writer does have some basic guidelines that will achieve productive communication.

Attitude: The writer's point of view.   The writer always has a point of view and it should be reflected in information writing. It may affect the reader's point of view, but that is *not* the purpose. Here, the writer's point of view provides clarity to the communication. Furthermore, it offers a personal approach to the communication—naturalness. Courtesy and tact are also a part of the writer's point of view. Courtesy and tact are considerably more noticeable in oral communication, but they have a significant role in writing. Sincerity is another part of the writer's point of view. Sincerity reflects a quality that is very important for developing the reader's opinion of the writer's credibility.

Clarity: The cornerstone of writing.   Clarity is reflected in the writer's knowledge of the subject. Placing the information in simple, short sentences for efficient comprehension is vital. Selecting words for specific meaning and eliminating ambiguity are essential. The vocabulary must be familiar to the reader, taking into consideration the reader's background and experience with the subject of the communication.

Clarity is also reflected in the organizational ability of the writer. If the writer creates a workable organization, the reader will be able to grasp the communication quickly and accurately.

Conciseness: Respecting the reader's time.   Unnecessary detail is the constant plague of written business communications. The details are too many and, quite often, unnecessary. Much valuable time is wasted for readers by writers who are careless about brevity. Repetition has a place in writing, and it belongs in the summary of written communications. Often writers repeat the same ideas from paragraph to paragraph.

Coherence: The writer's organizational flow.   All ideas should have some order. When order is estabished, the reader immediately begins to comprehend. If ideas are structured in time-order sequence, ascending or descending pattern, in a cause-and-effect, or in problem-and-solution structure, the essence of the message flows. It is easy to follow the relationship of multiple ideas in a simple communication.

Organizational flow functions well when information is placed in some type of divisional format. Planned structure allows the writer opportunity to expand or compress information when space or brevity are essential factors.

A writer can develop force with organizational flow. Individual ideas receive the proper emphasis and are presented to the reader one at a time. By placing the ideas of a message in an opening, or introduction, the writer prepares the reader for what is to come. The message should present one idea at a time, expressed clearly, with a proper transition that will carefully guide the reader on to the next main idea. And once all the ideas have been developed, a proper closing should summarize the key issues and signal the reader that the message is completed. All of this can be accomplished with planned organizational structure. Furthermore, flow can be supported by careful selection of the effective vocabulary.

After the writer has established the purpose of the communication, and selected the proper format, it is merely a matter of following a few basic guidelines. Being aware of point of view, realizing the significance of clarity, respecting the reader's time, and establishing some type of organizational flow will aid greatly to structure a written message.

WRITING TO PERSUADE

Writing persuasively is challenging for the business professional. Whether it is to be a memo, a formal letter, a report, or an elaborate contract, the writer must take time to analyze the intended reader(s). A clear understanding of writing to communicate is necessary in order to recognize the difference between information and persuasive writing. Persuasive writing, unlike information writing, is concerned with influencing the reader's point of view. This could range from stimulating the reader to make a change in a attitude, to coercing the reader to accept an issue. It takes more strategic planning for the writer to create a persuasive argument on paper.

Like informative writing, persuasive writing is easier for a writer who follows some basic guidelines. When using these guidelines, the writer will have to select the proper format, such as a letter, report, or memo, and then adapt it to the situational factors for sending a persuasive communication.

Stimulating interest: Starting on the right foot.   The opening paragraph in written persuasion must get things off on the right foot. The interest of the reader must be stimulated by the introduction. If the writer has some notion of the reader's attitude on the subject, it is much easier to stimulate interest. The conclusion, which normally comes at the end of a written communication, should appear right in the opening. By starting off with the conclusion, the reader will know immediately where the writer is aiming. This will eliminate any hidden fears, confusions, or possible misinterpretation on the part of the reader. This immediately places emphasis on clarity at the very beginning of the communication.

Continuity: Establishing organizational flow.   As in information writing, persuasive writing must have an organizational flow. By taking the topic and structuring it into a sequence or pattern, the writer will be sure that the reader is able to follow the flow.

Order of importance is an excellent way to structure the ideas in a persuasive communication. By starting with the most important idea and moving to the least important, the writer is setting up priorities and emphasis. In this manner, it is very easy for the reader to understand the rationale of the writer.

Cause and effect is another pattern of organization easy for the reader to follow and be influenced by. The writer can carefully establish all of the causes and then, one by one, describe each effect. This makes it very easy to show the relationship between cause and effect. It is the established relationship between the two that appears logical to the reader and that creates the positive attitude necessary for persuasion.

Problem and solution as an organizational pattern works very much like cause and effect, in that the relationship between the two is important. The solution, if it does eliminate the problem, in a practical, workable, or desirable manner, will gain strong acceptance from the reader.

Chronological, topical, and spatial patterns of organization can all be used in persuasive writing, but these depend on the relationship of the subject to the reader. Need/satisfaction is another common structural pattern, and it works well in persuasive writing. In this pattern, the writer establishes a need for the reader, and once this has been clearly explained, an idea is presented that will satisfy that need. Once the need is met, the writer can then set up some plan of action that will explain how this satisfaction will take place and offer benefits to the reader.

Credibility: A must for the writer and the content.

As the writer presents conclusions, their justification must be established. This justification is accomplished by presenting good evidence in an organized structure that will support the conclusions. If there is contrary evidence to these conclusions, it is better for the writer to deal with it openly rather than to overlook it. Not all contrary evidence need be included, but if it is evidence familiar to the reader, it is better for the writer to deal with it directly.

The content will have credibility if good examples are used to illustrate points. Furthermore, if the evidence is timely, accurate, and appropriate to the issues, it will be credible to the reader.

The writer must also appear credible to the reader. The credibility of the writer is reflected in the organization of the content. The openness of the writer's attitude toward the subject, the reader, and the situation will help to establish the writer's credibility. The smoothness of style, the clarity of details, the conciseness of data, and correct grammatical usage add to the writer's credibility.

Minimizing: Respecting the reader's time.

Persuasive writing should not have stylish extras and unnecessary details. Unnecessary details cost the reader time, and saving time for the reader can itself be a persuasive factor.

Long sentences are to be avoided. They confuse the reader and not only take up time, but may make the reader feel tricked or conned into accepting something. Contracts are a perfect example of the use of long sentences and the nondescriptive terms that tend to make readers distrusting. Short sentences are more appropriate. If these sentences are written in the present tense and the active voice instead of the passive, the communication appears straightforward and open. Readers who follow this type of writing maintain a willingness to be influenced. This type of writing is persuasively effective in letters, memos, contracts, news releases, or any type of written communication commonly used in business settings.

In the final analysis, persuasive writing can only be as effective as the writer creating the message. The purpose for persuading by written communication must be carefully supported with a clear writing style that is well organized around brevity of content.

A REVIEW OF KEY ISSUES

Written communication has distinct advantages over oral communication.
1. It is a more precise form of communication.
2. It is a more efficient form of communication.
3. It offers a personal convenience for the writer.
4. It allows for an exact replay of the message.

Written communication has a model to demonstrate its process:
Writer/sender—initiator of the message communication
Message—the content of the intended message
Message medium—format for message
Reader/receiver—the party for whom the message is intended
Message analysis—allows for written or unwritten response
Feedback reaction—originates in the mind of the reader/receiver
Unwritten message—verbal or nonverbal response
Writer message—prepared written response

Style:
Style can be viewed as the conscious and unconscious choices made among the options offered by a chosen language.

Functions of style for the writer:
1. It is a vehicle used to carry out a planned purpose.
2. It creates the patterns of the writer's thoughts.
3. It establishes the type and quality of language used.
4. It provides meaning that would be lost if message were merely summarized or outlined.
5. It creates a mood for the reader.

Functions of style for the reader:
1. It provides a means for an immediate reaction.
2. It indicates the expected feedback anticipated by the writer from the reader.

Writing for clarity:
1. Use visual/verbal images.
2. Organize ideas from the general to the specific.
3. Avoid grammatical errors.
4. Remove all unnecessary words.
5. Use the personal persona style whenever possible.

Selecting effective vocabulary
1. Use denotative definitions whenever possible.
2. Use positive and negative words carefully.
3. Avoid prejudice words.
4. Avoid using in-house words.
5. Avoid clichés.

When writing sentences:
1. Keep the sentence short.
2. Monitor the use of verb tenses.

3. Monitor the subject/verb agreement.
4. Use simple and direct word order.

When writing paragraphs:
1. Carefully plan the topic sentence.
2. Use cohesiveness to make the sentences relate.
3. Maintain continuity through the use of transitions.
4. In a series of paragraphs, use an opening and closing one.

Writing to dispense and search for information:
Attitude—be clear about your point of view
Clarity—cornerstone for informational data
Conciseness—respect the reader's time
Coherence—maintain an organizational flow

Writing to persuade:
Stimulate interest—start on the right foot
Continuity—establish specific organizational structure
Credibility—necessary for the writer and the content
Minimizing—respect the reader's time

EXPERIENCING EXPERIENCES

Many business people are afraid of writing. Like speaking skills, which only improve with practice, writing skills need to be worked on.

Because there are so many forms of written communication, from formal business letters to informal reports, a writer needs to practice each form. Even though a difference exists among the various forms, the need for effective writing skills remains equally important, no matter what form is selected for a message. If a writer can work well with one form, such as an office memorandum, chances are the writing style will be equally clear when used in some other form, such as a sales summary report.

The secret of developing an effective writing style is practice and experience. The carpenter who works regularly with set of specialized tools becomes more skillful. So it is with the writer. The more practice writing you do, the more skillful you will become in organizing information on paper.

These thoughts should be kept in mind as the following activities are considered.

ACTIVITY 1: Persuading With a Point of View

The following article will appear in the weekly employee newsletter for Future Communications, Inc. As one of the newsletter writers, you must edit and restructure the article.

No Self-Improvement, No Promotion

Employees, today, must be willing to take additional training classes for self-improvement if they expect to get promoted on their present jobs. A study was released from the federal government showing that 74% of the federal employees who took the time from their busy workday to attend a course for job self-improvement got a job promotion within six months of completing the requirements for the course for which they had signed up.

Since this is the only way job promotion appears to be popular and work well for the benefit of a business organization, we here at Future Communications, Inc., are going to start self-improvement training courses next month. Registration will start next week. Sign up and when you do, bring in a recommendation from your supervisor at the time of the signing.

This is the only way we here at Future Communications will consider you for a job promotion.

ACTIVITY 2: Dispensing Information

The following memorandum is to be sent to all departmental offices in your organization. Rewrite it in an effective and clear style.

```
Interoffice Memo XYZ Corporation

Date:    January 18, 1979

To:      All employees in all of the XYZ Corporate Offices

From:    The Communications Controller in Office 474

Re:      A New Procedure For Recording All Incoming Long Distance Calls

            as well as All Outgoing Long Distance Calls

This new procedure is different from the old one for both the incoming

and outgoing calls in the following procedural steps:

The Incoming calls:

1)  Each call should be recorded on the pink form using one of the code

      letters that follow.  (This is a new set of code descriptions from

      the ones we have been using here at XYZ.)

      S = sales order    C = customer complaint    I = sales information request

      OS = Order for shipment    IN = instate order    OUT = out of state order

The Outgoing Calls:

1)  Use the above newly revised code

2)  In the next column after the code, place company/client name and address

The Phone Call logs will be collected on the first and third Friday of every

month through the interoffice mail system.  If you have any questions call

me at 5699 between 8:30 a.m. and 4:45 p.m. on any day.

Respectfully,
Communication Controller
```

ACTIVITY 3: Searching for Information

The following grievance form has been designed for Company Communication, Inc. Rewrite and design it for collecting the proper information needed from such a written communication.

GRIEVANCE INFORMATION SHEET FORM

Employee: _____

Office Address: _____

Office Phone Number: _____ Office Position: _____

Discuss YOUR complaint briefly, but don't leave out any facts:

Why are YOU making this grievance at this time about this matter?

What do YOU want US to do about this grievance?

How do you suggest we carry out your suggested change or activity or procedure?

Date _____ Signature of the employee: _____

Your immediate boss: _____

EXERCISES

1. Select some mechanical office item such as a ballpoint pen, pencil sharpener, carbon paper, or paperweight, and write out explicit directions on how to use it. These directions should be written so clearly that another member of the class can pick up the directions and follow them without question.

2. Study the directions from the back of some packaged item. See if there is some way in which you can rewrite the directions to make them clearer for the reader.

3. Collect some of the posters from various bulletin boards around the campus. Study them and see how you might rewrite them for more efficient communication to the passing reader. Possibly your instructor will share some recent departmental or college office memos. Study them and see if there might be some ways of rewriting them more clearly.

4. Invite a writer for some business organization to your class to discuss the specific writing skills this person uses daily. Ask for tips on improving your writing skills.

NOTES

1. J. Harold Janis, *Writing and Communicating in Business.* New York: Macmillan, 1978.
2. David Edditt, Wilman Edditt, and Porter Q. Perrin, *Writer's Guide and Index to English,* 6th ed. Glenview, Ill.: Scott, Foresman, 1978.
3. Rudolf Flesch, *The Art of Plain Talk.* New York: Harper & Row, 1966.

CHAPTER ELEVEN

COMMUNICATING IN THE TRAINING ROOM

Training is an intricate part of any business or organization. Like all communication, training is an ongoing process that involves specifically planned interaction, in this case, between a trainer (instructor) and trainees (employee-students). Reviewing the communication process as described in Chapter 1 emphasizes four critical elements: speaker, message, channel, and receiver. These same four elements exist in the training process. The speaker becomes the trainer; the message is the content of skills and knowledge; the channel is the technical methodology used to present the content; and the receivers are the employees, who are referred to as trainees.

We have developed a training model[1] that is based on the classic communication model referred to in other chapters of this book. We call this a continuous-action training model because, like communication, it is ongoing and transactional. It continuously functions on two distinct levels: (1) The trainer communicates with the organization's management structure as the training cycle is in process; (2) the trainer communicates with the staff in carrying out the training functions; (3) the trainer communicates the preplanned content of specific programs to the trainees (employees) within the organization.

This model clearly reflects the high impact of communication in the training process. If the communication process breaks down, the negative impact on the training cycle is significant. This model reflects that at each step of the training cycle, an inherent communication action inputs to the organization's management

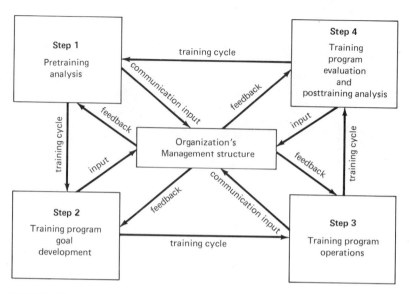

FIGURE 11-1 Continuous-action training model.

structure. This body of feedback to the decision makers consists of information essential to the developmental training cycle. This feedback controls each step in the training cycle as it progresses into the next step. In fact, this process is so similar to communication, that when the fourth step of program evaluation and posttraining analysis is completed, development continues actively, starting again with the first step of the training cycle. And like communication, the next activation of the new cycle begins using, as a working base, the information gained from the first experience.

In order for you to understand how vital the communication process is to training, as well as recognize the need for highly developed communication skills (reading, writing, speaking, and listening), we will examine each step of this model separately and in detail.

STEP ONE: PRETRAINING ANALYSIS

Identifying organizational problems is an ongoing job. The trainer, when looking at the organization's problems, separates behavioral problems from nonbehavioral ones. Only the behavioral problems are of concern to the trainer[2]; management deals with the nonbehavioral problems. As trainers examine these behavioral problems, they in effect become consultants to the organization's management, which necessitates open lines of direct communication.

The direct communication between an organization's management and its training staff requires an agreement of understanding. This is a commitment of responsibility and accountability by both parties, and it is the basis of this first

FIGURE 11-2   Communication skills in training situations are essential for positive results.

step in the cycle. It establishes the pattern of communication input and feedback that, as the model demonstrates, should occur during each step of the cycle.

The primary commitment of responsibility of the trainer should be to act as the communication disseminator for this training cycle. The responsibility requires constant open communication with the organization's management, the training department, the employees-trainees, the trainers' supervisors, and the organization's development planners. This commitment requires a great deal of report and memo writing, report and records reading, a constant listening awareness, and certainly, a great deal of presentational speaking as well as group interaction, using brainstorming, problem-solving, and decision-making activities frequently.

When behavioral problems come to the attention of the trainer, specific departments, jobs, and types of employees are studied. Work habits, skill requirements, knowledge levels, values, and attitudes are at the center of this search. This formal search is usually labeled "needs assessments." This is planned action by the trainer to determine, through surveys, questionnaires, interviews, focus groups, and work-site observations, what are the needs of employees in order to perform more productively. Needs-assessment plans and design instruments need to be tested. These trial testings need to be reported to the organization's management for input and feedback to determine the final form for both assessment instruments and plans for action.

Communication must be clear and direct between trainers and management during this first step of the cycle. A misunderstanding either of needs or of how to search out these needs would be disastrous at this stage of the cycle. Conducting surveys requires well-designed instruments that will collect usable information to use as a basis for future training plans. Interviewing people requires consistency, accuracy, and well-developed speaking and listening skills. Collecting the data in an organized format is necessary, and often, so is insuring confidentiality for the information source. The responsibility for sharing this collected information with management is the trainer's. Misuse or misinterpretation of this collected information, whether in written report form or an oral-presentation style, will interfere with the progressive development of the training cycle.

Most professionals will agree this first step is one of research and investigation. Reliability and validity of information is a high priority. Yet both these essential factors hinge on the level of the professional trainer's communication skill. The best-trained needs assessor will only be as effective for the organization as his or her communication skills permit.

Once needs are defined and documented, they must be recognized, understood, and endorsed by management. Only then is the professional trainer ready to move into the second step of the training cycle.

STEP TWO: TRAINING PROGRAM GOAL DEVELOPMENT

At this step, the trainer, in an effort to define or reevaluate present job descriptions, looks at specific jobs in the area where the organization has a recognized problem. The trainer determines what skill or competencies are essential to the performance of the specific job, or series of jobs, within this recognized problem area.[3] When skills, content knowledge, values, attitudes, and desired work behaviors can be defined for the specific job, the task of identifying desired job competencies or skill behaviors can begin.

Communication skills are critical at this stage, because much of data are generated through interviews, critical-incident checks, brainstorming, and formal or informal discussion groups. Specific training goals are created and then learning objectives are developed. Although input from management is critical, experienced employees often become a vital source of information for writing these objectives. Frequently, the information exchanged in this training step is highly technical. Trainers and management might not have the formal training to understand all of the details, yet both carry responsibility for creating and communicating these goals.

Training goals need to be correlated with the organization's goals. Some specific relationship should exist between the two. Trainers are responsible for articulating the similarities and sharing them with management, employees, and training peers. Frequently, informational conferences, management reports, quarterly organizational development presentations, and focus groups such as quality-circle activities are vehicles used for goal planning and communication.

Goal development in training is a critical step because it controls budget planning, calendar structuring and commitments to deadlines, human-resource researching, and long-range organizational planning. Once goals have been set, the trainer must plan how to communicate the goals to all of the necessary people.

These goals frequently are communicated in a variety of ways—company newsletters, management presentations, annual reports, bulletin-board notices, formal memos, and highly sophisticated internal public-relation campaigns. The speaking and writing skills of the trainer are put to task. But possibly the greatest challenge is to seek out accurate feedback and reaction to the goals. Listening, without bias, is essential. It becomes extremely difficult when the responses and incoming information is negative or personally critical.

Trainers may discover the feedback calls for reexamination of goals, as well as possibly developing completely new goals. When a point of agreement is reached concerning acceptable training goals, the trainer is ready to move on to the next step in the cycle.

STEP THREE: TRAINING PROGRAM OPERATIONS

When goals have been agreed on, then it is time to make plans for achieving them. This is the program planning and operations step, and the nature of this function is completely communicational.

The trainer creates units of information to share with trainees in formally planned settings in order to achieve certain goals. Some questions must be considered. How much content can be covered in a unit? Should there be a series of courses that will structure into some types of complex programs? What employees should study such a unit? It is a challenge to communicate specifically planned information for the distinct purpose of achieving mutually agreed-on goals. The trainer must have formal training or background in instructional communication. Speaking in public, facilitating small-group activities, holding question-and-answer sessions, leading demonstrations, processing classroom activities, and testing for comprehension of information are some of the trainer's major communication-based functions. There are many additional communication skill related responsibilities the trainer must be prepared to do, such as recording and reporting all of the training program and activities.

The accuracy and timeliness of communication with management in this part of the training cycle is a science and art all its own. Frequently, the organization's goals or the turnover of employees will radically change. This change affects training programs and operations. Sometimes the change is complex and requires fast action. A breakdown in communication between trainers and the organization's management in such a situation can be costly and anti-productive. Communication skills must continually function at their best for all parties concerned. The larger the organization and the more complex the training program, the greater is this need for accurate, timely communication.

Determining who will attend training sessions and on what days, as well as scheduling course times, often becomes a matter of game strategy. How many employees can be off the job and involved in training without interfering with organizational operations? How can the costs of training reflect profits for the organization? These are just a few of the questions the trainer must consider at this stage.

Planning the operations of training programs includes more than designing and implementing lesson plans for training sessions. It often covers numerous additional details like travel, lodging, meals, ordering supplies, textbooks, and audio-visual equipment, working with printers, negotiating details with contracted instructors, writing letters to prospective trainees, planning backup training, reserving rooms, and finding demonstration space. These activities require a wide variety of communication skills. Costs have to be carefully planned, budgets approved, and expenses justified. Communicating information about these activities to the financially responsible individuals within the organization takes time.

In this stage, quality control and productivity are given high priority in training. Trainers must also be sensitive to these considerations. Insuring quality control in training is difficult and requires planning and coordination. Effective communication is essential to maintain any type of quality control in the training room. Instructional communication that is not carefully preplanned for specific target groups will, in all probability, not provide quality control. Training objectives must be established, implemented, and periodically checked during the actual instructional communication. The speaking and listening ability of the instructor-trainer will have an effect on any control effort. Poor public-speaking skills, weak listening skills, and careless use of interpersonal skills will prevent the positive benefits of quality control in training.

Productivity, the critical success element in training, comes from accurately communicating the training goals and the skill content in the classroom. Behavior that is to be judged productive must be measurable. For mutual understanding in the minds of trainers and trainees, information must be specific and clearly worded.

Productivity for a training class is not easy to define. Free, open communication between instructor and employees will encourage and support a productive outcome for the training. The real test of productivity takes place after the training program is completed and the employees go back to the job. At this point, the training cycle moves its the fourth and final step.

STEP FOUR: TRAINING PROGRAM EVALUATION AND POSTTRAINING ANALYSIS

This last step in the cycle is challenging, because the quality control that was one factor in Step 3 is difficult to maintain. The trainer can more readily control the communication flow and quality in a training room. And for that reason, most trainers primarily do immediate training evaluation, right at the conclusion of a session.

Trainees usually are asked to evaluate the instructor, the course content, the manual or printed material used, and the instructional methods and activities employed. At times they are even asked to comment on food, travel arrangements, lodging, and other indirect but training-related issues. This type of evaluation is done through written surveys, private interviews, and focus-group actions. The trainer usually has responsibility for such assessment functions and, again, the quality of communication skills used in carrying out such action can affect the entire training cycle. If the assessment is done poorly, misinformation is collected. This information will be used for future decisions about training plans and strategies. The oral and written skills of the trainer affect the outcome of evaluation in such situations.

Another important area of evaluation is pretesting and posttraining. This responsibility is part of training functions and, likewise, is affected by communication behavior. Many training programs are designed with pretests and posttests. Trainees come into a program and begin by taking a pretest. At the completion of the program a posttest is given. The results of the two tests are compared and analyzed in order to determine whether or not training goals have been met. This is a common measure of productivity in training. Whether this type of testing is written, oral, or based on behavior demonstration, many communication skills are used to carry it out.

Frequently, trainers find their communication skills are challenged when pretesting and posttesting results must be provided to management. Whether their reports are written reports or oral presentations, trainers work with many facts and numbers. Accuracy of the information is essential, but frequently it is a matter of taking lots of details and condensing them into abbreviated essentials. These essentials are used to make important decisions and future plans regarding training action. Error at this point becomes costly.

The last part of this step is frequently referred to as posttraining analysis. The term refers to assessment activities scheduled after the training has been completed, when employees are back on the job. The organization needs to know if the employee has improved on the job since going through the training. Is there a greater output? Is it of better quality? These are some of the issues trainers must concern themselves with in the post-follow-up stage.

Communication skills at this point require a lot of work and patience. Frequently, there is significant paperwork in the form of surveys and questionnaires requesting information from the employees trained, their supervisors, or their subordinates. Sometimes formal or informal interviews are scheduled with these people, or focus-group meetings are planned. Collecting usable information from all these assessments is challenging and essential, but recording, tabulating, and assessing it is time-consuming. Then, frequently, it must be condensed to essentials and communicated to management; again, communications skills are needed to carry out the training function. This reporting requires clarity and accuracy. It is difficult to communicate on paper or verbally how human behaviors are changed in training and, furthermore, how this change has brought about better productivity for the organization.

The result of this fourth step determines where the training cycle will go. Like the communication model, training continues, good or bad; it develops or redevelops based on people's perceptions. The trainer must be able to function within this cycle. As simple as the training or communications models appear in this text, the reality of their functioning is complex and dynamic. If you wish to get involved in training activities within an organization, the following training axioms are worth your consideration.

COMMUNICATION TRAINING AXIOMS

Axioms are self-evident statements explicit to a specific subject. As professionals who must function with high-level communication skills, trainers should keep these axioms in mind.

> Training is the art and science of facilitating human resources for the development of job-performance skills and competencies.
> It is an art because it requires creativity and imagination.
> It is a science because it is based on research and proven theories.
> It is facilitation of human resources for performing training activities.
> It is based on a job performance that can be identified with specific communication behaviors considered essential to organizational development.
>
> Communication training is instruction in specific, knowledge-based skills and behaviors, to assist people to interact productively in achieving preplanned goals.
> It focuses on examination of four of the basic elements in communication: sender, message, channel and receiver.
> It examines these elements in specific communication situations, and these situations are grouped into four generic skill categories: reading, writing, speaking, and listening.
> It involves explaining and practicing these skills in generic situations that commonly occur in structured organizations that work toward some common goal or purpose.

To act on these axioms, trainers must be able to do the following:

1. They should be able to create and control the proper environment for learning experiences, so that the information they communicate will be retained and used on the job after leaving the training.
2. They should be able to use effective presentation skills, with clearly planned audio-visual supports, to communicate the information that must be transferred from trainer to trainee.

3. They should be able to interact with trainees in an interpersonal manner in order to foster motivation, information retention, and transfer of knowledge and skills to job duties.
4. They should be able to recognize and respond, react, and adapt to the dynamic situational needs of trainees with self-confidence and successful facilitation behaviors.
5. They should be able to guide groups into interaction to encourage group dynamics and synergy in a developmental process of willing participation.
6. They should be adaptable for creativity and change, in order to support productivity based on predetermined goals.
7. They should serve as a role models for communication skills and behaviors that are being taught and are considered necessary for individual and organizational development.
8. They should have some working experience with the instructional information, some formal training in the subject, positive attitudes about training others, a high standard of personal expectations, and enthusiasm that will motivate a desire to learn.

COMMUNICATION TRAINING SKILLS

Because speaking publicly before a group of trainees is a major part of the job, trainers are expected to develop these skills at a professional level. These skills should enhance the learning process and not detract from it. The human voice and body become the primary tools in this situation. It is often necessary to use visual aids when instructing a group of trainees. And likewise, their use should not detract from the instructional content! Practicing, use of videotape equipment, and professional-peer feedback are all ways for trainers to be certain of ongoing improvement. It is best to look at instructional communication skills in three categories of responsibility: vocal, visual, and psychological.

Vocal responsibilities. **Vocal pitch** should be comfortable and pleasant-sounding. It should not irritate the trainees' hearing, nor be so high or low that it is uncomfortable for the trainer to use for long periods of time.

Volume requires variety because many training sessions are long. But volume flexibility is essential, because some training is done on the job in noisy and distracting environments. Often volume must be used to maintain attention as well to emphasize technical content.

Speaking rate must vary frequently, because instruction of information demands a greater percentage of comprehension and retention. A slower rate is necessary if trainees are expected to write notes, perform activities, or work with machinery as they listen to the trainer.

Vocal inflection becomes significant, not because it is a way of entertaining the trainee's ear; rather, this vocal quality is used to place priority on instructional content. This helps present information in a series or sequence of actions. It can also separate critical information from less important details.

Articulation of the voice provides an aural clarity for trainees that will support the psychological clarity of the instructional content. This quality is vital when modeling performance information. It can also be used to simplify complex technical data when providing large amounts of information.

Projection of the voice is often important, because demonstration equipment is frequently operating during instruction. Some training settings do not always permit trainees to see the face of the trainer. For example, lowering lights in a room to show slides requires more vocal projection to compensate for lack of visible facial expression or gestures.

Some hints for achieving good vocal delivery are given in Box 11-1.

BOX 11-1   *HELPFUL HINTS FOR THE TRAINER TO CONTROL VOCAL RESPONSIBILITIES*

1. Open mouth wider whenever speaking before a training group.
2. Use yawning (as well as smiling) as an exercise for activating facial expression.
3. Rinse out mouth frequently with water, especially when training at dusty or noisy worksites.
4. Excellent phrase exercise for improving articulation: "Red leather, yellow leather."
5. Distinguish clearly between:
   "t" and "d"; "p" and "b"; "f" and "v"; "m" and "n."
6. Don't drop word end*ings*—e.g., *ing, ed, s, th, d, ng*
7. Inhale through the nose, short but deep breaths; use *total lung capacity*
8. Exhale through the mouth, controlled and much more slowly than you inhale.

Visual responsibilities.   For the trainer in the classroom, **eye contact** is critical. This is the major way to listen for trainee feedback. Watching faces for confused looks, questioning expressions, and glances of frustration is necessary for maintaining quality control over the content of the material. The eye contact of the trainer helps to establish positive interpersonal relations. This is especially important if trainees are required to attend the training program rather than requesting to be in it.

Facial expression provides the "messages between the lines" in a training environment. It emphasizes priorities and degrees of importance in the data, and it influences group attitudes about the training content. It is one of the best ways for the instructor to provide feedback, whether praise, encouragement, or challenge. It is used to select responders, rebuke, and assess answers to questions. It animates and enlivens the training process when the material gets difficult, boring, or tedious in long sessions such as on Friday afternoons.

Body movement and poise are always on display when standing in front of trainees. These qualities reflect the feeling of the trainer, but often the trainees interpret this as the feelings, beliefs, and values of the management in an organization. Poise and posture pose a very real health issue for professional trainers. Unlike schoolteachers, they conduct training sessions that may go on for long hours or several continuous days at a time. A trainer might be standing up for a solid-eight hour working day. Therefore, for conservation of energy and protection of the back and leg muscles, correct posture is essential—not only for an effective communication style, but also for health reasons.

Gestures are the human audio-visuals of Mother Nature. The arms, hands, and torso came into use long before slides, pointers, transparencies, and rear-screen projection. Use of gestures frequently takes the place of a huge piece of equipment that cannot be placed in the training room. And most important, gestures can take an intangible concept or theory and provide it with a visual image. Gestures also help a great deal in the pacing and timing of information. Trainers who tend to talk fast can use gestures to help slow their own speaking rate.

Some hints for fostering good visual communication are given in Box 11-2.

BOX 11-2   HELPFUL HINTS FOR THE TRAINER TO CONTROL VISUAL RESPONSIBILITIES

1. Exercise and keep the body healthy for the physical and psychological stamina needed in training.
2. To keep physical stress of body weight at a minimum, balance body equally on both feet when standing for a long time.
3. Move about the room some, trying not to "favor" one section of the class.
4. When a trainee has the focus of attention, sit on the edge of the instructor's table or desk to provide a "rest break" for the body.
5. When not using arms and hands, let them hang at side to avoid distracting gestures such as playing with a pencil or eyeglasses frame.
6. Avoid orchestrating with pens, rulers, and the like when gesturing, since this can look visually threatening, especially to front-row trainees.

Psychological responsibilities.   In this category, **credibility** is the most important quality. If the trainees do not trust or believe in the professional information presented by the trainer, rarely will that information serve a positive purpose back on the job. Credibility is displayed in the training room by avoiding overdependence on written notes. Frequently, if the voice is tense for any reason, the trainees will interpret this as not knowing the material. At times, maintaining credibility can appear as a visual quality if this trainer fails to display some poise when instructing the group. Small incidents like mixing up flip charts, slides out of correct sequence, or paging through a training manual for a certain major piece of information are examples of behavior that, in front of a group of trainees, can break down the credibility of the instructor.

Sincerity is another important quality. *Trainers must show concern for the trainee and the content of the program.* If attitudes of not caring or condescension appear in a training environment, it is difficult to remove them. Rapport, the psychological relationship between a speaker and audience, is very real in the training room. Effective rapport is brought about by the instructor's displaying positive attitudes. And most important, effective rapport has a direct effect on learning outcomes and on the use of the information back on the job.

Self-confidence is an important psychological quality because the trainer is a role model as well as a dispenser of information. This is especially true for trainers doing communication-related training. All of the above-mentioned qualities are influenced by the level of self-confidence displayed by the trainer. The display of self-confidence by the trainer frequently acts as one of the best motivators for adults to learn in the training room.

Some useful suggestions for carrying out these psychological responsibilities are given in Box 11-3.

BOX 11-3   HELPFUL HINTS FOR THE TRAINER TO CONTROL PSYCHOLOGICAL RESPONSIBILITIES

1. Display positiveness in word and action before, during, and after training sessions.
2. If discussions about organizational policies, politics, or personalities become part of the classroom activity, don't use this as a platform opportunity.
3. Dress appropriately for the training site, trainees, session content, and instructional demonstration demanded, rather than according to current fashions.
4. Use morning coffee opener, breaks, lunches, and related evening meals as valuable time to interpersonalize and develop positive attitudes that will carry back into the training class.
5. Be generous with praise and recognize contributions. Use responses to trainees' questions as a means for giving compliments along with the required information.
6. Each time the trainees are asked to perform activities, it is a good idea to "put oneself in the trainee's shoes, and see how they fit"—especially if there is a sense the expectation level is too high.

If the communication skills used in the training room are closely examined, one can see that professional trainers must use and model highly developed skills in their speaking, listening, and writing. The qualities and skills of effective speaking presented in our chapters on presentational speaking are essential for each trainer.

The training model presented in this chapter has attempted to display how similar training as a process is to communication. And as with communication skills, cognitive awareness only goes so far; practice and experience are essential for continual growth. This also holds true for training. At some point the trainer must do all of the behaviors discussed in the model and its action process. The real learning comes from experiencing the four steps of the training cycle, rather than reading about them.

A REVIEW OF KEY ISSUES

Training is an ongoing process that involves specially planned interaction between a trainer (instructor) and trainees (employees-students)

COMMUNICATION ELEMENTS	TRAINING ELEMENTS
Speaker (sender)	Trainer
Message	Content of skills and knowledge
Channel	Technical methodology
Receivers	Trainees-employees

Continuous-action training model
1. pretraining analysis
2. training-program goal development
3. training-program operations
4. training-program evaluation and posttraining analysis
Each of these steps requires the trainer to communicate with the management of the organization involved.

Pretraining analysis
    separation of behavioral from nonbehavioral problems
    development and testing of needs-assessment tools
    reporting of needs-assessment outcomes to management

Training-program goal development
    defining job description in terms of competencies and skills
    matching training goals to organizational goals
    getting goal commitments from management and communicating them to the organization

Training-program operations
    action planning, including seeking out human resources
    planning for budgets, calendars, and attendees
    developing course content and lesson plans
    designing support material with audio-visual aids
    maintaining quality control over the instruction

Training program evaluation and posttraining analysis
    evaluating the instructor, the content, and the support material
    designing and using pretesting and posttesting in effort to measure learning
    long-term assessment when the employee is back on the job (using questionnaires, interviews, focus groups, and observations on the job)

There are basic axioms for trainers, and following them demands specific communication skills.

Categories of communication skills for training
    vocal responsibilities
    visual responsibilities
    psychological responsibilities

EXPERIENCING EXPERIENCES

Training is a critical part of any organization or profession. This essential function, common to business professions particularly, is grounded in communication skills. As the chapter shows the comparison of training to communication, so does this chapter section stress experience as a way of hands-on learning of the chapter skills.

Such experiences in the classroom setting may appear difficult at first glance. Training and teaching have some likeness, but also some very important differences. It is important that the two are not confused or considered to be really the same thing.

The activities in this chapter have been specifically designed to prevent misunderstanding of training and teaching. The experiences to be obtained in this chapter should provide enough hands-on opportunity for the student to know how communication skills are basic to the training function. Furthermore, training might be a possible career for consideration by the student using this book in a business communications course. It is important to keep these activity objectives in mind when doing the following.

ACTIVITY 1: Training for the Professional Student

Step 1: Write a job description of one page or less of what your college expects of its freshmen students. List the requirements of skills they need to get through their first year of college. Put all the papers in a file.

Step 2: Divide the class into small groups of two and three persons representing the following college departments:
a.   admissions department
b.   student aid department
c.   academic counseling department
d.   student development department
e.   training department for freshman students

Step 3: Each department should randomly divide the file of job description papers, and working in its own group, come up with a list of skills that college freshmen should be trained to do during the opening orientation week in the fall.

The training department for freshman students will write up training-program units based on the skills lists of each department.

Step 4: The training group must interface and work with each of the other departments in this process, using the model presented in this chapter. This total process should continue over a 3 to 4 week period of time, using all of the business communication activities, skills, and formats suggested in the other chapters. By allowing fifteen to twenty minutes for two classes each week as interdepartmental meetings, this class activity can be accomplished.

Step 5: The objective of this activity is to have a training unit designed that all college freshmen would go through in orientation week. It must have approval and input from all five departments.

SUGGESTIONS:

1. Keep copies of all written communication between groups.
2. Audio or video all interdepartmental meetings.
3. Keep a log file of all documents generated by each department.
4. At the end of the activity, have the instructor and class together process the oral and written communication activities that transpired and correlate these activities with the final training product that was drafted and accepted. Look for such things as
   communication breakdowns
   management of communication time
   feedback processes
   forms of communication used as a basis for action

EXERCISES

1. Use persuasive and informative presentation assignments to carry out part of the above activity.

2. Invite college administrators who really work in these departments to come in and watch part of the interactions and offer critique comments to the class.

3. Work up a written document and really submit it to the college to examine as a possible way to help freshmen to get off to a positive start on your campus.

4. Invite an outside professional training consultant to class to examine the class's completed document and make observations.

5. Invite a professional trainer to the class to talk about the role of communication skills in this work. Hold a question-and-response forum with the professional about career considerations in the training field.

NOTES

1. Ronald C. Fetzer, *Train the Trainer.* Yellow Springs, Ohio: Fetzer Communications, 1983.
2. Ron Zemke, Linda Standke, and Phil Jones, *Designing and Delivering Cost-Effective Training,* Minneapolis: Lakewood Publications, 1982.
3. Leonard Nadler, *Designing Training Programs: The Critical Events Mode,* Reading, Mass.: Addison-Wesley, 1982.

CHAPTER TWELVE

COMMUNICATING WITH THE PUBLIC: THE SPEAKERS' BUREAU

Public communication in business is often left to public relations or public affairs departments. Businesses contract much of their public communication to advertising and public relations firms, a system that often seems to work effectively. But even with special departments and agencies to get the message to the public, communicating is every business person's responsibility.

Today, business often suffers from what Burns Roper refers to as the "tarnished image." He suggests that "the American public was once inclined to believe what it was told by authorities, even when what it was told was lies. In recent years, the American public has reached the point where it is inclined to disbelieve what it is told by authorities, even when what it is told is true."[1] There are, perhaps, many ways to polish the image of business, but to do a thorough job can take much time and effort. In this chapter, we focus on a practical way to solve this problem, regardless of the business or the particular company involved. We build on the concepts and ideas in the previous chapters. The concepts and principles for presentational speaking can be applied to the public relations efforts of a speakers' bureau, a dialog encounter, or a similar channel within a business. No matter what its size, every business must attract a degree of support from the public, and speakers' bureaus have a proven record for success in communicating with the public.

THE IMAGE A BUSINESS CREATES

The degree of attraction a business has with its public depends on the image it creates with its audience. Ascertaining the public images of a business becomes important to a company because a positive image correlates highly with the acceptance of the product or service offered. One large department store has built its entire business on the construction and maintenance of a good image—"sell the company through effective public communication and the products will naturally sell," one high-level executive explains.

Scott Cutlip and Allen Center, top experts on public relations, remind us that image-building is a concept of proven utility to business and must be pursued with diligence.[2] An image is the summing up of how persons perceive and react to companies. The importance of a business image lies in the fact that, whether they wish for it or not, large businesses do affect their social environment and are themselves affected by the image they create in the public's mind. We believe this is true for small business as well. Because the images of large and small businesses are affected by *both* public relations and advertising, some discussion of this relationship to business seems warranted.

Some years ago, a man was offered a position as a public relations manager with a firm based in Chicago. During the initial interviewing period, he asked the advertising manager of the firm: "Harry, what do you see as the real difference between public relations and advertising?" "Money!" snapped Harry. "We clearly buy our space for advertising and we have complete control over what is projected and where, which is not true for our public relations effort. We buy time on radio and television; we buy space in the newspapers; we buy displays to put in stores; we spend a great deal of money on buying space."

L. Roy Blumenthal writes from a similar viewpoint:

> Advertising is the use of paid space or time for the presentation of a sales message . . . public relations rarely uses paid space. Instead, the practice of public relations is the use of all communications media for the promotion and furtherance, subtle and overt, of a commercial property or a cause without the use of paid space. Although these two uses of communications media are closely related and very often overlap each other in broad campaigns, their techniques are vastly different.[3]

The routine techniques of public relations include speeches, news conferences, media interviews, news releases, newsletters, and annual reports. The activity you may have the greatest opportunity to experience in public relations is preparing and presenting speeches. We are not suggesting that you are unlikely to work in the other areas of public relations, because you may become a public relations or advertising specialist. But, to polish the image of business as part of the total public relations effort today, companies are asking employees who have confidence and skill in speaking to tell the "company story." Whether one is an engineer, an accountant, a production supervisor, or an executive secretary, one can help to increase the credibility and profit in business with the public. A significant way you can use your communication competence and affect the image of business through communication is through a speakers' bureau.

We want to show you what a speakers' bureau is, how one is formed, promoted, and maintained. We provide you with ideas about the kind of speech used to communicate with the public. *Remember, all of the ideas about presentational speaking, especially persuasive presentations, technical presentations, and conference leadership are tools to sort through and use when communicating with the public as a company spokesperson.*

A RHETORICAL SITUATION IN BUSINESS

A rhetorical situation exists when a problem arises that invites a particular communication response. Rhetoric is communication strategically designed to elicit a particular response—and so most business communication is rhetorical. Rhetoric uses shared symbolic interaction; it is instrumental to the creation of change, and it offers the audience a number of alternatives. The need for business to be attractive and credible in the public eye creates a number of rhetorical situations that can be treated effectively with expository and persuasive speaking. Many companies have turned to the speakers' bureau to handle this important area of their public communication.

Before viewing the speakers' bureau as a forum for expository and persuasive speaking, think of a rhetorical situation as providing the basis for communicating with the public. Lloyd Bitzer explains that a rhetorical situation may be defined "as a complex of persons, events, objects, and relations presenting an actual or potential exigence which can be completely or partially removed if discourse introduced into the situation can so constrain human decision or action so as to bring about significant modification of the exigence."[4] There are, then, three major constituents the speaker can address: exigence, audience, and constraints.

Essentially, *exigence* is an imperfection marked by urgency. Let's look at one instance in our current way of life that seems marked by urgency, at least to some members of the business community—the plight of the full-service gas station. As the proliferation of the self-service gas station continues, the full-service gas station disappears. Independent dealers and their Independent Dealers Association have become alarmed at the growing threat to full-service garages. They can sit quietly by, expecting the worst and hoping for the best, or they can do something, such as initiating an extensive campaign to encourage the public to want and demand full-service stations. As people try to fight inflation by turning to lower-priced fuel through self-service, oil companies increase the number of self-service stations. Those stations with attendants trained in auto repair begin to be abandoned.

In a rhetorical situation *audience* is a term that refers to those persons (listeners or readers) who can be influenced and who can provide the desired response to the message. For example, imagine the case of a county mental-health organization, expanding to meet the needs of a rising middle-class community. A number of community leaders and some groups in this upper-middle class city oppose the construction of a new clinic in the heart of their city. The city has tough zoning restrictions, and there is an obvious bias against the treatment of disturbed citizens "right downtown." The mental-health organization identifies its opposition and its supporters. Setting up a speakers' bureau and preparing fully for each audience, the organization takes its message to opponents and to supporters. Their speakers' words are further disseminated through the media and by word of mouth. An atmosphere is created in the city that gives the mental-health organization enough support to construct a new clinic exactly where it had been originally planned. The speakers have identified, analyzed, and adapted to their audiences effectively!

The spokespersons for the mental-health clinic discover, as they work their way around the communities, that discourse and response to it are shaped by the third constituent of a rhetorical situation—*constraints.* Constraints are persons, events, objects, and relations that are part of the situation simply because they have the power to defer the decision and action needed to modify the exigence. Let us look at another example—a funeral directors' association. The association decides it is necessary to lift the profile of the funeral business in all of the communities around the state. Apparently, public attitudes and beliefs have been swayed by television programs and books depicting the funeral business as insensitive and greedy. Both the reluctance of individual directors to encounter the public directly and a growing public bias against funeral directors have contributed the constraints the association faces in launching a speaking campaign. In addition, audiences often find themselves in a double-bind. On the one hand, many are interested in exploring the experiences of death and grief; and on the other hand, the discomfort caused by openly dealing with these subjects is inhibiting.

The standard sources of constraints are attitudes, beliefs, documents, facts, traditions, images, interests, motives, and the like. The funeral directors in our example have not previously undertaken a large unified public campaign, and they lack experience in speaking to the public. The public is reluctant, at first, to take the association's efforts seriously. As we can see, these constraints originate partly within the business, partly within the public opinion. As a business enters into a situation armed with a serious speaking program, five constituents affect the outcome—the business, the speaker, the exigence, the audience, and the constraints. An effective way to respond to a rhetorical situation is to participate in a carefully planned and managed speakers' bureau.

Currently, the public seems stung and strained by inflation, skeptical because of attempts by business and government to cover up questionable and illegal activities. But still people seem to want to learn about business, its motives, its problems, its goals, and its profits. Many businesses are sensitive to public desire. They want to provide information to create healthy understanding and good will. This is often accomplished through the use of company spokespersons.

Each of you may have an opportunity to communicate with the public through a speakers' bureau. And each of you will undoubtedly hear business communicators speak in public. Therefore, we want you to be able to identify rhetorical situations and be able to respond as an effective speaker and critical listener.

THE SPEAKERS' BUREAU

"How can a company improve its corporate image?" is a question posed on one industry's announcement to its management. Beneath the boldly printed question, the assistant vice-president of public affairs provides an answer: "We think one very helpful way is to establish a Company Speakers' Bureau and take our message to the people. So that's what we are doing. No project like this can be put together without the help of its management—so we are asking for your help. We are hoping that you will select a few of your most capable employees who are willing to be speakers." At the close of this announcement the exclamation read, "We can make this Speakers' Bureau a viable tool for improving relations with people if we have your cooperation."

The value and potential for creating understanding and good will with the public by using a speakers' bureau is summarized in a study by Patricia Nichols.[5] She points to reasons for having a speakers' bureau by listing seven principles expressed by one of the organizations she examined. Summarized, the list tells us:

1. Business needs a favorable climate and there exists a strong need for creating popular understanding of what business does, how, and why.
2. An effective speech is one that reaches a great many people beyond the immediate physical audience.
3. The appearance of business speakers at community events can demonstrate vividly a company's desire to be a good neighbor.
4. The personnel are as important as a business's products or services, and speaking in public permits personnel to be seen, heard, and known.
5. Face-to-face contact with the public can create more friendship than written words, for there is something especially attractive about getting information directly from a pleasant person.
6. The community's feelings and thoughts can be learned and addressed through a question-and-answer period at each speaking engagement.
7. Speakers can bring stature, prestige, and attractiveness to their business through participation in a speakers' bureau.

The speakers' bureau is a direct and highly personal way of reaching the public and building positive relations. For it to be effective, certain precautions and a high level of commitment are necessary for everyone involved with the formation and maintenance of the bureau.

LAUNCHING A SPEAKERS' BUREAU

You may work for a business that has a successful bureau or you may join an organization that needs a successful set of speakers but has made no effort to establish one. Or there may be no speakers' bureau but some genuine talk about forming one. While there are a great many speakers' bureaus in existence today in American business life, there are still plenty of companies that have yet to use this channel for communicating with the public.

One large industry recently decided the time had come to quit talking about establishing a bureau and set one up. Several high-level exectuives carefully examined the firm's organizational system to determine who should take the full responsibililty for establishing the bureau. The person chosen for the assignment was a manager, Jane, who was in charge of the Special Projects Division of the Public Affairs Department. She was given the task of getting real plans for a speakers' bureau on the drawing boards. Having no special training for this assignment and no frame of reference, she decided her best bet was to create a useful model and use it as a guide. A *key point to keep in minds is that the person in charge* (whether in public relations or consumer affairs or some other department in a business organization) *has to be self-motivating, highly responsible, and very much interested in public communication in the face-to-face setting.*

A model for the speakers' bureau.   The special-programs director followed two major approaches in the creation of the model we display in Figure 12-1. First, she found seven speakers' bureaus in three cities and spoke at length with those in charge of them, as well as with several speakers from each organization. Second, she located several communication experts at local colleges and a nearby university and spoke with them at length. Using her notes, she created her model and, from it, developed a highly effective speakers' bureau.

From the onset, a speakers' bureau must have top management's total support, and it must be assigned to a carefully chosen department, division, or section. One person, who, like Jane, has support from an advisory committee, should be appointed as director and coordinator of the bureau. This person must obtain a budget that reflects the strong support of the management team. He or she must recruit speakers, set up training programs, and work with advertising personnel to promote the bureau. Then there is the job to fill requests for speakers, and evaluate the speakers' efforts. There is a great deal to do in running an effective speakers' bureau. We have seen several organizations spend considerable time and energy forming and training a bureau, only to fall down by not using the speakers effectively.

One bureau we observed began by recruiting quite selectively the most self-motivated persons available in a business organization. These people were told they would receive high-quality instruction in public speaking on the company's time. A five-week course was designed by a professor of communication, specifically

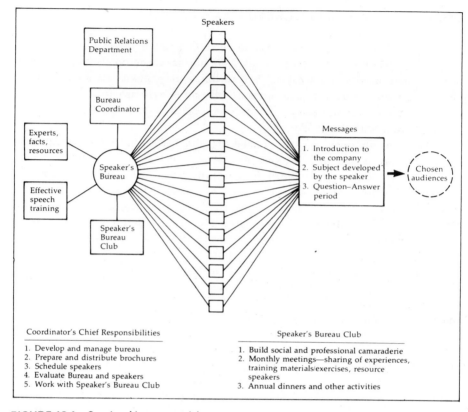

FIGURE 12-1   Speakers' bureau model.

shaped for the personnel of this firm. Forty-five persons applied for a place in the bureau, and fifteen were selected for the first training course. The course of instruction was similar to an advanced course in public speaking at the university. The class met for two hours twice a week, over a five-week period. The firm purchased color videotape equipment and refurbished a room specifically for the use of training and for practice sessions conducted by the bureau. A graduation ceremony was held at the end of the course, and a speakers' bureau club was formed to bring the fifteen together at least once a month to share experiences and enjoy camaraderie.

While this course was under way, the director of the bureau began the important task of designing a brochure to be mailed to those persons in the community who were most likely to request a speaker. With names from a number of sources, ranging from customer lists to newspapers to civic organizations, an initial mailing list was generated.

Announcement by mail—an effective introduction to the speakers' bureau.
One of the most effective ways to let the public know that business speakers are available is by distributing a simple, attractive brochure announcing the speakers'

bureau and the topics and programs available. This brochure should reach all the local service clubs, churches, schools, professional clubs and associations, and community action groups.

An attractive, easy-to-read mailer must be prepared in a format and style mirroring the business it represents. For example, one large grocery chain uses a miniature grocery bag to announce the availability of its speakers: "Groceries are our bag!" is the declaration broadly printed across the top front of the bag. The name, address, and telephone number of the coordinator is provided beneath the declaration, with the advice: "On the reverse side of this bag are a number of topics we can provide speakers to address . . . or given enough time we can tailor a program for you. These presentations are free to your organization and no commercial message is needed."

A brochure's attractiveness depends not only on design, color, and the quality of paper used, but on the titles of the speeches as well. If you shop for a book or a movie, you are often attracted by a title that is brief, provocative, and pertinent. We recently examined the titles of speeches offered by a speakers' bureau sponsored by a private counseling center. Here are some of the titles we found. How do you react to them?

1.   Psychological Intervention in Crisis Situations
2.   Crisis Points in Marriage—How They Start and What To Do About Them
3.   Why Should Anyone Be Moral?
4.   Born Again—Religion or Psychotherapy or Both?

FIGURE 12-2   Organizations find it necessary to create images and communicate them to specific publics.

5. Who Are You?—Facing Yourself Daily
6. Sex, Money, and Other Causes of Problems in Marriage
7. No Person is an Island—The Case for Group Therapy

We also came across a mailer sent out by a group of physicians representing several private clinics. This brochure mixed titles with topics in a lengthy list filling a page. Here we give nine and ask you to think about them. Does the list seem attractive to you?

1. Allergic Diseases in Children
2. Immunizations
3. A Surgeon's Approach to the Seriously Injured
4. Diabetes Mellitus
5. When To Call the Doctor
6. Heart Attack
7. Breast Lumps and Tumors
8. Cardiopulmonary Resuscitation
9. Psychiatric Diagnosis—What Can It Mean?

Finally, we share with you some information from a pamphlet mailed throughout the service area of a huge electric utility corporation. At the top of the brochure we found the following expression, underscoring the importance of communicating with the public: "Never before in the history of the electric utilities has there been a more demanding need to communicate with customers on a variety of subjects. For this reason we are pleased to offer this selection of programs to meet these needs as a public service."

Energy Decisions
Now is the time for utilities to examine their priorities for the uses of existing fuel sources and direct research into areas promising more abundant energy. A good overview of what is going on in the electric utility business today.

Pricing Electricity in Today's Economy
A basic explanation of the problems facing utilities as a result of rate-making. The speaker will look at the alternatives of peak load pricing, lifeline rates, summer peak load, summer-winter rate differential, and others, then answer any questions on the subject of rates.

The brochure describes four other speeches, four films, and two presentations available by special arrangements. The two presentations are described below.

How Utilities Use the Computer Today
A survey of the roles performed by computers . . . the new functions being developed and some of the possibilities for future expansion.

Residential Landscape Planning
Our company horticulturist will be available upon special request to talk on the following topics: foundation planting, privacy planting, flower gardening, home lawn management, and shrub and tree pruning.

The brochure concludes by making it easy to schedule a speech, film, or special program. The telephone numbers of eight offices in the service area are listed. All the brochures we have described are the size of long mailing envelopes. Each can easily fit into a coat pocket or handbag for quick reference.

Attracting audiences to obtain the service of a speakers' bureau is also accomplished through other standard forms of advertising: newspaper advertisement, radio announcements, and television spots. Perhaps the best time to advertise most frequently is late summer and early autumn, when most program chairpersons for clubs and organizations are busy planning programs for the year. Newspaper ads seem to create most attention when they are located on financial pages and in social sections. To avoid ads being buried among others a business ought to purchase space on Thursday or Sunday, when advertising is usually heaviest. One business that reported success in getting audiences purchased small notices placed on a half dozen pages. It bought space once a week for several weeks. Readers could not avoid noticing the little announcements.

A key source for making the public aware of the speaker's bureau is the use of a city's Chamber of Commerce services. Most chambers have a list of all of the clubs and social organizations in the community. Some even have a mailing list that contains names of club officers, frequently including the name of the program chairperson. This is a most valuable resource for making contacts through a speakers' bureau bulletin.

Another valuable source is to make speakers' bureau bulletins available to public school administrations and higher education institutions. Many teachers are seeking guest speakers for their classes. Business organizations have much to gain in public relations with these rich resources, but even greater value for future recruitment purposes when they work with high-school and college students in the classroom setting.

WHO USUALLY SPEAKS FOR BUSINESS?

We explained earlier how Jane recruited the speakers for the bureau she established, and the method she used is quite common. A speakers' bureau should boast a membership of highly competent, motivated, and dynamic speakers. Some businesses limit their company spokespersons to high-level executives, while other choose mainly from middle-management positions. Other businesses use a combination of both. A strong point about choosing speakers is made by James Durgan, of the St. Regis Paper Company: "Instead of using professional speakers, or even our own public relations department to deliver the message, we decided the best way to get across the St. Regis pollution control story was to let our own people in the mill and other operations tell it for us."[6]

Some companies, Patricia Nichols tells us, have "management only" speakers' bureaus because of management's anxiety about the misinterpretation of company policy and activities by lower-level employees. However, she explains, "Most companies like Kaiser Aluminum, . . . Alcoa, St. Regis, Eaton Corporation, and others have expanded their bureaus to include middle and lower level positions." Nichols points to one company that used both professional speakers and speakers from various employee levels: "Three full time speakers were selected and trained to speak to company employees, environmental and adversary groups, university and college groups, appear on television and radio programs, and train and coach other speakers. Then a speaker's task force of eighteen specially selected employees were trained to do all of the above with the exception of media appearances and the training." Besides this, Nichols explains, a general speakers' bureau of forty full-time employees was formed to speak to service groups and high-school audiences. Whether a complex bureau with several major speaking components is used, or several people are able and willing to speak upon request, a responsible business ought to be prepared without hesitation to provide speakers when asked to so.[7]

THE BUSINESS SPEECH
AND CHOSEN AUDIENCES

Many businesses prepare speeches to be delivered by spokespersons for the company. We argue that employees should prepare their own speeches. The message is to be based upon accurate facts and current policy made available through information provided by the business. Large business, or course, have corporate speechwriters, and these persons can serve important functions within their companies. You may find yourself someday working as a speechwriter, drafting messages to be edited, polished, and delivered by executives. However, the business speech can be a highly creative individual product, which is a reflection of a *person* as well as some facet of a *business.* We believe that each person in a speakers' bureau can and should prepare her or his message.

A business firm may decide what topics should be available to public audiences, and high-level executives can serve as gatekeepers to screen and check messages. Speech writers and researchers can prepare position papers and fact sheets to be used by speakers who write their own individual messages. For speeches to be delivered by members of the speakers' bureau, one business reviewed each speaker's outline. But the business speaker, unlike the actor or actress who is used to working with the words of others, is likely to feel most comfortable and confident delivering his or her own words.

A communication professor recently served a large business as an external consultant to train members of a growing speakers' bureau. Several executives decided it would be in the best interest of the company, as well as the speakers, if three speeches were prepared by professional writers. These speeches were to be used by the new members of the speaker's bureau. The consultant argued strongly against his position. Finally, he invited the executives to view the speakers in action, both on videotape and as they worked with their student audiences. He claimed, "What you will see that is most important is nice people, not polished orators, but nice people representing your company to the best of their ability. And when their audiences have long since left the speaking occasion, they will not remember a lot of the facts and figures presented, but they will remember whether the speaker they heard was an honest, genuine, and friendly person who had something personal and important to say about this business." In this case, the executives watched and listened to the speakers quite carefully. They ruled that each could prepare her or his own speech, and deliver it after it had been reviewed for accuracy and consistency.

There is a useful way in which information drafted by business writers and individuals in the speakers' bureau can be combined for effective public presentations. The company inserts into the introduction of the message a standard message about the company followed by the speaker's core idea and detailed information. This approach is illustrated in Box 12-1.

BOX 12-1   COMBINATION OF COMPANY'S AND SPEAKER'S MESSAGES

Creator	Part of Speech	Time
The company's writer	Opening remarks of the speakers	2 mins.
	Prepared remarks about the company	5 mins.
The speaker	Body of the speech—core idea and detail	25 mins.
	Conclusion—summary and closure	3 mins.
Total time: 30 minutes plus 15 minutes for a question-and-answer period		

A business frequently prefers to prepare speeches to be delivered by company spokespersons for three reasons: Business management has more confidence in what is to be said if it has complete control over the selection of words and ideas; business management feels the company should focus on selected topics, which should be treated exactly alike, regardless of which person goes out to speak for the company; and business management assumes that employees spend considerable time trying to construct speeches, time to be used in other responsibilities. While there is sense in these reasons, again, the average business speaker is more likely to feel comfortable and to project naturally if the speech is one he or she has written.

The public that becomes the immediate audience for business speakers can range from general civic groups to highly visible community organizations usually given significant press coverage. You could find yourself speaking to a variety of different audiences and go out once or twice weekly. On the other hand, you could also find yourself in a public-communication program that is highly selective in its audiences. One public information officer of a large business enterprise proclaimed to a group of executives trained in public speaking: "We won't speak to everyone who makes a request. We are going to be highly selective and speak to important audiences who are most likely to get good publicity." In either case, communicating with the public by speaking up for business is an important challenge for the business communicator. Try to be an active and effective public speaker. If there is a speakers' bureau where you become employed, try to join it; if there is not a speakers' bureau, try to establish one. The speakers' bureau can be a highly effective instrument to help create a favorable image of business, especially in times when the image of business seems tarnished.

THE DIALOG

The dialog is another method of communicating with the public and one that several business organizations have found to be quite successful. Armco, Inc., a large corporation that produces steel products, has used the dialog successfully for a number of years.

The dialog format does require that the speaker, or discussion leader, have some training. It is based on the principle that not all community groups wish to be spoken to, but often spoken with. Such discussions, which are designed around a conference-type setting, do require careful planning. When this planning is completed properly, the results of such a communication effort are most positive.

Business organizations that use the dialog concept train their employees in public speaking skills, but they place the focus of the training on conference-leadership skills. The thinking is that most managers, if successful on the job with their communication skills in conference settings, can also use these skills in a public relations capacity. These speaker-leaders must be able to act as group facilitators. As facilitators, it is their responsibility to get the dialog started with the host group, and then to encourage all members of this group to speak out.

There is great value in this dialog encounter. The public relations concept works as an interactive process. As in the speakers' bureau, the business organization brings information to the public, but the dialog also brings valuable communication back to the business organization from the public through the dialog leader.

Interactive public relations.   The dialog as a public relations tool became popular in the mid 1960s, when there was a lot of unrest in many segments of our society. Pollution, racial unrest, quality of public education, forms of censorship, and the ethics of an undeclared war were topics of real concern to society. All of these topics related to the business world. Very quickly, many business organizatins began to realize that society wanted to know what large corporations were doing about pollution. What were their policies on racial hiring practices? What was their contribution to public and higher education? Censorship and openness of public relations on radio and television were of grave concern. Many people wanted to know how businesses were contributing (or not contributing) to the war effort, or if veterans were being treated fairly in hiring and rehiring policies.

This was not an easy time for many large corporations. They quickly realized that the public wanted to communicate, not just listen. In the best interest of public relations, the dialog concept came into being. At first, it was tried on college campuses, a major source of unrest, but soon it spread to community groups. Company representatives, as speaker-facilitators, worked hard to take information to the public, but also attempted to collect ideas, attitudes, and beliefs from the public to take back to their organizations for study and consideration.

The immediate reaction from the public was a favorable one. "These business organizations really want to hear me out. They are concerned about what I think." This positiveness was most valuable for the growth and development of public relations.

A public relations communication process. The process of a dialog operates around the basic format as described in Box 12-2.

BOX 12-2   *THE DIALOG PROCESS*

A. Opening Remarks by Speaker (5 to 7 minutes)
   1. introduce business organizations
   2. introduce purpose for coming
   3. introduce the subject as requested by the group
B. The Dialog Encounter (30 to 45 minutes—usually determined by the host group)
   1. speaker acts as a facilitator
   2. provides opportunity for all participants to talk
   3. keep very brief notes of the encounter
C. Dialog Reaction (5 to 7 minutes)
   1. speaker reacts to the dialog in an editorial fashion
   2. openness and honestry are necessary in remarks
D. The Dialog Forum
   1. questions are fielded from the participants
   2. questions are asked of the participants by the facilitator or one another
E. Closing
   1. thank the group for being invited and participating
   2. offer the opportunity for a future return engagement

The dialog requires the speaker to have public speaking skills, question-and-answer skills, and especially conference-leadership skills. For the novice after completing some formal training, it is better to go out with the experienced person initially.

The dialog, when used appropriately, can be one of the most effective tools for communicating with the public.

PUBLICIZING THE DIALOG

Like the speakers' bureau, the dialog must be planned for an organized so that the public understands its purpose and values.

Most companies put out a dialog brochure. This publication explains the format, the purposes, and goals of such of such an activity, and usually has a section on the involvement of the requesting group.

A sample format might look like the one in Box 12-3, which was taken from an organization producing plastic products.

BOX 12-3   THE DIALOG

Why? This an opportunity for *you* to talk to us, to tell us how you feel about a particular subject. It is also your opportunity to ask us questions about this subject.

How? Our speaker, who has special interest in the topic that your group is currently concerned with, will come to your meeting and dialog with you informally.

When? You can call our Public Relations Representative at Plastics Diversified, 340 Weldon Road, Cincinnati, Ohio (513) 356-7859 to discuss your interests in such a program.

Where? We will come to your meeting location on a date that we can mutually schedule at *no* cost to your organization.

Subject	Dialog Leader	Time	Suggested Number of Participants
Inflation Tips for Cincinnati	Mel Belmore	90 mins.	12 to 18
Role of Plastic in the Future	Mary Taylor	60 mins.	15 to 20
Role of Women in Plastic Industry	Kathy Lenn	1-2 hrs.	12 to 16 (mixed group suggested)

Morning, afternoon, or evening programs can be planned if requests are sought 8 to 10 weeks in advance. Enclosed is a suggested program format, but the design of the program can be tailored to your group.

This sample copy was for a company starting out with the dialog as a public relations tool. Larger and more experienced companies can offer more diversified program formats on more topics of local community interest.

The dialog as a public relations tool is just now coming into its own. Large and small business organizations are recognizing the great value in this interactive communication with the local community or public at large. There is a great deal of room for expansion and development with this tool. For the business person who has highly developed and confident communications skills that he or she uses regularly on the job, the dialog will be a familiar activity. It will be a communication medium in which this successful business person is comfortable, but especially one in which such an individual can find great personal satisfaction and achievement.

A REVIEW OF KEY ISSUES

The concern of public relations is to communicate a positive image for the business organization to the local community or public at large.

The image of a business organization needs constant attention through its advertising and its public relations.
1. Advertising is the use of paid space.
2. Public relations is the use of all communication media for promotion without employing paid space or time.

Speaking from the lectern, persuasive presentations, technical presentations, and conference-leadership skills are all tools for communicating with the public.

The rhetorical situation in business is made up of the:
1. exigence—the problem facing the business organization as a member of the community at large
2. audience—the people concerned about the role of the business organization within their community
3. constraints—internal or external negative factors the business organization must, as a member of the community, deal with in a realistic way

The Speaker's Bureau offers seven valuable assets to the business organization:
1. informs the public about the organization's business
2. reaches the community at large
3. establishes a good-neighbor policy
4. personnel are as visible as its product
5. develops interpersonal relations with the public
6. receives feedback from the public
7. can bring stature and prestige to the organization

The Speakers' Bureau can be made available to the public in several ways:
1. publicized in an easy-to-read mailer
   a. showing colorful, creative planning and design
   b. introducing a variety of speaker topics
   c. containing the speech contents in preview

2. promoted through newspaper, radio, television
3. listed with the chamber of commerce
4. listed with public school and college administrations

The speaker's format should be thirty minutes of presentation followed by fifteen minutes of question-and-answer forum.

The dialog is based on principles of the conference and conference leadership, along with public-speaking skills.

The dialog has the special feature of interaction communication, from which the speaker-leader brings public opinions and ideas back to the business organization.

The dialog as a communication process contains:
1. the speaker's formal opening
2. a dialog encounter
3. a dialog reaction
4. a dialog forum
5. a formal closing

The dialog must be publicized with a carefully planned brochure that explains the process, the purpose, the format, and the values of such an interaction.

EXPERIENCING EXPERIENCES

Public relations work is a unique type of communication activity. Such work provides the individual with the challenge to use a wide variety of skills. It demands synthesis of all of the skills used in public speaking, persuasive speaking, technical presentations, conference participation, conference leadership, and the question-and-answer session.

The person who chooses to work in public relations in a business organization must regularly practice as well as know these skills. He or she must be able to pull these skills together and use them simulaneously in many situations. The key to success for working in such a challenging field is practical experience. You have already become aware of the situational factors involved in any communication act. You have been aware of the importance of analyzing these factors before attempting to plan or perform the communication. Public relations work requires an even greater in-depth analysis of these situational factors. Furthermore, it requires knoweldgeable flexibility in using the various communication skills in such a composite situation.

To prepare for such professional demands, you need to have experience and opportunities to put your skills to work. Professional public relations people stress the importance of experience because they know its significance in their career success. The following activities have been designed to provide a variety of experience for just this very reason. As you do this set of activities, try to adapt them to your community, or to some particular business organization in your local community. This will make these experiences of greater value to you.

ACTIVITY 1: The Speakers' Bureau Brochure

During this course, you and your classmates have given a number of speeches on a variety of topics. As a group, go back through these speeches and select the ten best. As a group design a brochure featuring these ten speakers and speeches. The brochures should include the following items:

1. brief synopsis of each of the ten speeches
2. brief comment on each speaker
3. the performing time for the speech
4. which speeches will be followed by a question-and-answer forum
5. which speeches will use visuals
6. the dates and times the speakers will be available
7. a cover that is attractive
8. a short paragraph stating your philosophy for providing such a service

Make up a mailing list and plan some method for distributing the brochure to the individuals on the list. Once the brochure has been laid out, print it up and distribute it. Have your classmate speakers go out in groups of two. One should be the speaker and the other should be a witness to the speaking engagement. The student who witnesses the performance should prepare a small oral report for the class, describing the situation and evaluating the communication event. This could be a good opportunity for you and your classmates to visit other classes on campus and discuss business communication as a professional career, or to talk to some of your local service clubs.

ACTIVITY 2: The Dialog Experiences

As a class, plan a dialog that focuses on several aspects of business communication as a professional career. You might wish to consider such topics as:

Business Communication in Our Community
The Role of Women in the Business World
The Role of the College Undergraduate in the Business World
The Need for Written Communication Skills in Business
Management Opportunities in Our Community
Interviewing for a Business Position in Our Community

Prepare a dialog brochure that includes the following:

1. attractive cover
2. a page of philosophy for providing a dialog activity on your campus
3. a page that lays out your dialog format

4. a page listing your themes and a short paragraph explaining each one
5. a list of classmates to operate each dialog (best to do it in pairs)
6. a list of the students available for each dialog theme
7. a list of dates, times, and running time for each dialog

When this brochure is prepared, send it to all the faculty on campus and start booking engagements. When the dialog partners meet with a group, two other members of class should go along so that they can come back to the class and report their observations of the dialog activity.

EXERCISES

1. Invite a professional public relations person to your class to speak about his or her job responsibilities. Students should preplan questions to ask this individual.

2. Students should go to all of the business organizations in the community and ask for any public relations material that is available. All of this material should be brought into class and be studied as a composite in an effort to determine the amount of public relations going on in your local community.

3. Have the class divide into groups of five to form speakers' bureaus. Each group should have at least one class period to speak to a simulated community audience. Students should choose the organization they are to represent, and each member of the group should contribute significantly to his or her bureau's presentation.

4. Look in all of the local classified ads and bring to class all of the public relations jobs advertised. Compare the various job requirements, work experience demands, and salaries offered by the business organizations in your community.

NOTES

1. Burns Roper, "The Tarnished Image of Business." *Public Relations Quarterly,* Summer 1977, p. 12.
2. Scott Cutlip and Allen H. Center, *Effective Public Relations,* 7th ed. Englewood Cliffs, N.J.: Prentice-Hall, p. 42.
3. L. Roy Blumenthal, *The Practice of Public Relations.* New York: Macmillan, 1972, p. 3.
4. Lloyd Bitzer, "The Rhetorical Situation." *Philosophy and Rhetoric,* Vol. 1 (1968), pp. 1-14.
5. Patricia Ann Nichols, "A Communication Study of Corporate Image and The Columbus and Southern Ohio Electric Company Speaker's Bureau," unpublished master's thesis, Ohio State University, 1978.
6. Nichols, p. 25.
7. Nichols, p. 25.

CHAPTER THIRTEEN

PREPARING
FOR A
PROFESSIONAL CAREER

Planning and structuring one's preparation for a career is a very serious activity. This process involves extensive use of the four basic communication skills: speaking, listening, reading, and writing. We have to first understand the process and then use these four skills to adapt it to our particular situation.

All of us have some kind of a personal philosophy that we use as our measuring stick when we plan our future. Whether this philosophy includes working to live or living to do some kind of work, searching for the right career is important for us all. Your search for this career in the right environment should be worth as much effort as you have put into your schooling. Reflect on the number of classes you have attended, the teachers you have studied with, and the many, many term projects or papers you have written. Surely you will come to the conclusion that career preparation work ought to be worth as much effort as necessary to make use of all your investment in learning.

Planning a career is not the simplest of tasks, and possibly at this point in your life, the whole subject of career preparation seems distant. We believe that whether you are starting, mid-way through, or on the last lap of your formal education, it is not too early to start preparing for your career.

The process that we are going to deal with in this chapter may not be the ideal method for preparing yourself for a future career. Like any process based on the use of specific skills, the steps presented here will need to be adapted to your

FIGURE 13-1   Interviews, site visits, and tours give the college student beginning a career or job search a large choice of options.

personal situation. How you use this process will, in part, depend on how well you are able to use your four communication skills of reading, writing, speaking, and listening. You can read this chapter and decide to consult a professional for additional career counselling, but when it comes down to the bottom line, you have to plan for your own career. It will be your responsibility to apply the guidelines and the suggested process to your personal goals and ambitions as they develop and change during your formal education. We assume that, at the moment, the business field is of major interest to you.

The career preparation for the person who is striving to enter into a professional field of business should include the following steps:

1. soul- and-goal searching
2. resume preparation
3. search for job information
4. job application
5. job interview

THE SOUL- AND GOAL-SEARCHING STEP

In order to deal with the first obvious question, "Where do I begin?" we believe that personal awareness is the starting point. This means that you have to begin with some soul-searching and then set goals for yourself. A good way to become aware of yourself is to do a personal inventory. Evaluate your assets and liabilities. Once you have done this, setting some specific goals will not be an impossible task. In order to assist you with this self-inventory technique, we provide the list of questions in Box 13-1. Give them serious thought, and then write the answers in clear statements on a sheet of paper so that you can assess them.

BOX 13-1   *GOAL-SEARCHING QUESTIONS*[1]

What are my real interests in life?
What kinds of people do I like to be around?
Do I have any special talents or abilities?
What kind of environment do I wish to live in?
Does my physical condition limit me in any way?
What does my education qualify me for?
What kind of work environment do I want?
What kind of jobs have I had in the past?
What did I like best about these jobs?
What did I like least about these jobs?
What kind of career opportunities do I want to consider?

As you look at your responses to the questions in Box 13-1, can you draw any conclusions? From this informal and brief soul-searching, can you draw any conclusions about a future career? At this point, you should be ready to establish some career-search goals. Look at these goals as you would an annual New Year's resolution list. This is your career-goal resolution list. Write these goals on paper. Put down a realistic date as your deadline to have achieved these goals. Make it practical, and allow yourself enough time. It might follow a format similar to the one in Box 13-2.

BOX 13-2   *CAREER-GOAL RESOLUTION LIST*

I, Jamie Dell, have decided that I want to look into business law as a possible career, and I am going to complete this list of goals by December 15, 1984:

1. I am going to the school library and look up material on business-law career possibilities.
2. I am going to talk to my college advisor and placement-office representatives.
3. I am going to write the local Chamber of Commerce for information about legal business careers in this community.
4. I am going to ask Mary Costaine if she thinks there would be time for me to talk to her brother when he comes home from school at Thanksgiving.
5. I am going to call a lawyer in the yellow pages to see if I can get a half-hour interview to ask questions.
6. I am going to write the federal government for career information regarding business law as a career.
7. I am going to call the local Bar Association to see if they have any free literature available.

As you compose your list, be realistic and establish a time frame that is reasonable and practical for your life style. Allowing enough time without procrastinating requires serious planning. Contrary to the popular slogan, opportunity does not knock at everyone's door.

While you are working on your career-goals resolution list, you can start work on the next step.

THE RESUME PREPARATION STEP

Like the soul- and goal-searching step, resume planning involves a reasonable time allowance. There are many types of professional agencies and placement services that will for a nominal fee put together a formal resume for you, but this is not as valuable to you as mailing your own resume. We contend that if you put your own resume together, you will do so with a very practical interest. You will put the personal element into it that an agency cannot, because no agency knows you the way you know yourself. Second, as you put the resume together, you will have a chance to get to know yourself even better. You may be pleasantly surprised to find out just what a talented person you are. You might realize some unique things about yourself that may have, until now, gone unnoticed.

A resume can be an abbreviated review of your education, your activities, job experiences, and reflected professional goals. (A resume that gives this information follows a biographical or chronological style.) This appears to be a lot of information to provide when you are told to keep it brief. You have seen movies about the life of a famous person created in well-documented detail. If necessary, a film editor could take such a two-hour movie, cut out the individual frames and end up with a series of color slides with the essence of vital information. A resume should attempt to do the same task. Employers do not have time to read lengthy resumes. Therefore, as you communicate information about yourself, you must be selective, yet accurate with the information. You are attempting to present a true, positive picture of who you are and what you are seeking to do in your career development. There are certain items that should be included in all resumes as you create your professional image. These basic items of information are provided in Box 13-3 in a format that you may want to consider as a model for designing your own resume. See Figures 13-2 and 13-3 for samples of this resume style.

In addition to this list of required items, we offer you a list of important but optional items (see Box 13-4). These items are only necessary in certain professional areas, ones that would apply for specially defined careers. We present these to you in a format that you may want to consider as you work on your resume design.

The resume can take a more function-oriented organization than is used in the biographical format just discussed. The functional resume focuses on the individual's skills, abilities, and life learning experiences. Preparing a resume of this type requires very careful planning of headings, such as "Communication Skills,"

BOX 13-3   SAMPLE RESUME FORM

RESUME

Full Name _____ Birthdate _____

Permanent Address _____
Temporary
Address _____ (college address if sending these out while at school) _____

Telephone: _____ (current home and school or business) _____

Health Status: _____ Military Status: _____ Marital Status: _____

Education: (or any formal training granting a certificate of completion)
   List institutions in reverse chronological order (most recent first)
   Institution, location, degree, and major area
   Date of graduation (year sufficient)

Previous Job Experience: (use reverse chronological order)
   Business name   Job title or description   Period of time held

List of References:
   Name   Relationship   Years known   Current address and phone
   (3 or 4 are quite adequate: 2 performance references; 1 or more character
   references)

Professional Goal Statement:
   One short and well-stated paragraph describing the career goals and ambitions that you would like to achieve during your lifetime. Keep this statement specific and avoid general comments that really don't say anything.
   Attempt to reflect some positive quality about your personality that you
   believe is one of your strongest assets.

"Supervisory Skills," "Sales Management Skills"; or the resume can provide the job title and then list the skills exercised while performing it. The functional resume is mostly for the individual who comes to a new job with some previous work experience. New graduates with little or limited work experience will have trouble using the functional resume style.

Employers and recruiters will accept either resume style, but many complain that functional resumes are often wordy to read. The resume writer gets wordy describing the job and the skills. Figures 13-4a and 13-4b are examples of functional resumes. No resume should be longer than two typed pages. The resume should be attractively laid out and typed neatly and accurately. It should be easy to read. Consider the resume from the employers' point of view. By the time they have finished reading it, they should have an accurate picture of you. A well-prepared resume should inform the employer whether or not you would be a possible candidate for the job opening.

This format should use descriptive words to provide necessary information, but should be structured in general terms so that it can be sent to a variety of

```
                              RESUME

                                for

                        Mary Joan Rhinehart

Permanent Address:  234 North Bay Drive, Manteca, California 67577

Temporary Address:  178 Bevis Dorm, Ohio State University, Columbus, OH 4321(

Telephone:          (school) 614/422-4545        (home) 871/332-4877

Health:  Excellent  Marital Status:  Single      Birthday:  February 12, 1959

EDUCATION:

  B.S. Degree (in progress)  Political Science Major  Ohio State University
                             French Minor             Columbus, Ohio
    (tentative graduation:  June, 1980)

  Graduate                   College preparatory      North Bay H.S.
                             major                    Manteca, California

  2 years (9th & 10th)       private school           Rosegate Academy
                                                      Manteca, California

WORK EXPERIENCE:

  Office secretary      Pol-Sci Dept. (part-time now) Ohio State University

  McDonald's waitress   1978-79 (part time)           Columbus, Ohio

  Playground aid        1977,78 (summers)             Manteca, California

REFERENCES:

  Martin Dolman,        academic advisor             35 Allen Hall, O.S.U.
     Professor          phone:  614/422/2234          132 17th St.
                                                      Columbus, Ohio 43201

  James Blumb           McDonald manager              1869 N. High Street
                        phone:  614/294-5565          Columbus, Ohio 43201

  Sue Angle             City Park Director            43 Elmo Park
                        phone:  871/334-5823          Manteca, Calif. 67577
```

FIGURE 13-2   Sample resume: biographical style.

CAREER GOAL:

Working with people is important to me and my job experience has

reinforced this belief. I have been interested in working in

government since I was the representative from our high school

to the state student government clinic in my senior year. My

interest has grown with my college education, and at this time

I feel I would like to start my working career in local govern-

ment work with the opportunity at some future date to work on a

masters in a specific area of local government administration.

HONORS, AWARDS:

Poli-Sci Club, President	Ohio State Club	1978-1979
Akerman Memorial Honor	Ohio State University	June, 1979
Voice of Democracy	Manteca City Winner	April, 1976
Girl's State Representative	North Bay High School	March, 1976

FIGURE 13-2 (cont.)

BOX 13-4 OPTIONAL RESUME ITEMS

Honors, Awards, Trophies (list these in reverse chronological order):
Award title (description optional)   Granting agent   Date received

Community Service (list in reverse chronological order):
Service description   Agency   Date completed

Professional Publications (list in reverse chronological order):
Title   Publisher   Date

Professional Memberships:
Organization name   Professional affiliation   Years member

Professional Workshops, Conferences (list in reverse chronological order):
Workshop title   Participation description   Location, date

Professional Consulting Experience (List in reverse chronological order),
Organization served   Description of consulting capacity   Date
(it is optional to include the location of the organization)

Hobbies, Interests, Activities:
Description   Location   Time involved   Date
Note: These should be listed sparingly and only in meaningful situations.

```
Marion G. Carroll       127 Longfellow Drive, Tiffin, Ohio 44883

Phone:  419/239-4675 (home)      Birth: 9/4/57      Health: good

Marital Status:  engaged

Education

Graduate, 1979      Tera Technical Institute      Fremont, Ohio 44812
                    2 yr. degree in Electro-
                    Automotive Repairman

Graduate, 1974      Columbia High School          Clay St., Tiffin, Ohio 44883

Work Experience

Garage Mechanic     part-time, 1973-75            Dell's Station, Rt. 53
                                                  Tiffin, Ohio 44883

Dish Washer         part-time, 1970-73            Howard Johnson's
                                                  Perry St., Tiffin, Ohio

References

Ray Ashbury         Electronics Instructor        Tera Technical Institute
                                                  Fremont, Ohio

Ellen Craft         Owner, Dell's Station         Tiffin, Ohio 44883
                                                  phone: 419/239-2232

Jay Cordon          Night Manager                 Howard Johnson's
                                                  Tiffin, Ohio 44883

Awards, Honors

Finch Electronics Honor    Tera Technical Institute    1979

Best Player, basketball    Columbia High School        1974

Career Ambition
```

   I would like to work as an auto electrician for some large company like General Motors that will give me a variety of experiences working with new model cars. I have had two years of experience and found ample opportunity to apply my theory coursework. I would like to go back to school at some future date after I am married and have purchased a house. I would like to continue to live in the northern part of Ohio near my family and my fiancee's family.

FIGURE 13-3   Sample resume: biographical style.

```
                                VITA

Jill McCarty                              Phone: 513/466-4598
23 Hammel Lane                            Birth: June 3, 1953
Dayton, Ohio  45402                       Married--2 children

Education:    Part-time graduate student, Wright State University, Dayton, OH
              Applied Behavioral Science
              B.A. University of Dayton, 1978.  Sociology major/Speech minor

Work Experience:
              Substitute teacher, Bishop Carroll High School, 1979-1982.
              Taught sociology and speech.  Assisted with debate team and
              coached girls' volleyball.  Taught one full semester as substitute
              for teacher on sick leave.

              Rikes Department Store 1976-1979 (part time/full time)

              Worked as sales clerk in children's wear one full year.
              Supervised two other clerks.  Left full-time position to complete
              undergraduate degree and continued for seasonal help on part-time
              basis.

              Secretary for Darnell's Insurance Agency 1970-1975
              Typed, filed insurance claims and reports, took pictures of
              property and accident sites, operated copy machine and word-
              processing unit.

Personal Interests:
              Completing M.A. degree in applied behavioral science
              Tentative graduation:  June 1983

              Thesis topic:  Sociological Factors Affecting the Retraining of
              Unemployed Workers in the Automotive Industry

Career Objective:
              To research for support information in company heavily involved in
              employee retraining.  The long-range goal would be to manage a
              company-wide training department for a large corporation.

References:   Available on request
```

FIGURE 13-4a   Sample resume: functional style.

employers. You should not have to redesign the resume for each employer or organization you apply to.

Look at all of the sample resumes in this chapter. After you have read them, see if you can determine what type of people might write such resumes. If you were an employer, would you consider any of these people as possible candidates for employment? This is precisely what you will expect others to do after reading your resume.

```
                        Personal Data Sheet

                                for

                          David R. Jacobs
                          435 Lane Avenue
                          St. Guiles, Ohio


OBJECTIVE:   Seeking a management position in personnel work, with a focus
             on recruiting college graduates in technical fields

EDUCATION:   B.S., Ohio State University, 1983
             Business Administration major with personnel management focus
             and a related core of courses in computer technology

EXPERIENCE:  Technical Institute Laboratory, 1981-1983

             Part-time work while in college.  Assisted in Computer Department
             with program planning, operations, and client evaluations.  Used
             variety of computer languages.

             Ohio State University Undergraduate Library 1979-1981

             Worked circulation desk, supervised four employees, interviewed
             candidates, and hired part-time student help.  Worked in the stacks
             and on book repairs.

             Barney's Dairy Isle, 1977-1979

             Worked the grill, service counter, and cleaned the parking lot.
             Ordered supplies, totaled employee time cards, and trained five
             new employees.

INTERESTS:   Personal:  hiking, rock collecting, traveling
             Professional:  working with people and helping them to do their jobs
             in a satisfying manner

REFERENCES:  Dr. John Lane, 432 Raft Hall, Ohio State University 614/422-4532

             Mrs. Mary Stolt, OSU, Reference Library 614/422-5778

             Mr. Jay Rinehart, Technical Institute Laboratory 614/453-1121

             Mr. Bill Barney, St. Guiles, Ohio 513/786-5631

HIRING ISSUES:  Willing to relocate immediately
                Would enjoy traveling on the job
                Willing to accept a job not in career goal area if there is
                potential for moving into that area
```

FIGURE 13-4b   Sample resume: functional style.

Reflect on these sample resumes. Do they give you adequate information? Did you notice that not all references in the resumes provided phone numbers? Could there be a reason? Do the career objectives reflect serious thinking? Is it necessary to mention when one is engaged? Should part-time work be listed? Is there a difference between "excellent" and "good" health? These are some of the questions that might come to mind if these resumes were viewed by a personnel director.

Do you know enough about the candidate to decide whether or not you would want to interview them for a job opening? These would be the very questions employers would be faced with if any of these resumes were sent to them. Certainly, if these resumes did not present a positive self-image, the opportunity would end at this point. You should create an accurate image in your resume—but also a positive one.

Once you have composed your resume, have someone else look it over for spelling, grammar, and structural errors. Be careful to select confident reference sources. Check the accuracy of your dates and descriptive information. The resume should be typed on good-quality white paper, and then have it printed professionally on good-quality white or ivory paper. It is always important to have additional copies so they are readily available when you need them. You can always add information you believe to be important. If you want to indicate that a graduation date is upcoming, merely indicate the date, or that the degree is "in progress."

Let us direct our attention to the references needed for a resume. This is one area that most young people are very confused by. There are two basic kinds of references: performance references and character references. The character reference provides information about the personality traits, attesting to the positive credibility of an individual's attitudes, beliefs, or values. The performance references indicate a person's ability to perform specific skills or to use certain knowledge in specific job areas. It is important to have two or three performance references and one or two character references on your resume. The performance references are of more concern to an employer, but they like to have access to both types. Former employers, teachers, job supervisors, and administrators are good sources for performance references, while ministers, family physicians, officers in social organizations, community-service personnel, and teachers are often good sources for character references.

References can be categorized into two groups: confidential and open. This distinction is required by law. All references or recommendations are open unless you sign a paper relinquishing your right to see the recommendation. If you agree to this procedure, it is then considered a confidential reference. According to a study conducted by Michael Carey, 72 percent of 381 employers surveyed indicated they preferred the confidential reference and placed more credibility in it.[2]

Today, many employers prefer to telephone the reference person, because this is faster than writing a letter and requires fewer demands on all the parties involved.

For this reason, you should always try to include a current phone number with each reference listed on your resume.

As a last thought, once you have completed your first resume, always keep it in your personal file. The resume is one item that you will want to keep updated as long as you are concerned about a career. This is an item that might frequently be requested of you as you do speaking engagements, consulting assignments, and other professional activities in conjunction with your regular job assignments.

THE SEARCH FOR JOB-CAREER INFORMATION

As you continue on your soul- and-goal resolution list, and after you have drafted your resume, you will want to start collecting job-source information. The sooner you begin this third step in the career preparation process, the more quickly will you become aware of the efficiency of following these five steps. You do not want to feel rushed because graduation may be near and you are in need of money. If the urgency for a job is immediate, this factor will greatly influence your efforts. This decision-making phase is one of the more difficult activities in career preparation, and time is a vital factor. You need time to search for information, talk to people, do reflective thinking, and compare viewpoints from a variety of sources.

The obvious start for sources of job career information is with **relatives, friends, and neighbors.** These sources should not be viewed as a means to get a job

FIGURE 13-5   The placement center gives the student beginning a career or job search a large choice of options.

with minimal effort. Rather, view them as people who know you as a person, ones who can offer you advice on the basis of what they know about you personally. It is amazing how many young people take up careers in the same professional areas as their parents. They can see the personal satisfaction displayed by their parents. Here is a way to get first-hand information about the specifics of a particular profession. Even when you hear young people say they would never go into the same profession as one of their parents, they are no doubt basing this on the information they have discovered about this field through the family structure. Such a decision would reflect constructive use of first-hand information.

Colleges and universities usually have **placement services** for their students, graduates, and alumni. Many students fail to recognize this valuable service. College placement services provide counseling, reference and resume formats and forms, career literature, job listings, and on-campus and off-campus interviews. As you get involved with your career preparation, investigate this service and find out how it operates on your campus.

The most common source of job possibilities are the **want ads** in your local newspaper. Most people looking for immediate jobs use this source. For career preparation, however, we do not consider this one of the better sources. It allows you very little reflective thinking and preparation time for the amount of investment you have in your education. Employers use the daily newspapers because they can fill job openings quickly. That hiring process is somewhat different from the process we are concerned with here.

Another resource you should give serious consideration is the **professional journal and trade magazine.** These publications specialize in specific career areas and announce job opportunities based on the current market demand in their area of specialization. If you have a special interest, you can go to any library and look at their listing of such publications, or at least find out from the librarian what ones are in print. Try to find one or two of these sources and scan them. If you feel they are of help to your goals, subscribe to them for a few months. In this way you can follow the specialized job market and study its growth patterns. You will have a resource list of possible job openings if you wish to start applying. This can be one of the most valuable ways for you to achieve your goal-resolution list's activities.

Another valuable resource is **craft- and trade-union literature.** These publications are difficult to find in libraries, but telephone or city directories can lead you to the organizations. They usually are very willing to provide literature and information. Sometimes this same information can be found in counseling services at technical or vocational schools.

The **federal government**, through the printing services of the Superintendent of Documents, provides much literature about career information. The United States Civil Service Commission specializes in providing just this type of career information. At the end of this chapter, you will find some addresses.

We consider one of the best ways to obtain resources for job and career information is to go to the direct source—to the horse's mouth, so to speak. Search out **practicing professionals** in the field in which you are interested, and ask them for information. Young people trying to make career decisions often look at the professional as the person who has "made it," far removed from the common person—an untouchable. Rarely is this the situation. Most professionals enjoy sharing information about their professional activities. Those truly involved in their work are concerned about the future growth and development of their field, and they want to see young, ambitious, and concerned people come into their professional areas. Because these professionals are busy and often have schedules that place limits on their time, it is a courtesy to call or write for an appointment. Ask for an interview and tell them why. Of course, it is your responsibility to make the most from such a valuable opportunity. You should prepare! Write out specific questions for such an interview, questions that you would like specific information about. And last, remember that this is a formal appointment with time limitations and that you should respect it. We have found that many of our students got their professional start from just such interviews.

Once you believe that you have exhausted the available resources for job-career opportunities, make a progress check. Look over your goal-resolution list, check your resume, and look over all of the information you have collected in your search. Do you believe you have enough information to start formally applying for jobs? If you do, then you are ready to move to the next step in this career preparation process.

APPLYING FOR JOBS

There are two techniques to use when applying for jobs: One is to apply in person and request the organization's application form to fill out; the second is to apply by mail with a formal letter of application.

Applying in person.   When applying for a job in person, you will receive some type of printed form. You should read the entire form before starting to fill it out. When you begin to fill it out, use blue or black ink, and print the information. If you are permitted to take the form home, it is better to type the information.

Fill out the form by answering all the questions, and if one does not pertain to you, write in "not applicable." It looks bad to merely cross out the question. If you feel some of the questions are too personal or you feel negative about them, do not take it on yourself to write in critical remarks. If there is not enough space to give a complete answer to your satisfaction, finish the response on the back of the sheet if it is blank, or on a separate sheet if the form has printing. Be careful to correctly label all of your responses so that they match the proper questions.

When you have completed the form, and as you turn it in, it is your responsibility to request an interview. You may be able to get one the same day, but more often you will have to return on another day for the interview. It is important to keep in mind that the person who reviews your application is meeting you for the first time by means of that printed form. Therefore, the image that you create by how you respond to the requested information is what the reviewer will perceive about you. Certainly, you will want this to be a positive image.

Applying by mail. The second technique is to apply by mail, which involves drafting a formal letter and mailing it with a copy of your resume to the intended organization or agency. When applying for jobs in this fashion, there are two forms of letter applications: solicited and unsolicited. The solicited letter (Figure 13-6) is applying for a job position or opening that has been announced or publicly advertised. The unsolicited letter (Figure 13-7) is applying for a position with an organization, business, agency, or corporation that has *not* advertised a specific job opening. Rather, you have decided to contact them and ask them to consider you if such a position should open. No doubt, you will want to send application letters of both types as a part of your career preparation. The unsolicited letters are very frequently used by graduating students when they want to work within specific fields or in certain regions in the country. The solicited letter will have a more specific content than the unsolicited letter. Some students make the mistake of drafting one general unsolicited letter, and then make one hundred copies to sent out to lists of employers. This is not recommended, simply because the "form letter" is too impersonal and often creates a negative impression with employers or personnel directors. Even with the form-letter approach, you will still have to type each inside address and salutation and sign each form. If all of the letters do not go out together, then you have to also fill in the date. The dating of the letter is a vital issue. Most employees file and look at all applications in chronological order, according to the mailing date of the letter.

Certain basic items should be dealt with in letters of application. Some require more detail than others, depending on whether they are solicited or unsolicited. We have tried to present these items in Box 13-5 to indicate their importance in each type of letter.

The application letter should comply with standard business-letter form. Regular business-size (8½ X 11) white or ivory bond stationery should be used with a business-size envelope. Block paragraph style is the popularly accepted typing format. You should proofread the letter very carefully for grammar, spelling, and sentence structure.

Do you notice good and bad points in either of the letters? If you were the employer in either situation, would you consider either one of these applicants for a formal interview? What impressions do these letters leave in your mind?

Letters of application do take time to compose. Writing several practice letters will help to sharpen your letter communicating skills. The self-image you create in your letter is very significant, as you can see from the sample letters. You may find it helpful to draft a letter of application and then put it aside for a few days. Come back to it a day or two later and reread it. Does it have the same meaning, your intended meaning, as the first draft? Every letter of application that you send out should have a carbon or photocopy in your files. You will not be able to

143 East Lial Acre
Superior, WI 44880

4/23/79

Mr. Lloyd Filmore
Personnel Manager
Milikin Market Researchers
19 Ardmore Ave.
Syracuse, New York 13201

Dear Mr. Filmore:

Your company announced an opening in the recent issue of <u>Training</u>
magazine for a market researcher. I would like this job.

In June of this year I will graduate from the University of Wisconsin
here in Superior with a BS degree in marketing research. I would
like this job because I do have some experience working with one of
the local public utilities and your ad mentioned that most of your
clients are public utility companies.

Even though I am only 22, I believe you will find that my academic
course work is good and that my summer job experiences gave me the
opportunity to work with some of the classroom theory in a realistic
work setting.

Even though your company is a long way from me I would be willing to
move to New York. My being young, single, and excited about traveling all are reasons for you to consider me for the job.

I would like to have an interview as soon as possible. I have a
spring break next week and that would be a perfect time for me to
come to Syracuse.

I will be eagerly waiting to hear from you.

Respectfully yours,

Todd Jackson

Todd Jackson

FIGURE 13-6   Solicited application letter.

remember the details of all your letters, especially if you are sending out several at
a time. You may want to refer to your copy of the letter, especially if you are
asked to come for an interview.

12 Tamerick Circle
Sunset, Utah 34551

May 14, 1979

Director of Personnel
Farm Bureau CoOp, Inc.
Bountiful, Utah 34589

Dear Director:

I am interested in working with your organization focusing on the agricultural concerns of farmers in Utah. I am finishing my second year as a vocational agriculture major at the Sunset branch of the University of Utah.

I have worked on my father's farm since I was a child and have had a great deal of experience working with John Deere farming equipment. I have also worked for many of the neighboring farmers.

In college I majored in crop rotation and soil conservation study areas. I would very much like an opportunity to experiment with some of the new theories I have been introduced to.

At present, finances force me to suspend my studies and go to work, but I want to make this work a positive and profitable experience so that I can go back to school and finish my degree. I have found that I could work a forty-hour week for your company and attend Saturday morning classes at the main campus which is only about eight miles from your work site. In this manner I could serve you as a full-time employee and still work on my career goal of getting my college degree.

I am very willing to come down to Bountiful for a job interview. I will be anxiously waiting to hear from you on this matter.

Thank you for your consideration.

Respectfully,

Janice Sneed

Janice Sneed

FIGURE 13-7   Unsolicited application letter.

It is best to allow two to three weeks for a response to your letters. If by the end of three weeks you have not heard it, it would be appropriate to call. If you feel there are conflicts with other applications and interview possibilities, it is not

BOX 13-5   BASIC ITEMS FOR LETTERS OF APPLICATION

Letter Item	Solicited Letter of Application	Unsolicited Letter of Application
Letter head and date	Include	Include
Inside address	Specific name, use a use a job title	Specific name unnecessary, departmentally directed
Salutation	"Dear," using proper name	Dear Employer, Dear Personnel Staff Person
State purpose of letter	Mention specific job position advertised	Include a job description for which you are interested in this organization
Educational preparation	Give precise degrees, dates, and institution	Provide general field degree in; express the latitude of degree training
Job experience	Describe how previous jobs prepared you for this one	Describe the latitude of experience obtained from your various previous job experiences
Personal career goals	Relate them specifically to the job opening	Relate them generally to the job description stated in the purpose of the letter
Geographic location on job	Mention if a long distance from present location	Mention if a long distance from present location
Mention of the desire for interview	Ask for specific details with possible suggested date or locations	Describe your general availability for interview indicating your eagerness to hear in near future
Complimentary closing	Sincerely yours,	Respectfully yours,
Typed and written signature	Yes	Yes
Resume enclosed	Yes	Yes

improper to call and inquire about your letter of application, explaining why you found it necessary to call rather than wait for a written reply. You should not jump to negative conclusions if you do not hear immediately about a letter of application. There could be many reasons why the response is slow in returning.

Acting on impulse could create a very negative impression about you with the employer.

We realize this waiting period in your career preparation is an upsetting one. Therefore, we offer a suggestion to get through this period. You can make the time pass more quickly if you start to concern yourself with the next step of your career preparation process.

THE JOB INTERVIEW

For many young people, the job-interview step is the most frightening. This step involves significant use of speaking communication skills. Time is another factor in the interview step. Up to this point, taking plenty of time to do the job right was strongly encouraged. Unfortunately, most interviews are appointments that are usually confined to strict time limitations. And last, in all of the previous steps you had the opportunity to do a second draft, to rethink, or to ask for a second opinion from another person. The interview does not allow this luxury. The job interview is a "one-shot" deal, and you must do it right the first time, because rarely is there a second chance. With these points in mind, we recommend that you give time and serious reflection to the preparation of the impending job interview. While you are waiting for the response to your letter is the ideal time for the interview preparation.

In the **first phase** of preparation, you can begin to collect all of the standard data you will need before, during, and immediately after the interview. It is good to have available your social security number, birth certificate, draft card, driver's license, union or trade card, special diplomas, military discharge papers, or any other information that might relate to the job for which you are applying.

In the **second phase** of preparation, check your resume. This is particularly important if you are a graduating senior and have received any special honors or awards since you sent copies of the resume out. Several months can pass from the time the resume was drafted until the job interview; possibly, some special experience, part-time job, or publication could be added to the resume, and you would want to mention it in the interview.

In the **third phase**, you should try to find out the specifics of the interview: the day, time, length of appointment, number of people to be involved during the interview, and if the interview will take place in two parts. One part may involve exchange of information between you and the employer/interviewer, and there may be a second part in which you will be asked to demonstrate your skills or the depth of your knowledge or the latitude of your working experiences. Find out if the employer/interviewer is expecting you to bring anything to the interview appointment, such as a professional portfolio or samples of your work.

Once you know what to expect during the formal interview, you can then plan your performance. You can write out the questions that you will want to ask the interviewer in order to obtain information you want about the job. As an applicant, you have rights and a responsibility to your career goals. You should not hesitate to ask questions, because you are at this interview to gather as much information about the employer as he or she is about you. Consider some of the subjects in Box 13-6, which lists information that you will before you agree to accept the position.

BOX 13-6   TOPICS FOR APPLICANT'S INTERVIEW QUESTIONS

1. Job description, responsibilities
2. Salary, employee benefits, insurance, sick leave, etc.
3. Vacation time, holidays, payroll procedures
4. Dress code, social behaviors, social responsibilities
5. Type of work environment, people, and equipment that you would work with on a regular basis
6. Opportunity for advancement, on the job training
7. Attitude toward self-improvement; additional schooling or degrees
8. Cross-country moving, local housing, travel expenses
9. Community involvement relating to the job

Once you have determined the questions that you want to ask the employer/interviewer, you will want to think about dressing for the interview. There are several popular paperbacks that provide guidelines on how to dress for success in the business community. You could get yourself very involved in this particular phase of career preparation and lose sight of what you are trying to do. This is not to imply that we think how to dress for a job interview is not relevant. Two general guidelines will serve you in making effective choices in your clothing. (1) Wear clothing that you can function in with comfort. Clothing that is too tight or constricting to body movement should never be worn for a formal job interview, even if it is the current fashion. The muscles working with the natural tensions in the body do not need the added problem of dealing with ill-fitted clothing. (2) Don't select clothing that will call undue attention to itself. You are not trying to be a fashion plate or to demonstrate your expensive taste. Rather, you are trying to demonstrate your abilities and qualification for the job position. Remember that it is as possible to overdress as to underdress for a job interview. If you are worried about what to wear, you can "case" the place out inconspicuously a few days before the interview, or ask some professional person who has a similar position in a similar organization to help you. If travel is involved, take enough clothing for the changes you will need. For example, if the interview is in the morning with an afternoon tour followed by an evening dinner engagement, you would want to freshen up and change for dinner. Don't forget to allow for the different climates that you might possibly face traveling across the country for an interview.

The night before the interview, get a good night's sleep, and rise early enough to really get yourself awake for a morning interview. It is good to have some type of light, but warm food. Your nerves will naturally be a bit tense, and either an empty or overstuffed stomach will add to the nervous tension. Nervous tension is not all bad. You will get adrenaline to work during the interview. This adrenaline will help you maintain a high energy level.

Go alone to the interview; do not take a friend with you. If you are driving, park your car so that you don't have to worry about small chores like feeding a meter.

Walk confidently into the waiting room a few minutes early with pen, paper, resume, and list of questions all placed in a hard-cover notebook on which you can jot notes in case there is no desk or table in the interview room. Many interviewers believe large pieces of furniture such as desks or tables act as a barrier to effective interpersonal communications. If you pass a water fountain and have a moment to moisten your lips, do so if it will make you feel more comfortable. Do not chew gum or suck breath mints. Just use your toothbrush before you show up and you won't have to worry.

As the interview gets underway, start off with a relaxed voice. It is good to start with some light conversation, and most interviewers usually do this, but if they choose not to, follow their cue on this issue. Try not to interrupt the interviewer. You will have an opportunity to talk. Listen carefully, jot down a note or two if you feel it is important. That merely indicates you are listening and that your intentions are serious. When you respond to a question, pause for a moment and think before you speak, then give your answer. The moment or two that you take to collect your thoughts for a good answer reflects the effectiveness and organization of your response.

Usually the interviewer will provide some type of closing with a summary and ask if you have any questions. Usually the interviewer ends by reaffirming the date when you will be notified about the job. This is a good time for you to thank the interviewer for the opportunity and agree to the notification by an agreed-on date. This is very crucial to you if you have other interviews or job offers.

ADDITIONAL CAREER PREPARATIONS

At this point, you have completed the career preparation process as we have presented it in this chapter. There are some other areas related to this process that we should concern outselves with while we are on the subject.

Since preparing a professional portfolio is a necessary part of preparing for a career in certain professions, we will discuss this now. If you are considering a career such as engineering, photography, architecture, graphic design, or one of the performing arts, you will probably need to show a professional portfolio before, during, or in rare cases, after the interview.

We will provide you with some general guidelines in putting together this portfolio, but if you need particular information, you will have to research this during your career-resource information step. The basic purpose of the portfolio is to show what you can do with your specific skills and to show what training and experiences you already have in the specific field.

The cover of a portfolio is important, because it will reflect, in part, your professional attitude about your career. The portfolio should open to a copy of your resume as an introduction to your background. Most work is presented in drawings, draftings, photographs, or slides. All of this material can be organized and placed in fitted plastic sleeves. The plastic sheets for color slides even have frosted backs to diffuse the light and make it very easy to view the slides without carrying along a hand viewer. Original letters, awards, magazine or newspaper articles or special color programs can all be kept clean in plastic sleeves that can be purchased in any office-supply store.

Material should be recorded in chronological sequence for clear organization as well as for demonstrating the development of your skills and talents. The important thing is to prevent the portfolio from looking like a scrapbook of memories. You want it to have a professional image. Because you invest money in a portfolio, you should carry it with you to interviews rather than mailing it. If you must mail it, do so by registered mail for your own protection. If you are going to have slides and photographs made, have a set of copies just in case.

CAREER PREPARATION AND THE LAW

The recent changes in laws regulating hiring practices are also of concern to you. You should know your rights as an applicant. You have rights regarding certain issues:

1. Race, religion, creed, and sex may not be used as a basis for discrimination in hiring.
2. You do not have to indicate race, religion, creed, or sex on an applicant form.
3. You do not have to provide a photograph of yourself on an application form or resume.
4. You do not have to provide confidential references as a prerequisite for a job application or interview.
5. If you agree to provide confidential references, you must sign a statement to that fact before the reference is written.
6. The criteria used to evaluate candidates must be open knowledge to all concerned in the hiring procedure.[3]

If you have followed the procedure we suggest, or one similar to it, why didn't you get the job? This is one of the questions most frequently asked by young people who have spent time going through the career preparation process. A simple answer can be formed by taking a good look at the job market and then at the rate of unemployment in this country today.

There is another answer and it comes from a study conducted by Frank Endicott.[4] This researcher conducted a survey of 186 job recruiters. He asked them to list what they considered their most frequently used reasons for not hiring job applicants. These are the significant results:

Inadequate personality, poor attitude, lack of poise and confidence	124	67%
Poor scholastic records without explanation	99	53%
Lack of goals, poorly motivated, indecisive	80	43%
Lack of enthusiasm, drive, initiative	50	26%
Inability to express self, poor speech	45	25%
Unrealistic salary demands, more interest in salary than in the job itself	39	22%

Interviewers and employers look for the personality qualities that indicate leadership ability and interpersonal cooperation and communication with others. Achievement is an important quality because it is an indicator of the potential of the person. Obviously, these are some of the things that you should be concerned with in your resume and in your letters of application.

Thinking over what we have emphasized in this chapter, you should be conscious of the importance of timing in career preparation. Time should be used for effective preparation in presenting yourself to others in a way that will help you achieve your career goals. The professional image that we have talked about in this chapter is reflected in your creation, planning, and thinking. You are the one who must now take your basic communication skills of reading, writing, speaking, and listening and apply them to this career-preparation process.

A REVIEW OF KEY ISSUES

Career preparation requires that you use the four basic communication skills of reading, writing, speaking, and listening.

The first step in this professional career preparation is referred to as the soul and goal search, in which you should concern yourself with discovering and defining your interests in career possibilities.

The second step is to design your resume, using either the biographical or the functional style that will describe your professional image in a very accurate manner; there are also optional items that you may want to include, depending on your specific area of interest.

The next step is the search for career information by investigating all of the available sources and resources. This is an effort to open up the search rather than to narrow the focus.

The next step is applying for various jobs by mail or in person. This requires extensive use of writing skills so that you can communicate your career goals and skills.

The last step is the job interview, in which you are gathering information as well as providing information for the employer/interviewer.

The professional portfolio is a necessary item for some people in certain career areas; it requires additional planning or organization.

As an applicant, you have certain rights, under law, that are for your protection when you venture into your job search.

Unfortunately, some people don't get the job after all of the work, and often the reasons are to be found in the applicant. With some simple awareness and preparation, these negative aspects can be avoided.

EXPERIENCING EXPERIENCES

Career preparation is the first big step for many young people venturing out into the world as an adult. It is frightening to some degree. Take a look at the job market, the percentage of unemployment, and the number of individuals under-qualified and overqualified for their jobs; you are viewing a very frightening picture.

As a student, you have spent a great deal of effort and time reading, writing, studying, discussing, and testing a wide variety of information with the goal in mind to find a job and work to support yourself. You probably included in this plan a job that you would enjoy. At this point in your thinking, the dream may not be quite so idealistic. Now you are more prepared to face reality and also find satisfaction in a job. One of the definite advantages of formal education is that you can experiment with reality in the classroom. Furthermore, you have time on your side as you experiment with the complex process we know as learning. And certainly, no one would argue that experiencing is not a vital part of this process.

As you look over the last section of the chapter, notice the values in experiencing some of the skills and working with some of the knowledge that you have been exposed to. This final part of the career preparation process could very well be one of the most significant in this book, in this course, and maybe even in your life! Experience with freedom, and experience freely, without fear.

ACTIVITY 1: Your Resume

Directions: Using this form as a guide, draft your resume. After you have completed it, hand it to a classmate to proofread and offer critical remarks.

Name _____

Permanent address _____

Temporary address _____

Phone _____ Birth _____ Health _____

Marital status _____ No. of dependents _____ Military _____

Education:

Work experience:

References:

Career goal statement:

Selected listing of optional items:

ACTIVITY 2: Resume Analysis Form

Directions: When the resumes are completed, they should be exchanged and analyzed, using the following form, and then returned to the original owner.

Resume for _____

Rating + 1 = poor   2 = adequate   3 = great

Address information   _____ Reason:

Birth, health, marital,
military status infor-
mation   _____ Reason:

Education information _____ Reason:

Work experience
information   _____ Reason:

Career goal statement _____ Reason:

Optional items   _____ Reason:

Additional comments about spelling, grammar, punctuation, and general format:

Reviewer: _____

ACTIVITY 3: Applying For the Right Kind of Job

Directions: Read all of the following advertisements for various jobs. Select one on the basis of your interests, educational training, and previous job experience. Draft a formal letter of application; assume the job is real and apply it to your real career situation.

Direction: Give your application letter and resume to your "employer." Classmate/employer should respond by formal letter and offer an interview to applicant. The interviews should be conducted in class and be reviewed by classmates.

A young executive type needed for a market research position. Salary is negotiable and good benefits. Experience preferred but unnecessary with evidence of formal education. Write Joseph Williams, Personnel Director, Advertising Consultants, Inc., Box 43, Springdale, Mass. 49712.

Technicians, draftspersons with formal training needed for creative work with small but fast-growing company. E.O.E. Write Dale Casto, 5612 Ellen Lane, Conover, Ind. 61230.

Ambitious individual willing to travel, but interested in quick advancement to do various types of sales work. Will provide three weeks of extensive in-house training. All expenses paid to large city of home office. Some college desired. Contact Debra Hailman, P.O. Box 6787, San Francisco, Calif. 90234.

College graduates, variety of openings with General Electric Corporation in sales, purchasing, public relations, engineering design, and laboratory development. Sales competitive and excellent fringe benefits. Opening located in 18 different states. Interviews to be conducted in New York, May; Chicago, June; and Houston, July. Write to General Electric, Main Offices, Schenectady, N.Y. 21239.

Large Metro hospital needs LPNs, RNs, lab technicians, medical secretaries, and bookkeepers. Excellent health benefits. Salaries range from 11,800 to 23,500 based on training and experience. Write to Marla Frankert, St. Jude's Hospital, Beverly Hills, CA 90211. Deadline: May 30. Equal opportunity employer.

Corporate lawyer for large firm. Heavy travel schedule but excellent salary. Opportunity for advancement. Degree required with major in corporate law. Write Blackburn, Blackburn, and Willard Assoc., Handcock Building, Plaza Circle, Decatur, GA 30030. References required.

Teachers with high-school certification in history, foreign languages, science, art, and math for Cleveland City Schools. Starting salary 14,200. Equal opportunity employer. Advanced degree work encouraged with board remuneration. Experience not necessary but references required. Apply Board Building, Cleveland Avenue, Cleveland, OH 26488.

ACTIVITY 4: Employer/Interviewer Info Sheet

(Assigned employer/classmate should fill out *before* interview so that it can be used during class interview.)

Name and address of company/organization:

Name of interviewer/employer:

Official position of interviewer/employer:

Create the necessary additional details of the job description:

Make list of candidate qualities you are searching for:

List any specific requirements demanded for the job:

Indicate the strategy you intend to follow during the interview:

ACTIVITY 5: Interview Analysis by Observer

Interview for the job of: _____

Between employer: _____; applicant: _____

Rating Scale: 1 = poor; 2 = fair; 3 = average; 4 = good; 5 = excellent

Employer: **Comments:**

Made applicant feel at ease: 1   2   3   4   5   _____

Asked worthwhile questions: 1   2   3   4   5   _____

Listening ability: 1   2   3   4   5   _____

Verbal skills: 1   2   3   4   5   _____

Adequacy answering the
  applicant's questions: 1   2   3   4   5   _____

Brought interview to closure: 1   2   3   4   5   _____

Applicant

Self-confidence, poise   1   2   3   4   5   _____

Completeness of answers   1   2   3   4   5   _____

Appropriateness of
  questions   1   2   3   4   5   _____

Ability to listen   1   2   3   4   5   _____

Quality of career goals
  expressed: 1   2   3   4   5   _____

Suggestions for improvement for both:

Critiquer: _____

EXERCISES

1. After role playing the interviews, hold class discussions to discuss openly the written remarks of the observers.

2. Each member of the class should select a profession, go to the yellow pages to find a phone number, and call for an interview appointment. Each member should come back to the class and give an oral report about the information collected during the actual interview.

3. Bring in the job ads from local newspapers and trade magazines or professional journals. Compare how they are written and how they attempt to appeal to applicants.

4. Invite career counselors or job recruiters into the class as guest speakers. Plan a list of questions for them.

5. Invite a staff member from the Student Placement Service on your campus to come to your class for a question-and-answer dialog.

SOURCES OF CAREER INFORMATION

American Federation of Information
  Processing Societies
210 Summit Avenue
Montvale, NJ 07645

Institute of Electrical and Electronic
  Engineers
345 East 47 Street
New York, NY 10017

National Art Education Association
National Education Association
1916 Association Drive
Reston, VA 22091

Speech Communication Association
5105 Blacklick Road
Annandale, VA 22003

American Institute for Design and
  Drafting
3119 Price Road
Bartlesville, OK 74003

American Newspaper Publishers
11600 Sunrise Valley Drive
Reston, VA 22091

Professional Photographers of
  America, Inc.
1090 Executive Way
Des Plaines, IL 60018

National Alliance of Television &
  Electronics Service Association
5908 South Troy Street
Chicago, IL 60629

American Hospital Association
840 North Lake Shore Drive
Chicago, IL 60611

American Occupational Therapy
  Association
6000 Executive Boulevard
Rockville, MD 20852

American Society for Training and
  Development
600 Maryland Avenue
Suite 305
Washington, D.C. 20024

American Optometric Association
7000 Chippewa Street
St. Louis, MO 63119

American Fund for Dental Education
211 East Chicago Avenue
Chicago, IL 60611

American Medical Technologists
710 Higgins Road
Park Ridge, IL 60068

Office of Personnel
Veterans Administration
Washington, D.C 20420

National Highway Traffic
  Administration
400 Seventh Street SW
Washington, D.C. 20590

American Medical Record Association
John Hancock Center
Suite 1850
875 North Michigan Avenue
Chicago, IL 60611

ANA Committee on Nursing Careers
American Nurses Association
2420 Pershing Road
Kansas City, MO 64108

American Bankers Association
Bank Personnel Division
1120 Connecticut Avenue NW
Washington, D.C. 20036

National Association of Accountants
419 Third Avenue
New York, NY 10022

National Shorthand Reporters
  Association
2361 South Jefferson Davis Highway
Arlington, VA 22202

American Bar Association
1155 East 60th Street
Chicago, IL 60637

Society of American Foresters
1010 16th Street NW
Washington, D.C 20036

National Oceanography Association
1900 L Street NW
Washington, D.C. 20036

American Veterinary Medical
 Association
939 North Meacham Road
Schaumberg, IL 60172

Manpower Development Staff
401 M Street SW
Washington, D.C. 20460

Department of Human Resources
 Development
Mail Control Unit
800 Capital Mall
Sacramento, CA 95814

NOTES

1. Marilyn Hutchinson and Sue Spooner, *Job Search Barometer*. Bethlehem, Pa.: College Placement Council, 1975.
2. Michael Carey, "Placement Credentials as a Screening Device." *Journal of College Placement,* Winter 1977, p. 30.
3. Miami University Career Planning and Placement Publication. Oxford, Ohio, 1978.
4. Frank Endicott, Questions Frequently Asked During the Employment Interview.

INDEX